To 'Kev' and 'Dick' (you know who you are)
and to Mum, for teaching me to recognise
the real heroes in our lives.

# AUTHOR'S NOTE

My pen name is Holly Hill and the following pages are mostly true, although my friends tell me I am prone both to understatement and exaggeration. A neuropsychologist once told me I have an 'underdeveloped hypothalamus', which means, among other things, that I have a weak risk response. In other words, I often should feel more scared than I do. Believe me, this can lead you to do some pretty bizarre things.

I have used pseudonyms and changed other details to protect the identity of people mentioned in the book. Please respect their privacy – we all carry the burden of their guilt in one way or another.

# CHAPTER 1

It was a 'John' who introduced me to my life of Dicks.

I met John at Jason's party. Jason worked for a small investment company that did very well. Amazingly well, in fact. Jason's
income just seemed to keep on doubling while the rest of us
looked on with undisguised envy. I had known Jason since my
Newcastle University days, when I did psychology and he did
engineering. Jason was often found passed out on our lounge
room floor in the mornings clutching an empty bottle of Jack
Daniel's. This was a feat in itself because Jason was well over
six foot tall and our tiny lounge room was probably only about
five square.

Jason was best known for his fabulous parties, and that
night's was no exception – people were littered throughout the
Federation house in various states of inebriation.

I was in the main bedroom with a group of people sprawled
on Jason's king-sized waterbed. (Jason always had waterbeds
because he reckoned the new-fangled 'zero partner disturb-
ance' beds were sacrilegious and ought to be banned by the
Church. He liked his partners *awake*.) We weren't having a sex
romp or anything. It was just three or four talkatively tipsy

people having a toke and solving all of the world's problems in one conversation.

Feeling chuffed with my contribution, but faintly concerned about whether I had over-simplified with my answer 'Succumb', I walked out of the bedroom just as John walked in the front door.

It was like every worn cliché. Our eyes met and I was instantly attracted to him, without even seeing the rest. His eyes were an intense blue and there was a whole lot going on behind them. Whoever said the eyes are the windows to the soul was probably a God-botherer. Let's face it, the eyes are the windows to the brain, just as nature intended.

Introductions naturally followed and I was amazed to learn this person of the blue eyes was Jason's boss. Apparently he was a 'very rich and powerful man' who was not only a financial backer of Jason's investment company but also the computer genius who had written the program that had made the investments so successful. 'A mad genius' was how Jason had described this man who was gazing at me so intensely. I drowned in those eyes that night. I was like a rabbit trapped in a spotlight. And it wasn't just the eyes. That brain.

I would like to be able to describe what John was wearing and what he said to me. But all I can remember are those blue eyes and the fact that he was attracted to me too. In fact, so obvious was our attraction that Jason pulled me aside at one point and told me John was married.

Married! My mood plummeted. John was off limits, an 'untouchable'. I was no marriage-wrecker. The last thing I wanted to do was come between a married man and his wife. Perhaps they'd been childhood sweethearts and were one of those couples that still went everywhere holding hands. Maybe they even had children.

But I couldn't help myself. This might be my only chance to ever get to know a blue-eyed, zillionaire genius.

The party was one of those all-nighters only people with

high tolerances for excess can endure. My friends and I believed that moderation should be in moderation. In other words, we occasionally binged.

Anyway, a bunch of us were still going strong about 6 a.m. when the final guests started to leave. So I invited John, Jason and Susan around to my place to watch the spectacular sunrise my apartment was privy to.

Susan was one of my very few women friends in Sydney and one of the only true bisexuals I knew. She quite literally alternated between men and women, all of them highly exotic creatures who worshipped the ground Susan trod on. I guess most of us worshipped Susan – she was a far better clinical psychologist than I ever hoped to be, and was drop-dead gorgeous with long, spectacular legs and a smile that could melt a sociopath (and often did). Although she hadn't gone to university with us, she had partnered another friend of ours for many years and now I saw her more than the original friend. I always feel like a traitor when that happens.

My unit was located right in the middle of Darlinghurst, a well-known entertainment strip between Sydney's CBD and its red-light district. The streets were lined with cafés, restaurants, pubs and nightclubs, all well within staggering distance of my place. After the taxi dropped us off, we all trooped into the lift, up to the seventeenth floor and into my apartment, a tiny studio with plate-glass windows facing the north-east. It had been my home and refuge for about six months, ever since I'd moved back to Sydney from my home town of Port Stephens. I'd lived in Sydney before about five years earlier, but had fled to grieve when half my friends died of HIV/AIDS. Now I was back, and making up for lost time.

I made drinks for everyone and Jason passed around a joint. I could make up a conversation to recount, but it'd mostly be shit. Bullshit, that is. We were all pretty far gone. No-one says anything clever after they've been up for twenty-four hours.

John sat beside me on the couch, rubbing whatever part of

my anatomy he could decently reach in mixed company. Being a rather intellectual lot, we continued to solve the problems of the world, although I suspect our solutions might have been a tad impractical. For example, if religion of any kind was banned and everyone started worshipping the planet instead, like Susan suggested, I'm sure there'd be hell to pay. Pardon the pun.

When John started to give me a back massage and I generously offered to take my shirt off for better access, Susan and Jason quickly made to leave.

'No, no!' I almost screamed, wanting them to stay because I feared John would leave with them and he hadn't found the tattoo at the base of my spine yet. 'Please stay, I'm enjoying the conversation.'

I gave Susan the 'Urgent Eye' (you know what I mean – a kind of wide-eyed grimace as you mouth nonsense words that you hope can't be seen by the other person). Luckily for me, Susan was quite used to translating non-verbal grimaces and she hastily sat down again, realising it was make-or-break time for me and Blue Eyes.

I might not remember much of what our little group said that morning, but I sure remember the massage. Not only did it seem to last forever, John seemed compelled to continue, almost as if the need to massage was a physical tic or obsessive-compulsive movement. Two rounds of coffee, half an ounce of pot, and almost a bottle of vodka later, I was ready for Jason and Susan to leave. By now John had well and truly discovered the tattoo on my back and even whispered to me that he'd always wanted to make love to a girl with a tattoo but had never had the chance.

I refrained from saying I'd never made love to a married man before and until now, it had been a point of pride.

This time I gave Susan the 'OK, You Can Go Now' eye and, bless her cotton socks, she had Jason shuffled out the door before John could even think about removing his cramped fingers from the bowl of iced water I'd put them in. But we didn't leap into each other's arms, as all the novels and films seem to have it: rather, we explored each other's intellect. I'd never met a certified genius before, but soon discovered the gift of the gab thwarts genius any day. While John delivered quality of conversation, I delivered quantity, thereby ensuring some conversational 'gems' through sheer number of words generated (the monkeys typing in a room theory), which the genius in him thoughtfully remembered and discarded the rest.

I probably should reveal at this point that I am gifted in what I describe as 'conversational bluffery'. It's probably derived from being both psychologist and writer – if those two professions don't give you the gift of the gab, you're in the wrong job. I guess they also explain my need for catharsis and the urge to tell all to the world – dangerous traits for an adventurer into the human psyche!

I also have a terrible short-term memory. So over the years, I'd written down my various psychological and literary insights in a small book. My new genius friend didn't need to know that I had only produced them, on average, at the rate of a couple a year.

'I tend to jot down what I'm thinking,' I told him, producing the notebook. 'These are the most recent thoughts.'

And so I was able to produce at least thirty musings with varying degrees of insightfulness. They included such life-changing observations as 'Can the dead see you when you have sex?', which was about as original as lunch at McDonald's but had bothered me when my father died. Likewise, 'the loneliness of a crowd' had been a symptom of the grief I had felt then. Some related to my work: 'A delusion is merely a thought that has snowballed' seemed to impress John enormously. Individually, they didn't seem like much, but reading them out together, I somehow managed to convince this married blue-eyed genius that I had a halfway decent IQ and a philosophical nature.

For his part, he told me he believed the world, and everyone in it, could be reduced to a set of numbers, and that by doing so you could predict just about anything, given a large enough sample size. Apparently the computer program he had written rested on this theory and was one of the most successful investment software programs in the world.

To my amazement, despite his wealth John also spoke about how unhappy he was with his life and how, for him, the world was a boring and unfulfilling place. He told me he'd realised he didn't love his wife ten days after he married her, and the birth of his children had only made things worse.

How a zillionaire with two children could *possibly* be bored and unfulfilled was completely beyond me, and only added to my fascination for the man. I was out to impress, so I quoted the latest sci-fi novel I was reading and gave him a sketchy account of how I believed worm holes could quite reasonably be accessed to travel across space and time. (Thank goodness for sci-fi novels, I say – they can always be relied upon for some interesting adjunct to conversation!) When that led him to talking about quantum physics I managed to nod in all the right places, although he pretty much lost me after the first couple of sentences.

When he asked if he could kiss me, it seemed quite reasonable that I would reply in the affirmative, and I did. I suspect he was relieved at a break from my conversational bluffery more than anything else, although the poor man could just have been horny.

I guess I should also mention that I'm lucky enough to be considered darned attractive. How this came about, I'm not sure. At school I was the tall, pale, awkward girl who was always the wallflower and didn't even get to *touch* the male species until I was sixteen and lucky enough to spin the bottle at a guy who also had big metal railway tracks on his teeth.

Then, somehow, someway, when all the boys got taller and I stopped trying to appear shorter, the pear-shaped hunchback turned into an alright kind of gal. The straw-bleached hair (yep, the household stuff – we'd done it in the toilets at school) turned out to be soft and auburn, and the tendency to fat was merely excessive after-school snacking. Even more surprisingly, I moved gracefully and confidently without a hint of curvature of the spine!

That kiss was one of the most erotic encounters of my life. I gazed deep into his mad blue genius eyes and explored his lips with my own. I should mention here that I have big, puffy Angelina Jolie lips on an equally big mouth. As you can imagine, both mouth and lips get me into trouble regularly.

This is probably also a good place to explain that I am an advocate of the pash and dash. The philosophy is thus: one pashes, then one dashes. Every good girl has done it. For one thing, it's far better to be considered a prick tease than a slut. Plus, it doesn't mean anything – just another type of interaction with a pair of lips you find attractive. It's also an excellent way to startle someone. One minute they're deep in conversation with you and the next, you've got your tongue down their throat. (Or vice versa.)

But so good was the kiss with John that it immediately high-lighted one of the principal flaws of the pash and dash: sometimes, it is difficult – if not impossible – to dash after the pash. In this case, I wasn't going anywhere. And neither was John. Not for a while, anyway.

I would like to say that what followed was a morning of the most intense and passionate sex I'd ever had, but in reality we were both far too sleep deprived and he had a guilt-ridden soft-on for most of the time. Of course, I didn't let on that I thought his penis flaccidity was marriage-related; rather, I used all of the bluffery I could muster and somehow managed to convince him that he was the sexiest man alive.

This was really saying something, because in reality my blue-eyed man was several cans short of a six pack. John was very squat and very short, a bit like a cube. He had pale skin scattered with moles that looked suspiciously like melanomas, very fine red hair cut short to disguise premature baldness, and big, thick black spectacle frames that even Prada couldn't make attractive.

Did I wonder why someone who could afford Prada would choose to wear big, thick black spectacle frames? No! I was the rejected wallflower, remember. I had before me a real, live, unhappy rich man who was living proof that Richie Rich wasn't just a character in a comic. So I decided then and there that I would prove to John that the world was a thrilling, beautiful, glamorous, roller-coaster ride and it was his Goddess-given duty to darn well enjoy it. After all, money didn't grow on trees.

Or so I thought.

I won't bore you with all of the lovey-dovey details. The fact is, I genuinely thought it was love. For the first time in my life, I didn't want to change a single thing about the person I adored. In my eyes, he was the most beautiful man I'd ever seen.

But I'm honest enough to admit this was the first time I'd been with a man who offered to wave his magic wand and bring to reality anything I desired. I remember walking past a row of exclusive shops one day and John offered to buy me anything I wanted. He told me that $5 for me was about $500 for him. It was an extraordinary thing to say to a person who didn't get her first pair of Levi's until she could afford them herself. In the end, I chose a $350 pair of knickers and a matching bra. They weren't even the most expensive set in the shop. John wanted me to choose two. Instead, I described how I'd once offered the same deal to my three-year-old niece and been tremendously relieved when she'd picked a $2 bubble-blower.

It's a strange predicament, being able to pick anything from a shop. Trying not to notice the price tags. Hoping that you don't pick the most expensive thing. Wondering what the staff are thinking. Cringing when your companion pays for something so sexy on your behalf. It was a very strange feeling.

My whole life, I had always bought my own things: clothes, make-up, underwear. And now here was a married man buying my most intimate garments on his credit card. A black Amex, at that. I hadn't even realised there was anything beyond platinum.

At some points in your life, you cross boundaries that cannot be re-crossed. In sport, I think they call them 'back court': non-negotiable benchmarks of experience beyond which lies failure to progress. I had once accepted a 'pick of the jewellery store' from a best friend, but that was very different from a 'pick of the lingerie store' from a married man. I'd crossed a line, and suddenly it was *hot* that this man was buying me expensive presents and making me feel like a kept woman. It was amazingly, who'd-have-thoughtingly sexy. And there was more to come.

For the record, I didn't ask for a single thing. I still can't imagine asking for something hideously expensive, let alone demanding it, as we are led to believe some people do. But I didn't have to. John looked around my life, saw what I needed, and suddenly I had a fabulous camera, a high-powered telescope, a beefed-up computer, a high-tech DVD player (that I still can't set the time or record on) and more bling than a hip-hop convention.

They were heady days for a mostly unsophisticated girl so recently returned from life in a small coastal town. When John wasn't around, I'd walk down Oxford Street smiling a sexy smile generated by a vastly increased sense of self-worth. (Perhaps 'ghastly inflated' might be a better description, but I didn't know that then.) I was so flattered that a man like John was telling me he loved me. I felt so incredibly *proud*.

It made me horny too. When I went out with my friends, I would flirt like hell with any poor man who happened to be straightish and able to carry off a song or two on the dance floor. These teased souls got the pumpkin treatment in the wee small hours, and John would later reap the benefits of my pent-up desires. He was the only man for me: no-one else even came close.

So when John suggested I give up my work as a psychologist and go on the 'Mistress Plan' in order to be more available to him, I didn't hesitate. In fact, I rejoiced! I'd been working for the Department of Corrective Services and my client load included several rapists, a home invader and one of the major witnesses for a paedophilia inquiry. Counselling gave them a better chance at parole. I could practically feel their eyes roll when I called them up and tried to be cheerful.

It was so nice to actually *help* John. To soothe his troubled hurts when he came home, or say the right things when he wanted to vent about his wife or his work. I stocked the fridge with the foods John loved to eat and started to purchase gourmet coffees. I took him on adventures and to dance parties and he met people he would otherwise never have come into contact with. And all the while he was grateful, saying he couldn't believe he had met a person like me. That I was indeed the perfect woman. That he loved me unconditionally.

To hear a man such as John utter those words and more took me to heights of happiness that I had never known existed. It just felt so good that little ol' me was helping big ol' John. He would walk into my apartment stressed, unhappy and sometimes even suicidal. He would walk out again relaxed and happy with a smile on his face. We texted each other dozens of times a day, and he jokingly described the time he spent with his family as 'boot camp' in comparison with the time he spent with me. I taught him how to love life again. How to see the beauty in the world. How to appreciate his wonderful children. So great were my levels of support for him that I would have cheerfully told you that *he* owed *me* and I didn't feel in his debt at all. I was *earning* my keep.

I told myself and anyone who'd listen that the man of my dreams was in a 'messy separation' and would shortly wake up next to me every morning. I believed I would become the perfect stepmother to his children and we would sail yachts and live in exotic locations together. I'd imagine myself on his arm at fabulous parties, dressed in Versace with my hair done by someone with only a first name. We would vacation in Europe for months at a time, and I would leave little presents under park benches for vagrants to find. I'd finally have time to write novels and achieve my life-long dream of becoming a successful writer. Most importantly, I'd be making a very rich, powerful man happy. Little old me. I would achieve what a zillion dollars was incapable of.

*That* was the buzz. It wasn't the presents; it wasn't having the world placed at my feet; and it wasn't being able to go into a shop and buy anything at all. It was the fact that the daughter of Mrs South Port Stephens was more valued by this man than all of the money in the world.

I began to consider him the only true love I had ever known. I sang in the shower and around the house. I gave $5 notes to beggars. I smiled and laughed to myself as I walked down the street – and people smiled back! – I identified with the lyrics in songs. I thought his annoying habits were endearing. I would have given my life for his children, even though I hadn't met them yet. I opened up my heart and joyously offered John my soul.

I even started a novel about some audacious little old ladies I'd always dreamed of writing. I had planned it for nearly a decade and it was simply a matter of putting pen to paper. It didn't flow as freely as I'd expected, but I had the rest of my life to complete it. I wasn't in a hurry. Cloud Nine had so many other things to offer.

The trouble with being so very, very 'up' is that there is an awfully long way to fall.

When I met John for the second time, his first statement was: 'I'm not going to leave my wife'. Six months later, they had separated and he was mentally divvying up a $20 million estate. But when his wife threatened to kill herself and his children if he didn't return to her, he transferred $4000 into my account and I never spoke to or saw him again. At bloody Christmas-time too.

Our last meeting was when I gave him a stack of presents I couldn't really afford and he gave me glandular fever. I spent two fevered weeks in bed wondering why he didn't return my calls.

On 10 January I finally heard from him. By email. Five cold sentences, probably proofed by his wife. He said he'd returned to Charlene 'for the sake of the children' and that one of her conditions was that he never speak to me or contact me again. He sent some of my things back to me by Australia Post and didn't even include so much as a comp slip.

I cried so much it was a wonder I didn't dehydrate. I didn't leave my bed for another three long weeks. I remember sobbing to Susan that anyone could give me expensive presents, but none of them could give me John. I finally convinced her to phone him after I'd had a full-on anxiety attack. That was when I learned about Charlene's ultimatum. What a cow.

My friends couldn't understand it. They thought I should be grateful and pointed out the presents I'd received. I was incensed at their reaction. I had considered John to be my one true love. The money had nothing to do with it.

So from the dizzying heights of ecstasy I plummeted to the depths of vaguely suicidal depression. I was also jobless and flat broke. My mortgage and rent alone were $1300 a fortnight. I'd leased my unit in Port Stephens to a single-mother acquaintance who had recently split with her boyfriend and was doing it tough. With John's encouragement, I had generously offered her a twelve-month lease at a paltry $150 a week. My mortgage payments were nearly double that but John had said he'd subsidise me. Now, after two weeks in bed sick and another three weeks of moping, I had $300 in the bank and a week and a half to find at least another grand. Social security would give me a whole $400 a fortnight.

And so I did what everyone does in times of hardship: I started eating at the homes of friends.

# CHAPTER 2

'You're a psychologist – perform an assessment on yourself,' Kev told me, tired of hearing me moan about my jobless state and pending financial doom. 'What skills do you have? What do you do best? Where do you want to work? How do you want to work?'

Kev was another university friend and had shared the same house where Jason had spent so much time on the lounge room floor. One of the reasons we'd all clicked was because most of us were 'mature age' students. I'd done a couple of years as a cadet journalist and Kev had worked as a lab technician. Now he was an eminent scientist at the Institute of Molecular Biology and well on his way to finding a cure for heart disease. Ours was one of those friendships where we could say absolutely anything to each other and still remain friends. We knew all the dark secrets because we'd been there for most of them. I always said that if Kev chopped someone up into a million pieces and microwaved them, I'd hold his hand in court.

I sighed and tried to list what I did best. 'I'm a bloody good psychologist if people give the profession a chance. I hope I'm intelligent, although I'm very vague. I'm good at entertaining. I enjoy cooking. I like to spoil people, make them feel good about themselves. I'm pretty good at treating depression, or my clients seem to think so. But it'd be nice to work from home. I want to be able to write my novel. Novels, plural. As for physical attributes, I dunno – I'm pretty lucky in that department, I guess. So far, that is. What else? I want to travel. I like spending most of my income on clothes and beauty. Hah. Funny that. I like spending time with my gay friends without having a boy-friend insist on always coming along. I like . . .'

I trailed off and looked at Kev.

'What else?' he prodded. 'What do you want out of life?'

'I don't know,' I said grumpily. I sighed again. 'I like men. A man. One man. I'm definitely a one-man girl – the sex is better that way. Someone like John. Definitely no love! Not just yet anyway. Enough money for play. Sex. Dancing. Adventures. Entertaining. Keeping myself well maintained. Helping people with their problems. Pilates. Writing. Did I already say that? I probably said sex too. I dunno – that's it, I think.'

Kev was busily scribbling down my various answers. He stared at his jottings for a moment and then a huge smile spread across his face. He sat back in his chair and looked at me again, still smiling broadly, leaving me wondering if he should have smoked that last joint.

'What?' I said. I was over the fun and games. I just wanted to know what was so blatantly obvious that my best friend of twenty years was grinning like a Cheshire cat.

Kev just kept grinning. It was highly annoying.

'What?' I repeated, more sharply this time.

'Are you sure you want to hear it?' he said. 'You might not be open-minded enough.'

Bloody Kev. He knew me too well. I took the bait. Don't you hate that? Tricked by your own principles!

'Open-minded!' I spluttered. 'Of course I'm open-minded! I might be from the country, but I've been hanging around with you lot for over twenty years now. I've got a completely open mind, thank you very much.'

By 'you lot', I meant gay men. Kev was gay, as were most of my city friends. I did have straight friends, but they were mostly still in Port Stephens with teenage children and divorce settlements. My theory was that I was safe for queens and they were safe for me: the perfect recipe for harmless flirtation and outlandish behaviour. I also lived in Darlinghurst. That might have had a tad to do with it.

I glared at Kev.

'OK, OK,' he said, still grinning. 'You're not going to like it very much but I'll tell you anyway.'

He took a deep breath and looked at me.

'Why don't you become an escort? Get yourself a sugar daddy – some rich, married dude. You're beautiful and educated and you're good fun to be around. You have wonderful clothes. You can carry yourself anywhere. I suspect you'd be good in the sack – I could be wrong – either way, you could probably bluff it out. Your passport is current. You're well-informed. You're a babe! Some man is going to pay through the nose for the privilege of being with you, especially if you're recently hurt and not likely to fall in love again for a while. You can't hurt a heart that's already broken. You enjoy sex. If you found another man, you'd just be giving it away for free anyway. And then you'd probably have to be dishonest, because you wouldn't be able to tell him there's no chance of love.'

'Why not?' I demanded. 'I could get myself a fuck buddy. You guys all have them. Why not me?'

Kev regarded me sadly. 'Holly, do you honestly think you're the type of person that doesn't want the dinners and the spooning and the spoiling? You love those things. Fuck buddies are just for sex. You want a boyfriend without the strings. In my book, that's an *affair*.'

I stared at Kev. It could have been one of his funny jokes;

sometimes it was difficult to know whether he was serious or not. But Kev wasn't laughing.

An affair. A sugar daddy. I rolled the words off my tongue. It was so wicked. So irresistibly naughty. It was the kind of thing whispered in high school locker rooms and giggled about in playgrounds. We'd all joked about having a sugar daddy but no-one ever went through with finding one.

A strange ripple of excitement went through me as I thought about applicants applying for the position formerly held by John. It would almost be like revenge: I could replace him with a better model and yet be no threat to a marriage. A John who was *safe*.

I felt a boundary falling away. I think it had something to do with morality.

'Having a sugar daddy would just be another job,' Kev said. 'Sometimes you mightn't want to see him, but you'd have to anyway. There'd have to be chemistry, but that's the easy part for you – you can have anyone you want. Why not make a living out of it?'

'But would someone want me enough to pay for me?' I asked. 'There's a big difference between lusting after some-one and supporting them financially.'

'Is there? Isn't that what marriage is for? If anything, this is better than marriage because it has all of the benefits and none of the problems.' He laughed. 'It's probably a hell of a lot more honest too,' he said, reaching for the remains of the joint in the ashtray and lighting it.

One never knows how truly broadminded one is until one's broadmindedness is tested. This was my test. Sexual favours in return for money. Egad. My best friend was suggesting I become a prostitute!

'Kev,' I said, in that special guarded tone we used when one of us was So Wrong. 'You are –'

I shut my mouth. Apart from the wife issue – which was huge – I couldn't think of anything wrong with the idea. A case load with just one client. It suited my abilities, my money problems, my man problems, my sex problems, my writing aspirations. Sweet Goddess, it was so logical it was perfect!

'But I'm supposed to be a good girl,' I argued. 'My mother would say it was wrong; she'd remind me about the wives, for sure. She went through it herself with Dad. He'd sleep with anything that moved. Mental abuse, she called it. It was years before she trusted men again.'

But I could be different, I thought. I could do it as a service. I could help the men to help their wives. I might actually save marriages, not destroy them. The last thing I wanted was another John on my hands.

'Then Mum would lecture me about the ethics of the sex industry and tell me I was disempowering myself,' I continued aloud. 'She's right. It's impossible. I can't sell myself. I'm a professional. I've worked forty-hour weeks for the past seventeen years. I have a reputation to uphold. I even have a mortgage. You can't get any more respectable than that. No chance. Sorry, Kev, but you're way out of line this time.'

I glared at him for emphasis. Kev just grinned.

'It's crazy. It's wrong. I just can't do it,' I muttered, as if trying to convince myself.

'I'm sorry, Holly, but you're judging something you haven't even tried. You've always said you're open to new experiences, but I guess only the very open-minded could do this one. You'd never dare.' He raised his eyebrows mischievously.

I grabbed the joint from him and drew on it hard. He was waving a red rag to a bull with his stupid dare. Kev and I were going to out-devious each other one day and end up spontaneously combusting on barstools in a country bowling club drinking glasses of crème de menthe. I was reminded of the time I dragged the entire party out of our house to cheer Kev on while he vomited in the backyard. The bigger the hurl, the louder the cheer. Friends do that to each other. Friends like ours, anyway.

'But it's so wrong!'

Kev just shrugged.

The thing was, I knew I was being narrow-minded and, shit, I hated that. Not only did I hate narrow-mindedness, I was stupid enough to tell anyone within earshot how much I hated it. Loudly. Curse my mouth. I made a mental note to keep my opinions about anything even vaguely controversial to myself. Goddess help me if anyone ever remembered what I'd said once about dwarves.

My brain was in a state of shock because, deep down, I knew what Kev had said was true. Such a job *would* be perfect. It was the stigma that was the problem. But I was a psychologist. I was supposed to teach people how to cope with stigma. Not being able to face it myself would make me a hypocrite.

I took a long, deep breath and gazed at Kev.

'Doing what I do best,' I mused aloud. 'A set of attributes. Selection criteria. Thinking non-judgementally. Making $1000 by Tuesday to pay my mortgage. Another John. This time in a more honest way. I've already been on the Mistress Plan once – why not a second time? I've got to tell you, it's a possibility, Kev. If I am going to be truly non-judgemental, maybe this is a perfect solution.'

'Please tell me you're not serious,' Kev said, staring at me with wide eyes.

I began to feel excitement stirring. Maybe it was possible.

I grinned evilly at Kev.

'You're going to do it, aren't you?' he said, watching me closely. 'I was only joking.'

'Yeah, right,' I said. 'But jokes aren't so funny if they're based on the truth. You've made a very good suggestion, Kev. And if I do this, I'm going to remember you as my first pimp. My best friend. Thanks for that. Do you want twenty per cent of the takings?'

Kev didn't even have the grace to look horrified. Instead, he gave a wicked laugh.

Somebody stop us, I thought. This one was going to be hard to pay back. The pranks and dares got more outlandish every year. Maybe we really were going to end up dying together. We joked about it often enough. But if I went ahead and did it, if I got a sugar daddy and was good at it, Kev would have to eat his prank.

Suddenly I needed to be somewhere else. Where my brain could whirr wildly away in peace and not be caught up in plotting against Kev too. The funny thing was, there was a new spring in my step as I walked down the stairs. Finally, I had an option. It might not be a great option, but I was better off than yesterday. The world seemed like a brighter place.

By the time I got back to Darlinghurst, I'd worked out the hypothetical advertisement in my head:

Sugar Daddy sought by attractive, educated, well-spoken, 35-year-old professional woman. I live in Darlinghurst, in an air-conditioned unit on the seventeenth floor with fantastic skyline views to the harbour. The block features very discreet and secure undercover guest parking, although I have a reliable car and am prepared to travel to surrounding suburbs. I am aiming for exclusivity so will (theoretically) be available to you 24/7. I am single and don't have any children. Most of my friends are gay. I am a fabulous cook and can provide gourmet meals should you require them. I will enjoy keeping the fridge stocked with your favourite foods and beverages – there is nothing better than spoiling a person and whisking your needs straight out of your head and into reality. I am a qualified psychologist so I make an excellent listener and have a great love for intellectual conversation. I also enjoy socialising and am a beautiful, clever and charming companion in just about any situation. I LOVE sex and there's not much I don't enjoy. I also give a great massage! I will require a generous weekly allowance in return for all of the above.

I flung myself at my computer as soon as I got home, practically ranting with impatience as it took a whole minute to warm up. Then I googled 'Sugar Daddy Wanted'. Of the 117 supposedly Australian references, there was only one local website dealing with the employment of sugar daddies. Called 'Persona', it appeared to be mostly free classified advertisements, a large proportion of which fitted into the Personals category. There were five people already advertising for a sugar daddy, all of them men seeking men. I didn't click on them. I didn't even search through the site. To be honest, I didn't want to. Perhaps it was because I didn't want to see the kind of person I was considering becoming. Or maybe I was frightened of knowing my competition. But it was probably because I didn't want to think too much about what I was doing.

Instead, I followed the wizard's prompts to place my own ad, cursing when it was slow or I'd typed the wrong thing. A terrible sense of urgency took over. I couldn't get the words out fast enough. An all-encompassing need to get my hypothetical ad drafted just in case I wanted to hypothetically post it and follow through on this crazy, hypothetical thing.

It took me five minutes to type the ad and an hour to proof it. I re-read it at least ten times out loud. I took out the part about my gay friends, as I didn't want a boyfriend involved in my social life anyway, and I added a photo taken at a masked dance party a couple of months earlier. It was a truly beautiful mask that I had lucked upon in a local Venetian store. All golden twirls and diamantes, with me looking anonymously sexy beneath it.

Anonymously sexy. I pondered that. It was no wonder the internet was such a hit: it was the perfect vehicle for faceless sex. Or lies. I'd put my age as thirty-five. I was actually thirty-nine, but the reality was, I appeared younger. Didn't that make my lie more honest than the truth?

Sarcasm aside, my heart was pounding. I was considering entering the sex industry, crossing a forbidden threshold. I told myself a mistake was just a lesson with hindsight. Then I took a deep breath and posted the ad.

I returned to the homepage and ran a search on my criteria. Yep. There I was. My photo was huge. I should have realised it would be much bigger than the words. How embarrassment, as Effie would say.

I read the ad several more times, then I ran another search, this time just scrolling through the personals to see what else there was. Not a single other advertisement like mine. The men seeking men were only a couple of lines each and certainly no sexy photos in masks. Whoops.

I ran a general search using Yahoo and key words. Thirty-six hits later, I was at the end of the list and there was no sign of my ad. I was kind of relieved. Maybe it hadn't made the search engines.

Before logging out, I checked my mailbox. Oh my goodness, there was a response already! From a 'Snakeboy' with the subject line 'Sugared Daddy'. Holy shit.

I did what every sane person does in times of stress. I ran away. I turned off my computer, got under my doona and shivered as if it wasn't the middle of summer. But the really worrying thing was that the shivers didn't feel bad at all. They were shivers of excitement.

I was out of control. What was I doing? I was selling out feminism. Had prostitution been one of my soapboxes? I couldn't remember. I even knew all the words to 'I am A Woman'. Were feminists against prostitution or for it? I couldn't remember that either. I guessed they supported whatever empowered the woman.

Whatever empowered the woman. So that's what this strange feeling was – empowerment! How bizarre. Who'd have thought such a thing could possibly feel empowering? But I was the employer. I was the one doing the hiring. That made me the boss. I was selecting them, and I could also sack them, I thought. I am choosing my mate and he is going to pay for the privilege. What's so wrong about that?

A low, sexy moan escaped me. I felt incredibly turned on. Whoa. That shouldn't be happening, should it? I thought about the unknown response sitting in my inbox and making me as horny as hell. I couldn't understand what was making me react in such a way! I was meant to be turning on the men, not the other way around. I felt hotter and sexier than I had ever felt before. John had never made me feel like this, and I'd been in love with him. I'd never got off on porn in my life! Yet here I was, the daughter of Mrs South Port Stephens, feeling horny because I'd put myself up for sale to rich men.

Darn that 'I'm bitter, twisted and sick' button I'd worn at high school. And the 'We are the people our parents warn us against' badge. (Mum, to her great credit, faithfully replaced them on my tunic every time she washed and ironed it, and it was a good twelve months before they started to rust and make stains on my uniform.) Maybe I had somehow fated myself with those buttons. Maybe I was finally on life's true path. Maybe this was why I was a late maturer sexually – if I had been like this at eighteen, I would have been locked up!

And so I stopped worrying and did what any potentially bad girl does in a stressful situation. I masturbated.

Interestingly, I slept with the grace of angels that night. I was proud of myself: not only had I faced my own limits of open-mindedness and burst through them, I had found a logical solution to a dire predicament. I had been so busy trying not to judge other people that I had almost forgotten to not judge myself.

# CHAPTER 3

The next morning, there was a long list of responses to my advertisement. What did these men do? Spend half the night on their computers when they were supposed to be spooning their wives? A lot of them had reply times of 2 a.m. or later! Perhaps insomnia was more widespread than I thought.

I gazed at my monitor and the inbox full of unexciting user names. Not a single 'Axe-Wielding Maniac' amongst them. It was the subject lines that made me cringe:

*I will be your sugar daddy*

*A man for all reasons*

*Horny as hell*

*Casual employment*

Taking a very deep breath, I clicked on the first one. Once. Could a Trojan-horse-thingy be triggered merely by selecting a message? What would happen once I hit the reply button? Should I update my spyware? Did the site give them my personal email address? Oh good grief, my name is in that address! It's a common name. Get over it.

I gritted my teeth and prepared myself to read all the sick and twisted replies that such an act of sheer audacity and pure hussiness surely deserved. What if they wanted to have sex with me first? No way! Payment in advance. What if I was a dud fuck? How would I feel? What if they stalked me or raped me? Would clicking on their replies somehow grant them access to my innermost secrets and desires?

I opened the first message.

Hello to you, I am a profesional male in my mid 40s. Tall with an athletic medium build. It would be a pleasure to discuss your needs further with you. Do you either have a contact number or if you prefer please call on ——. Looking foward to it. David

Not so bad. Couldn't spell, though. I opened the next few.

I always like the chase, spontanaity and the unexpected and you sound like an adventurer as well. I like the location as well. I am near Town Hall . . . is that handy for you? Please let me know and we can move quickly. Cheers Barry

hi there, you are so beautiful. what nationality are you? i am single and 19. would i be able to see you? i can send you a pic if you like. thanks :)

hey i want to be your suger daddy. what do you expect? what are the conditions? bill

Hi, saw your ad. I am in my 30s and would be keen on speaking to you further on what sort of arrangement you want. live in / live out / occasional visit / etc. Also, what are you thinking in terms of $$$? Cheers, Marcus

Am looking for a good time tonight, what are you up for? Hamish

It was almost a let-down in a way. I felt relieved, but disconcerted at the same time. How strange that we were merely adults discussing a business arrangement. It seemed so incredibly civilised! None of them seemed to be lustful louts looking for virtual prey that they could trace through the telephone lines and spy on through air-conditioning vents. They were just ordinary men writing business emails, responding to what I was beginning to suspect was a rather extraordinary offer.

I wished I'd searched the term 'sugar daddy' itself and found out what the expectations were. Surely the world must be full of educated, attractive women with wallflower tendencies and surprisingly good posture who sold themselves on free classifieds websites.

One world-wide Google search later, I was scrolling through exactly ten definitions of 'sugar daddy'. 'A gentleman who spoils a woman with pampering and gifts, often money, in return for sexual and other favours' was the consensus.

Then I studied the people who were advertising. There were distressingly few. Most of the ads said things like 'Sugar daddy needed to pamper me' and provided a phone number. None were as detailed as mine. What was more, I'd assumed *I* had to do the pampering. Apparently *he* was the one that was supposed to do that. I'd got it completely the wrong way around.

I laughed at myself. I had stumbled upon an entirely new concept: *they* buy the spoiling and the pampering. Why not? A new profession is born out of Kev's bloody open-mindedness. Unemployment problems are solved. Men are happy. Wives are grateful that their discarded lover's attentions are being diverted. I didn't even want him for keeps; I just wanted to borrow him for a while. LOCAL WOMAN ABOLISHES ALL STIGMA, the Port Stephens news headlines would proclaim. ALL WARS CEASE. EVERYONE HAPPY.

I smiled to myself. I had somehow captured these men's imaginations. Imagination was such a wonderful place to be. Then I thought, darn their imagination! It was mine that needed capturing. Capturing and putting in someone else's body for a while. What was it cooking up now? I must be kinky!

Perverted, at least. Why was I feeling so fantastic? When would the guilt kick in?

I opened another response.

Hello, I just was a bit fascinated by your advertisement and was wondering why you were seeking financial compensation for everything you listed when you are also a qualified psychologist as well as working in PR in the past? Excuse me if that's a bit personal, I don't actually expect an answer, but I'm not trying to be rude at all, I really am curious . . . Secondly, I thought of a fairly ludicrous proposition for you if you'd indulge me for a moment . . . I am 30 years old, and have a whole lot of trouble ever meeting any women who I find intellectually stimulating, especially of my own age, and my interests are actually in areas such as psychology, spirituality, philosophy and such, and a dream scenario in a way would be to have a smart and success- ful, slightly older Sugar 'Mama'! Now, given you're seeking the opposite, this is probably where you'll click on the 'close' button to read a message from a well-heeled lonely gentleman in his 50s, but honestly, before you do, you have a beautiful smile in your photograph and if everything you said in your ad is true, then you must be intelligent and interesting too, if for no other reason than having placed this ad! Being interested in things that I often don't share with girls my age, it's often very frustrating because also I am a very sexual creature as well. So: is there any way you would be interested in any type of arrangement with an intellectually starved guy who has a lot of sensual and erotic energy to offer as well as anything else? I also love giving massages and would love to experiment with varying forms of sensuality and intimacy with a suitable woman who knows what she likes and does not like . . . Perhaps you could teach me what you like and vice versa? Well, anyhow, reading some books written in the past, I sometimes came across mentions of situations where women were given allowances by men and had furnished studios etc, but also sometimes where a woman would have a suitable younger man come in and provide company and laughter and sex and fun, in exchange not for money necessarily, but just as a way of giving something to the man, teaching him things and providing an outlet and perhaps guidance in aspects of his life, and in return she got to have the company of someone smart, artistic and young who was full of enthusiasm!

Goodbye for now, and probably for ever as I won't hear from you I suspect, but it would really be exciting to see what you might have to say about my crazy proposition, which I hope you don't find rude or too outrageous . . . It is late at night, and I don't know you at all, but your ad just really hit some kind of nerve in my imagination and I couldn't resist, and I can say that I am good fun and a very fast learner with almost everything! Thanks. Goodbye again.

Then there was the other end of the spectrum:

Hi. Would you be interested in roleplaying as mom. If so, let me know and we can talk further. Chemistry awaits. Snakeboy.

It was amazingly easy to sort the wheat from the chaff. There was something about the 'executese' language wealthy men used – even if they wrote only a sentence, it showed. How strange that all of these amazing men wanted something only I could provide! It was no different from internet dating. Proposals for coffee in a public place. An obsession with 'chemistry'. Was that a politeism for was I good-looking enough? Sexy enough?

All day, I worked on a standard reply. This time I would include the price. *My* price. I fretted over that. How much was I worth? I had negotiated half a dozen salaries in boardrooms and hoped I drove a hard bargain, but strongly suspected I was a pushover. This was different. My rent and mortgage were $650 a week. I needed money urgently. I also had to maintain a champagne lifestyle if I was going to entertain these men in the manner to which they were accustomed. So I took a deep breath and mentally placed a $1000-a-week sticker on my forehead. I needed $1000-a-week minimum to live, I said. Cash. In advance.

Hi _____. I have been working for many years in high-level corporate positions and took the past three months off to write a novel. Unfortunately, my savings have run out mid-manuscript and I am determined to finish it. I am both open-minded and a lateral thinker – hence the idea to do what I do best (spoil people), support myself and continue writing all at the same time.

As per my ad, I live in Darlinghurst in an apartment on the top floor of my building with fantastic skyline views. I will provide a keycard to my undercover guest parking, which means you get 24/7 parking in Darlinghurst whenever you want it. I have a reliable car and am prepared to travel to surrounding suburbs, although I would prefer to mostly meet you in my own home. I am aiming for exclusivity (i.e. I'm a one-man girl!) so will (theoretically) be available to you 24/7. However, I would prefer to see you mainly on weekdays, although would be willing to go away for weekends, etc.

I am single and don't have any children. I am also a fabulous cook and can provide gourmet meals should you require them. I really enjoy hosting guests and am well known for my fabulous dinner parties. (I also like nothing better than arranging a gourmet picnic in the sunshine.) I will enjoy keeping the fridge stocked with your favourite foods and beverages and creating a comfortable space for you to relax and unwind. I am a qualified psychologist so I make an excellent listener and have a great love for intellectual conversation. I believe that reality is based on perception and that you can change your reality merely by altering your perception of it. I used to specialise in treating depression and improving motivation and self-esteem. I enjoy socialising and am a charming companion in any situation – either one on one or networking a room at an important black-tie function. I LOVE sex and am very open-minded. If you have any fantasies, we might have fun fulfilling them!

I cost a minimum of $1000 a week to live and would require this in advance (Moet and lobster meals extra!). It may also be a good idea to make the first week a trial.

Cheers, Holly

I cut and pasted the reply to all of my enquirers and hoped they wouldn't be rolling on the floor laughing (ROTFL) at my expense.

I would like to say now came the wait, but there wasn't a wait at all – some of them replied immediately, plus there was a constant stream of new enquiries, to which I replied with my $1000 message.

I spent most of the next twenty-four hours at the computer. Night and day were equally busy. Emails flew.

Many who couldn't afford $1000, or baulked at the arrangement, simply didn't email back. This in itself amazed me: not a single person abused me for my audacity or price. If they did reply again, it was with politely worded disappointment and regret.

I was left with a much smaller group of men who indicated they were still interested. The money inserted a barrier between the haves and the have nots. The men who came back to me were educated and not at all aghast at the thought of paying someone a grand a week to be at their beck and call. They were replying to my emails between important meetings with the members of the board. How could someone with so much money in their pocket be bored? How could they not gaze out their cityscape windows and gasp at what was available to them? How was it that an ordinary woman sitting in a tiny apartment could so distract them from their important lives?

Above all, I couldn't help wondering what had happened to morality and fidelity. They had always been so important to me. When was I going to start feeling nervous or bad about this?

Normally my conscience ran riot; why was it being so quiet now?

I gave up wondering and began to individually tailor my responses.

Hi Holly, What a delightful proposition. How fascinatin'. I am thinking I should buy you lunch so we can mentally undress each other with witty conversation fuelled by the anticipation of possible sexual inevitability. Realistically, it's a lot easier for me to know I can arrange for your living expenses to be met than it is for you to know I am the one you want paying them. For me an issue bigger than meeting expenses is to be sure I won't want to buy you outright. I have attached a pic. You can see I am an older-than-you-are guy, by some years. Let me know if lunch sounds like a good idea to you. Cheers, Roger

Hi Roger, To be completely honest, I have a lot of self-worth – I'm not sure that you could afford to buy me outright ;0 Thank you for your photo. You appear to be an extremely attractive man. I have absolutely no problem with older men – in fact, I find them far sexier than younger ones because (and this is probably inherent in being a psychologist) I find stimulation of the intellect to be one of the greatest turn-ons of all. (Not to mention the fact that you make far superior lovers!) Besides, age is one of those states of perception I was talking about. I have not a single regret in my life (the nasty things provided valuable lessons) and would not trade a year of learning merely for a numerical value. Lunch sounds wonderful – weekdays are best for me. I attach a couple of photos of myself to return the favour. Cheers, Holly

And another:

Hi there, Have read your ad with interest and would like to offer the following option. You appear to be looking for a 'full-time' situation and I am sure you will get many responses. However, if none of your respondents matches your expectations and you are prepared to look at a 'part-time' (e.g. 1 or 2 days per week) arrangement then I would be very happy to put myself forward. Although I am in a committed relationship I am not intending to change this, at least not in the short-term. We are still very close friends, but the physical activity has dropped off recently – the result of some medical conditions my partner has endured recently which have diminished her sex drive. Hence I am searching for an alternative, discreet arrangement for which I am prepared to pay. About myself: I am a 50-something, university-educated guy who only works part-time these days. My days in corporate life ended a few years back and I lead a less stressful lifestyle working for myself to pay the bills and keep my mind active. The two children are grown-up and no longer at home. I live in an apartment close to the city. I am 5'10'', 80 kgs, well travelled, fit, a good conversationalist and have a good sense of humour, so others tell me. My ex also claimed that my best feature was my legs – maybe that does not say much about the rest though! Please let me know if my suggestion is of interest and if you would like to discuss it in more detail. Good luck in your quest. Regards, Mel

Dear Mel, I am terribly sorry, but I am offering exclusivity to the person I eventually choose and would not be in a position to engage in any 'part-time' endeavours. This is mainly because I have always been a one-man-at-a-time girl and would find it incredibly difficult to juggle the needs of several people at once. You do, however, sound like a wonderful person and I am confident you will find the woman you seek. Good luck for the future and best wishes in your search. Cheers, Holly

They all sounded so surprisingly nice. Out of the hundred or so emails I received, the only one I didn't reply to was Snakeboy's and that was mainly because of his user name – I'd always been afraid of snakes.

So, with barely any money to my name, no food in the

cupboards, a desk full of unpaid bills and a mortgage repay-
ment due in a week, I embarked upon the first steps of a career
that the whole of society frowns upon. The naughtiest job I
could possibly think of but with the potential to be the most
rewarding. I was not only smashing personal boundaries, I was
also embracing social stigma for the very first time in my life.
Me, the girl who had only had fiercely monogamous partnerships and a country-girl upbringing. And the really weird thing
about it was that I still felt like a good person inside. Was this
the greatest cover-up of all time? Were women so oppressed
that we had denied ourselves the very thing that would
empower us? After all, when you thought about it, the host
should always have more power than the guest.

Most importantly, I had finally found men like John. If only
he knew how much I missed him.


When I walked down to the shops I couldn't wipe the smile off
my face. I felt sexier than I had in years. I masturbated several
times a day. Nearly every man looked at me when I swept past.
For the first time in my life, I looked back. I'd always felt slightly
violated before; now I gave them a secret, sexy glimpse of a
smile instead. A smile that came from the realisation that men
wanted to pay to be with me. I was desirable. I was wanted. I
wasn't a joke. I was a commodity.

I continued to respond to the enquiries. In the end, my
advertisement scored a total of 11,000 hits. Some of the more
promising ones turned out to be let-downs, while some of the
less attractive offers were merely a result of English being their
second language.

The long-awaited reply from 'Roger' finally came. I grinned
with wicked delight at his words. It felt exhilarating to be
discussing such matters. Once again, I was amazed at my
reaction. What if I'd read these very words two years ago in Port
Stephens? What would I have thought then? I would have been

horrified, probably. But here I was, the same person, discussing fetishes like they were endearing personal hobbies.

Hi Holly, The exploration of the mind of a woman is such a wonderful thing. One can tingle and pulse with a woman's nipple at one's fingertips, but a woman's mind in full flight is captivating. I find your training as a psychologist at once alluring and daunting. I once found myself in the bedroom of a charming Brisbane woman following a night's frivolities. Approximately coincident with us undressing, she told me she was a sex therapist or some such. It is the only time in my life that I have experienced erectile dysfunction – despite the naked and willing presence of a woman with commendable physical qualities! I have often wondered whether it could have been the rather outdated furniture in her bedroom that was the cause.

My reference to owning you was not to belittle or question your self-worth. A man completely won over by a woman seeks her ownership, as I see it, however that manifests itself. I have over the past 10 years or so taken a keen interest in the various activities that fall under the generic heading of BDSM. I have found it of interest more for the philosophies that lie behind the motivations of those who practise it than for the physical activities. That is not to say that I have not enjoyed tying a naked woman bent at the waist chest down on a table with her arms raised above her head and fastened to the far end, then taking the cane to her bare behind, and then as her bottom quivers from the shock of the pain, taking advantage of her vulnerability and surprising wetness for my selfish pleasure. At the heart of BDSM is the essential notion of domination and submission, and it seems to me that this is an issue that everyone should focus on when a relationship is formed. For me, in my stage of life, I very much favour the role of the dominant, and enjoy the company of a woman submissive by choice and nature. At the extreme is the notion of master and slave – to the extent that the law allows – and it was in that sense somewhat self-indulgently I referred to possibly wanting to buy you outright. People who like BDSM are very boring to people who don't and I am not committed to either BDSM or vanilla. Like you, I am supposing, I like to be fluid in philosophical thought.

I have an office in North Sydney. I have quite a lot on this week and at this stage only Friday looks like a starter for lunch. I look forward to it happening as soon as it can be made to happen. I hope you can wait until then. I am sure you are overwhelmed with replies to your Persona ad. Your pics were much appreciated and admired. I see how beautiful you are. Cheers, Roger

Hi Roger, I am humbled yet at the same time strangely excited by your response (amidst concern for my bedroom furniture). :) I say humbled because I am proud to say that I have never said no to a new experience, but I have yet to say yes to this one – not because of existing prejudices, but rather because of a lack of opportunity. To be honest, you have made me feel narrow-minded for perhaps one of the first times in my life. It is not a pleasant feeling and is one I will have to change . . . However, whether you would be willing to accommodate a BDSM 'virgin' (with doubtful bedroom furniture) is another question entirely! For the record, I certainly wasn't offended by your offer to buy me outright – if one has true self-worth such a statement is flattering rather than insulting and I was merely concerned for your bank balance :) Indeed, as an observer of human nature, best friend of gay men and former confidante of some of Sydney's worst psychotics, I have heard many shocking things. But the thought of a quivering bottom resonates – perhaps the vulnerability of a first timer would further increase your pleasure . . . I have always agreed it is a fine line between pleasure and pain.

I would still be delighted to have lunch with you. Cheers, Holly

By the end of the week, I had set up meetings with five men, all of whom sounded educated, successful and able to afford me.

# CHAPTER 4

Hello, I would like to enquire as to your advertisement for the position of Sugar Daddy. I am a 42 year old man, and am currently living in the western suburbs. Firstly i would like to point out that your issue of a generous weekly allowance is of no concern to me, as i am currently employed in a fairly senior position with a major Sydney law firm. Due to the nature of my profession, ones reputation is invaluable, and as such i would prefer to remain anonymous for the moment. The main drawcard of your advertisement is that you state that you are an articulate and educated woman, a fact which I hope proves to be true, as i value intelligence highly in a woman. I presume that you have a high sex drive, this would be a mandatory requirement for me and as such i do not wish to proceed with this if you do not. I would like to hear more about your background and interests, and i would also like to see some more photos of you. If you would be kind enough to oblige I would at least like to see a full body shot, and a photo of your face minus a mask. Essentially what i am looking for is an attractive, intelligent woman, who can ease the stress of a long day, minus the attachments and responsibilities that a relationship carries. I hope that this is what you are offering. If you have not already acquired someone to fulfil your needs, please reply as promptly as possible with the answers to my queries and requests, and we shall take things from there. Warmest regards, David

Dear David, Relieving the stress of a long day minus attachments is indeed what I am offering. To be completely honest with you, I have been recently badly hurt in love and it is one of the reasons why I am proposing such an arrangement – I enjoy spoiling a man but I want to do so without the risks of love. Please find attached photos. The best way to go forward would be to meet somewhere 'neutral' and discuss things face to face. Cheers, Holly

Dear Holly, Thank you for your photos, you are a gorgeous creature indeed. Things are very busy for me at work at the moment – would you mind terribly driving out to the west and meeting at my local on Friday over a couple of drinks? David

Dear David, Whilst I envisage most of the arrangement being conducted in my own home, I would be delighted to have drinks with you. When and where do you propose? Cheers, Holly

As I drove out to Parramatta I tried not to think too much about the man I was about to meet. Surely he was a pervert.

It was hard to believe I was driving to an unknown pub to meet a stranger who wanted to buy me. Not just my professional skills. He was going to pay for all of the other things I did well too. Like cooking, and massages, and conversation. And sex.

*Whoosh!*

I had manicured and pedicured myself to perfection and washed my hair earlier in the day – along with the sheets, the windows, the bathroom and even my little bedside drawer that was full of condoms past their use-by dates. I knew David wasn't coming to my place, but it was more of a symbolic cleansing than anything else.

I pushed down my self-doubts and thought about my wonderful gift of conversational bluffery. I took deep breaths and convinced myself I was doing the right thing. Even the worst possible outcome would be a learning experience. Suffering develops your character and all that. Embrace your lessons, Holly. For the first time I'd get to be the chooser rather than the choosee. I'd had relationships before, but this was the first time I'd got to conduct interviews. The final decision was up to me.

The girl in my bedroom mirror had seemed gorgeous but I still found it difficult to believe she was me. What if they didn't think me good-looking? What if they judged me to have an average face? What if they considered me too old? Maybe they were impotent. Maybe they'd want receipts so they could claim me on MBF.

What was it about me that these men desired? Maybe I was conducting the only real 'full service' on the planet. With every little bit of me. Multiple dimension employment. I should start an agency.

As I drove, thoughts raced through my mind. Don't let him drug you; don't give away any freebies; don't get into his car; stay in the public eye; ask the barman not to let you leave with him if you appear unconscious; smile a lot.

Leaving more than enough time for traffic, minor road collapses and terrorist attacks, I arrived forty-five minutes early after a near-perfect run. The road went right past our meeting place. It was just as well. I had a severe map-reading deficiency and was totally unable to drive and turn the Gregory's around at the same time.

I cased out the pub from the KFC opposite. I sat and ate popcorn chicken and drank Diet Coke and hoped that I wasn't smudging my lipstick. I watched the pub's car park start to fill. A man in a suit paced out the front. Was it him? I hoped not. He appeared old and stressed. Worse still, I thought he belonged to the old Holden nearby. People who had old

Holdens couldn't afford $1000 a week, not if they drove them, anyway. Rich men kept mint-condition Holdens in the garage alongside Harley Davidsons and other things they rarely used.

At 6.45 p.m. the man in the suit disappeared inside. Please, don't let it be him.

At 6.55 I checked my lipstick again in the toilets then drove to my rendezvous. Rendezvous! Now there was a word that I hadn't used often in my life. It was so very, very new! I was tingling all over with excitement.

I entered the car park, did a perfect reverse park, checked my lippy again and walked inside: 7 p.m. on the dot.

The place was a dive. The beer garden looked like the Port Stephens Bowling Club during the finals for the Ladies Major Singles. I should know. I'd been to every one for the past five years. Once I got drunk there with Mum and we carved it on the dance floor at three in the afternoon. It was Mother's Day, and when all the other mothers saw how much fun mine was having, they wanted to dance too. There was even a lady with a walking frame having a bit of a wiggle. Was that why alcohol was so popular – because it impaired our judgement? On the other hand, we were *supposed* to be non-judgemental. It didn't make sense.

I scanned the main room with ease. I'd been meeting people in pubs for more years than I cared to admit. I walked up to the bar, doing the old 'scan the room and look-at-your-watch' trick. This announces to the gathered throng that you are not a Nigel-No-Friends and that you are, in fact, meeting someone at a pre-arranged time. Whether or not this is true is irrelevant. It allows you to suss everyone out and no-one hassles you. Pub etiquette.

As I stood waiting to be served, I continued to search the bar. There was one man sitting by himself, but he was finishing dinner, so I got my own vodka and soda (to avoid being drugged) and propped myself on a stool facing the door. I felt like the proverbial shag on a rock. It was wall-to-wall flannelette shirts and I was like a creature from another planet in my trendiest inner-city attire: tight black trousers, loose-flowing, long filmy black top showing off the merest hint of cleavage, and shiny black patent-leather shoes.

Zero points for clothes and venue choice. Note to self: never meet in a bar again. Never meet beyond walking distance of home. I'm conducting the interviews; they can come to me.

Trying to seem casual, I texted David telling him I was 'here'. In a couple of moments he replied and said he was running a few minutes late. I quaffed my vodka nervously and reminded myself not to let him buy me a drink.

I flicked my hair over my shoulders and picked at my fingernails. I must have rearranged myself on the stool a thousand times.

Then David walked in.

I knew it was him immediately. The look of a man searching for someone is very different from the look of the man who has already found them.

He wasn't the man in the suit. He didn't look like a pervert. Come to think of it, he didn't even appear particularly affluent. He was dressed in very ordinary black trousers and a generic polo shirt. His shoes were highly polished but unspectacular. He had sandy thinning hair and a slim build with a small beer belly. His skin had that slightly reddened look of a man who'd spent too many years in the sun before realising what it was doing to his capillaries. I'd never been good with ages but I guessed he was in his mid to late fifties.

'Holly?' he asked, looking pleased at what he saw. That in itself was a relief. *This will be a positive experience* started like a mantra in my head. Anything can be positive with enough hindsight, even only for the fact that you're still alive and you've chosen not to die yet.

He was so very ordinary. So very unassuming. I could walk all over this man and I wouldn't be chopped into little pieces. I was glad I hadn't asked the barman to keep an eye on us.

'Hi! How are you? Why don't you get a drink? I'm fine.' I nodded at my glass and watched him walk over to the bar.

During my relationship with John, I'd met a lot of his friends, most of whom were in the millionaire to zillionaire bracket. There was something about the walk, the movements, the style of dress of wealthy men and David wasn't exhibiting any of them. I hoped he could afford me. I tried to recall his reaction to my price. Maybe he'd just wanted to meet me, to see the woman who had the audacity to charge men $1000 a week.

As I studied him, it was hard not to judge him. I told myself I had no right. I was a woman who couldn't pay her bills and had to be nice to strange men who appeared obsessed with sex far later than Nature intended. This was not about judgements, I reminded myself. This was about survival.

When David returned from the bar we took a couple of lounges in the corner and I began the bluffery perfected so long ago with John. I prattled on about things that had seemed to attract John, like the beauty of the world and what a thrilling place it was. David was very unforthcoming. I hoped he was captivated, but perhaps he was just amazed that I could babble so much.

When he offered to get us another drink I asked for a still water (so I could see any pills at the bottom) and watched his hands closely while he was at the bar. I needn't have worried. Anyone into spiking drinks and raping women sure wouldn't have been able to do it at this pub. The place had more light than the Sydney Cricket Ground.

I gave him one of my best smiles when he returned but I couldn't help thinking there was none of the 'chemistry' that so many of my correspondents had alluded to. I hoped he wasn't the best of a bad bunch.

'So what kind of sex do you enjoy?' David asked suddenly, leaning forward as if to catch every word of my reply.

I would like to say I was thrown by this question, but I'd been expecting it and my answer was well-rehearsed.

'Well, I'm into most things,' I told him. 'Except pain and animals. And I don't like the thought of anyone too young. But I think sex is healthy. Babies aside, it's about pleasure and having orgasms. It's about getting your rocks off. I sometimes wish women could think about sex more like men do; maybe then there'd be a lot fewer cheating husbands.'

Curse my big mouth! He probably was a cheating husband. Note to self: don't use the 'C' word again!

'Yeah. My wife's a bit like that,' David told me gloomily. 'Getting a screw out of her is like extracting teeth. Frigid bitch. We've been on and off for a long time now, but she's still taking me for every dollar I've got.'

I cringed. Where was the politeness of his emails? Maybe he only *wrote* Executese and couldn't speak it. I couldn't help leaping to her defence. 'But what about your children? They're yours too. Surely you're happy to pay for them?'

'We couldn't have any,' he replied. 'Besides, I made my bucks before I met her fucking twenty years ago! Apparently she's still entitled to half of it, though. Stupid cow.' He glowered into his drink.

So his wife was like me, but less honest about it. She was getting money from this man she didn't love for services she wasn't even performing. It was no wonder I had found marriage so elusive; or maybe men just didn't want to risk divorce any more.

'Maybe she deserves the money for looking after you,' I couldn't help saying. 'Twenty years is a long time. Perhaps she's just bored. It's no wonder when you think about it. I mean, the average erect penis is, what, about 15 centimetres long? Let's be generous and call it 20. And a normal fuck is what – a hundred thrusts? That means the average root is 2 metres long! And if you fuck the same penis say three times a week? That's 6 metres! Multiply that by roughly fifty weeks a year and you've got a whopping 300 metres. So if you've been married faithfully for twenty years, it means your wife's had 6 kilometres of the same cock – it's no wonder she's over it! When you think about it, you wouldn't want to travel up and down the same stretch of road over and over again – why on earth would you want to do the same thing with a penis?'

I studied David closely. My psychobabble was working – he was grinning broadly and enjoying the analogy.

'You should talk to my fucking wife,' he said. 'By the way, do you swallow?' He leaned forward and licked his lips, staring at my chest.

Darn my hint of cleavage!

'Sure,' I lied. 'There's not too much I won't put in my mouth.'

It was true. Well, kind of. But I hoped it wasn't my foot again.

'I'll bet you do.' He leered at me. I didn't dare glance at his crotch but I was willing to bet he had a hard-on.

'Well . . . er . . . I'm going to have to go shortly,' I said, wincing inwardly. 'A couple of quick questions. Do you want me to come out here all the time or can you meet at my place? Are you interested in daytimes or evenings?'

I'd thought about these things a lot. I wanted someone who would come to my place, preferably during the day. Someone with a wife to go home to. Someone who wouldn't be constantly camped on my doorstep. Someone I wouldn't have to get half-drunk with to enjoy their company. Someone who didn't need me to drive anywhere.

'Definitely evenings,' David replied. 'And some stayovers at my place, so we can have all night.'

He licked his lips again – I hadn't noticed how thin they were until now. It was hard not to grimace.

'Er . . . what about meals? Would you like me to cook for you as well? What do you like to eat?'

'Italian. Pasta,' he said. 'But I'm mostly interested in the sex.'

He probably didn't realise you could eat women too. I suspected this man wasn't good for the hips or the lips.

'Well, you've got my telephone number. You've met me. Have a think about it. I've got some more . . . meetings next week. I'll let you know my decision by next Friday. I want whoever it is to start on the following Monday – $1000 payable in advance.'

Phew. I'd said it! All of the things a lady isn't supposed to say. Sex for money and all that. Good girls were meant to get those things by marrying and then shutting their legs 6 kilometres later.

'I'll think about it over the weekend,' said David. 'In fact, I'll be thinking about you a lot from now on.'

I gave him a quick peck on the lips, trying to hide my disdain, and he walked out ahead of me. I went to the ladies' toilet, replaced my lipstick and washed my hands in the same way a surgeon might before performing open-heart surgery without gloves. Then I sat on the loo for a while with my chin in my hands and hoped that I hadn't made a terrible mistake.

As I headed back down the M4, my phone beeped. It was David. 'I forgot to ask you, wanna fuck?' he said.

I gagged.

'Sorry, but how do I know if you're genuine?' I replied coolly. 'I need to see your money in my account first. I'm on the freeway, I've got to go.'

It was the last I ever heard from him.

# CHAPTER 5

Please contact me. I am interested to chat about an arrangement. Richard

I sent him my standard reply. His response was almost immediate:

Hi Holly. Thanks for the reply. Yes, I am interested. It must be exclusive as I have a very prestigious position in a major financial company. Before I call you, could you send me a couple of photos? Best wishes, Richard

Hi Richard, I have attached a couple of photos for you. Being new to this, I do not have more explicit ones. Exclusivity and discretion will be very much guaranteed. Cheers, Holly

Holly, Thank you. I was not expecting explicit photos. You appear attractive and quite petite. Nice. Are you available to meet up this morning over a coffee for a chat? If so, I will ring to arrange. Best wishes, Richard

I walked into this second meeting with some trepidation. I desperately hoped he wouldn't be another David. This time, I'd arranged to meet within 50 metres of my apartment, at a Starbucks. Up there with McDonald's and town halls as pre-arranged meeting places between people who don't know each other.

Once again, I'd dressed very carefully, taking an entirely different approach to the one I had with David. This time I wanted to appear businesslike rather than sexy. This was about earning an income, after all.

Richard was standing out the front looking at his watch. He seemed stressed, as if the person he was meeting was running late, yet I was exactly on time. He might have had a neon light flashing over his head so obvious was he amongst the morning café-goers.

I breezed up to him. 'Richard?' I asked.

He looked happy and relieved. 'Call me Dick. All my friends do,' he said in an American accent. 'Let's go in, shall we?'

A John called Dick! Kev was going to love this.

He led me in the door and squinted up at the menu board, eventually getting out a pair of spectacles and putting them on. I smiled to myself. I'd done exactly the same thing before I got contact lenses. He continued to act on edge. How bizarre that he wanted to impress me and that I clearly made him nervous! I hated to admit it, but it felt bloody good after all those years in offices when men like him had made *me* nervous and always made a point of correcting my work. I think it was at that point I really began to enjoy myself. It was so good to have the upper hand for once.

Dick was everything that David was not. Although he was dressed in casuals (his day off), his watch was expensive and the ubiquitous polo shirt was Ralph Lauren. But still he didn't move like John did. He lacked the 'I Can Buy You Or Anything You Have' look that came from years of privilege. I suspected that Dick had worked too hard for his privilege to come naturally yet. Maybe that's where I came in.

We sat down on one of the couches and I arranged myself in what I hoped was an alluring pose, but really served to hide the stain I had just noticed on one of my thighs. Darn the cost of dry-cleaning. I wore a pair of white sailor pants that had cost me a whopping $500, but were now worth every penny, and a chocolate silk blouse with a camisole underneath. Did I hang my self-esteem on the price of my clothes? Probably.

I needn't have worried about David-like tendencies or my clothes. It started to dawn on me that this man wasn't so interested in the physical; rather, he was starved of the intellectual. No doubt the chairperson of many a working committee, he succumbed to my management of our meeting like a work-experience student at his very first staff gathering. How odd.

'What do you want out of this?' I asked him after some small talk. 'How do you see it working?'

'To be honest, one of the main things I need is some nice chat between meetings,' he drawled. 'Maybe you can help me with some of your psychology. Everyone always wants a piece of me – maybe you can help me figure out how to keep them all happy.'

'But what about sex?' I replied, astounded. 'Surely you want that as part of the deal?'

He looked taken aback. 'Well, I'm still very sexually active and that will definitely be part of it, but it's not the main reason. I could get a prostitute if I just wanted that.'

Wow. Who'd have thought? Maybe I was on the right track, after all.

To change the subject, I launched into a discussion about the Starbucks we were in and how this was the first time I had ever been in one, whilst inwardly planning to ensure all of my future meetings were conducted in cafés such as these and not pubs in the western suburbs.

Dick appeared quite transfixed. 'So, have you done this before?' he asked, changing the subject again.

'No. It's like I said in my email – I was working professionally up until November last year and I took three months off to work at home on a novel. I'm only midway through and it's taking longer than I expected. My money's run out and I haven't found another job yet.'

I grimaced, remembering my job at the department – too many clients and an anal dictator at the helm. 'It was terrible, Dick,' I confided. 'I'd look at the senior women and there was no way I wanted to become like them. I'd study them during meetings and their mouths were always turned down at the corners.' I performed it for him: the reverse smile. The way my mouth would have become if I'd stayed.

'So I came up with this idea,' I went on. 'Well, a friend helped, actually. He was the one who first suggested it. I was complaining about going back to the office so we worked out all of the things I do best.' I rattled them off. 'Cooking, sex, dressing well, looking after guests, socialising. And I can work from home. When he first suggested it I was shocked, but now I think it's just a logical, honest solution to my financial woes.'

Dick studied me.

'What about you?' I asked. 'Why does someone like you need someone like me?'

He looked pained. 'Same old story, I suppose.' (I noticed his accent got stronger when he was uncomfortable.) 'I met my wife when I was on holiday here in the late seventies. We just don't seem to share the same interests any more. I'm still very interested in sex, like I said, and she ... well ... isn't. I can barely remember the last time we slept together. And every time I talk about work she seems to turn off. All she's interested in these days is looking after the kids.'

'Have you ever talked to her about it?' I asked him. 'Told her how you feel?'

'Yeah. Lots of times. I even bought a Sunseeker a year ago and suggested we motor over to California and see my parents. She didn't want to leave the kiddies. Suggested I go alone.' He sighed.

'I have a theory about that,' I told him, smiling. 'You can't really blame women. They're just sick of the same penis all the time.'

I launched into my penis mileage theory. Dick tried to debate me on the average size of a man's penis and made me get all my figures all messed up, but he was still as impressed as David had been.

'I'd like to think I'm helping marriages,' I told him. 'If you're happier, she'll be happier.'

He smiled at me and this time it felt good. This time I'd met someone I could live with. Until he went home to his wife, that was.

'How many people are you interviewing?' Dick asked.

'I've got another few to go,' I replied cautiously. 'They seem to be a lot like you are, really. A lot of my psych clients had similar problems: men whose wives were no longer interested in them sexually; men who wanted someone to listen to them. The whole sugar daddy thing has been very empowering. I thought it'd feel sleazy. But I must admit, I'm kinda enjoying myself.' I smiled at him shyly.

'Well, I'd be grateful if you'd consider me among the contenders,' he replied, rather formally. 'The money isn't a problem and I'd be happy to start the . . . er . . . arrangement on Monday. I should warn you, though, I'm new to this. Forgive me if I seem a bit nervous. I'm not normally like this at all.'

I grinned. 'That makes both of us. But what say we make the first week a trial? That way, no-one loses face if it doesn't turn out.'

Dick looked relieved.

'Yeah. That'll work,' he replied. 'I must say, it's been a pleasure to meet you.'

He glanced at his watch.

'I'll let you know by Friday,' I told him.

I got out of my chair feeling incredibly buoyed. Dick put his arm around me protectively as we approached the door and

I gave him a slightly lingering farewell kiss on the lips. Let him dwell on that, I thought.

I smiled all the way home. I was pretty sure I'd found my man!

# CHAPTER 6

Hi there, I am a 29-year-old male business professional living and working in Sydney. I have a keen appreciation of the finer things in life and am a great admirer of intellectual pursuits. I also believe that the largest sex organ is the human brain and the imagination therein. I must confess that I am intrigued by your proposal and would love to meet up for coffee and a chat. If things work out, then that's OK and if not, that's OK too and we part friends. I spend 3 days a week near the CBD in consultations and hence any decent café you suggest would be a good rendezvous. Ciao, Mahut

I had sent him the standard reply. Once again, his response was almost immediate, adding to my growing suspicion that these men were negotiating their sex lives on company time.

Hi Holly, Yes I would definitely like to meet up with you. How are you placed tomorrow at 3 p.m? Bye, Mahut

Hi Mahut, 3 p.m. tomorrow is no problem. I can meet you anywhere you would like — either in the city or in Darlinghurst.

Alternatively, I have a car and can drive somewhere further afield. I enclose a couple of photos so you can recognise me. Cheers, Holly

Hi Holly, 3 p.m. in the city sounds good. Perhaps we can meet near Broadway, say near UTS as there is plenty of parking in the area . . . and some good cafés. If you give me your number, I can call you if I am running late. Bye, Mahut

Hi Mahut, Where exactly at Broadway? At this stage I am not sure if you are genuine or not, so I would prefer to meet you at an exact time and place before I start providing my phone number (especially since you haven't offered yours!). I am always on time. Cheers, Holly

Hi Holly, I am genuine. We can meet at the Bella Café at the Broadway Shopping Centre. My phone number is ——. Unlike you, I am never 100% sure whether I will make an appointment on time. This is because of traffic, parking, meeting going beyond schedule and myriad other factors outside my control. Please feel free to give me a call before 3 p.m. Looking forward to meeting you. Mahut

Hi Mahut, I apologise for my caution – I got a lot of crank phone calls on the weekend after giving my number to someone prematurely! I would be happy to meet you at the Bella Café at around 3 p.m. I have sent a text message to your phone (hence giving you my number). I look forward to meeting you too. Cheers, Holly

I grinned as I drove to our rendezvous (that word again). It was difficult to tell whether the sense of power I got from the meetings and the emails was typical of my new career or whether it was something any woman interviewing men for sex would experience. I strongly suspected the latter; I had interviewed thousands of people both as a journalist and a psychologist and had never even remotely felt a sense of empowerment.

Perhaps it was because I was learning more about men right now than from a lifetime's worth of dating. The more approaches I received, the more powerful I felt. It raised big questions about what I'd been taught about women and sex. In my upbringing, sexual naivety was a virtue.

I was also going into the meeting with Mahut from a whole different perspective. I already had a candidate in mind. Dick was an excellent option – a normal, nice, civilised man. Even if he was from America.

I parked my car deep within the shopping centre's parking station, mentally ticking through Mahut's possible questions, viewing the whole thing like another interview.

I entered the centre near the women's toilets, which I considered a good omen. Conduct a lipstick check at all available opportunities, I say, especially when negotiating $1000 deals possibly dependent on appearance. I dashed into the toilet and fluffed. Nothing was awry, as I'd expected. It was a girl thing.

I calmed myself and located the café Mahut had specified on a map guide. It was situated just under one of the escalators. I floated down in what I hoped was a graceful way.

Mahut was pacing out the front. There was absolutely, positively no mistaking a rich guy called Mahut in this crowd. He was of Indian appearance with dark olive skin and collar-length blue-black hair. He was about 6'4" and I estimated weighed 100 kilograms, possibly more, but he looked solid rather than fat. He was dressed and oiled to perfection. I had known many gay men but this man put them all to shame. Mahut was not only spectacularly attractive; he was draped in the finest cloth imaginable for a man's suit. It was blue silk with a rough finish and a light blue sheen that matched his perfectly knotted tie. His hands were manicured and he wore some gold jewellery, but not too much. His shoes were highly polished without so much as a speck of dust on them. I felt like running forward and squashing the soles of my own shoes all over them, like we used to do to kids with new sneakers at school. He was so statuesque. So in control. He emanated a wonderful, positive aura. I immediately thought I was incredibly lucky merely to meet this man, let alone be audacious enough to charge him for the privilege of my company!

Unlike Dick and David, Mahut just smiled when he saw me and escorted me to a table without even confirming my name. When he asked what I'd like to order, he spoke in a beautiful sing-song voice with a heavy Indian accent.

Mahut and I didn't start with the weather. Or even the traffic. Somehow we immediately launched into an excited debate about whether you can change your reality simply by altering your perception of it. We didn't stop talking for the next two hours.

It turned out he was a very educated man. Not only did he have degrees in philosophy and literature, he was also – can you believe it – a rocket scientist! I almost cracked up. Getting fucked by a rocket scientist, and an immaculate, gorgeous one at that. That would be a good one to stuff it to Kev. I couldn't wipe the smile off my face as I sat and listened to Mahut state his case.

He was only twenty-nine years old and worked very long days making lots of money, but was too tired to go out in the evenings to search for a mate.

'I do not have time to court a woman,' he said. 'I do not want to have to go through the stages of finding her, wooing her, of being careful not to offend her, of meeting all her friends and having to have dinner with her family. All that and more must be done before I can even make love to her. Besides, I do not want to be married yet. Even if I were to do all of these things, I still might not find the one I seek. It is easier that I shorten the process and do it this way.'

'Less hoop-jumping,' I offered.

He cocked his head at me, looking puzzled.

'It means having to go through a whole series of steps to get to an end result. You seem to be saying that you want to go straight into a relationship without having to go through all of the stages.'

He nodded. 'That is exactly it,' he said in that wonderful voice. 'I do not want to travel through the hoops.'

'So what about this hoopless woman?' I asked. 'What do you want her to do?'

'I want to have a nice time with her. I want to be able to pursue intellectual debate. I would like to have sex with her sometimes but certainly not all times. I want to have someone to take to dinner and to the cinema and concerts. It would be nice to finish work and have a home-cooked meal occasionally. These are the things that I desire. In themselves they are not difficult, but it is the finding of the person that is the hard part.'

A small flicker of concern passed through me. It sounded like Mahut wanted a girlfriend, not a mistress. The trouble was, I wasn't ready for a boyfriend. Boyfriends led to love. Right now I wanted to be empty inside. I wanted to safeguard my wounded heart, not put it in the face of danger.

'I'm sorry if this is rude, but why not an Indian girl? There was a lady at my old office – she was from India. She used to run a match-making business. She showed me some of the people once. She said that Indian families always preferred their sons and daughters to marry other Indian people. Some of them even still have arranged marriages.'

Mahut laughed. 'I come from a very poor family in India. The only reason I am so educated is because I have a rich uncle who sponsored me. But I have paid him back every cent and more. My family are very proud of me. They do not care who I marry, so long as I am happy. They would indeed prefer for me to see Indian girls, but women from my culture have . . . what did you say? . . . hoops. I do not have time for hoops and my parents would not like to see me lonely.'

'So why did you choose Australia? It's a very long way from India. You must miss them – your family, I mean.'

'India has a very strong class system,' he replied. 'Even though I am very educated, I would not do so well. Better that I go to another country. Australia is a good country. I like it here very much. But perhaps I will go to another country if my work demands it. That is the good thing about being a consultant for the military – you go to many countries and observe what they are doing. Sometimes you can teach them. Sometimes they teach you. That is the nature of life.'

He shrugged and finished his coffee.

I had a terrible feeling I could fall for this man. And unlike John, he was very, very available. I wondered how his family would react if he appeared in India with me on his arm.

Good grief. What was I thinking? I was supposed to be paying the bills, not planning a wedding!

Mahut walked me back to my car, holding my hand in the crook of his arm. Normally, I would have baulked at the idea of showing any of my interviewees my little black Barina. To my naive way of thinking, baddies must surely be able to ascertain everything about a person just by running a check on their registration plates. I envisaged the check being run by some equally evil computer nerd, who hacked into police files just so his mate could chop women like me into a million pieces. But with Mahut, it seemed like the most natural thing in the world. Even when he insisted on giving me his arm, I considered it gallant rather than weird.

'What star sign are you?' he asked as we walked along.

'Leo,' I told him. 'I'm also a fire horse in the Chinese system.'

Of course I didn't mention that John had also been a Leo and we'd called each other 'Lionheart'. Nor did I reveal that John had given me a first-edition copy of *Elsa: The Story of a Lioness* by Joy Adamson and it was one of my most treasured possessions.

Then I realised what I'd said. What a fool! I was so hopeless at lying. So much for being thirty-five – now he'd know how old I really was!

'In China, all the male fire horses were killed,' I babbled nervously. 'Apparently the emperors thought they were a threat, or something. A bit like Moses, really. But that's about the extent of what I know. Apparently fire horses are pretty rare. What sign are you?'

'I'm a Scorpio,' he replied.

I nodded wisely. I knew absolutely nothing about Scorpios. Come to think of it, I didn't know very much about any of the signs. All I could think about was the fact that he might have busted me for my lie about my age. Surely an Indian rocket scientist wise beyond his years would immediately know fire horses were born in 1966. I didn't want this wonderful man to think I was a liar. The urge to confess was all-consuming.

Keep your mouth shut, Holly, I told myself.

I blushed. I couldn't help it. I could feel it rising up my face like a reddening disease creeping up to my hairline, betraying my lie and me. If Mahut had asked me about astrology, there was a strong possibility he was interested in it and would realise I had lied about my age. He knew. He knew!

'Er . . . I must tell you . . . I lied in the ad. I'm er . . . actually turning forty this year,' I said.

Mahut stopped and gazed at me. 'As in years?' he said, still clasping my hand in his arm.

I found myself staring at his vest. How many 29-year-old men wore three-piece suits?

'Er . . . yeah. I was born in 1966. I guess thirty-five sounds a lot younger, for some reason – funny about that. At least I keep getting better with each passing year. Slow learners always do.'

I laughed at my own joke and watched him closely to see if he got it. Nope. Rocket scientists probably didn't even know what slow learners were. Maybe they thought they were learners without legs.

We resumed our courtly promenade around the grey concrete car park and I started to wonder *what* I was getting better at. Perhaps I'd reached my peak. The prospect of diminishing returns is a terrible thing to face. When you think about it, it's the longest way to fall. Still, I wasn't about to admit that to a rocket scientist!

'I mean, I'm getting better at things like conversation and cooking and knowing what my body likes and dislikes. I know the foods I enjoy. When to call it a night at the pub. I even know how to make someone happy. I guess the best thing about getting older is that you spend less time making mistakes,' I said.

Mahut just patted my hand affectionately and remained silent.

We negotiated our way around the trolley collector. If there'd been a puddle anywhere, I was sure Mahut would have taken off his jacket and insisted I walk on it. It didn't matter that his suit was probably worth a couple of grand and my shoes had been on special at Williams the Shoeman.

'I can honestly say I haven't regretted a single year,' I continued. 'Or a single moment, for that matter. Even the bad things were only hard lessons. I like who I am now, so I can't change the bad things because then I might not be that person. I'm proud of my age. But I'm also a realist. Describing myself as thirty-five was a business decision. I'm sorry if I misled you.'

But it was as if he hadn't heard a word I'd said. Instead he paused and raised my hand to his lips and kissed the back of it, staring deep into my eyes.

'Please select me to be your consort,' Mahut said. 'I will treat you better than you have ever been treated before. I am not like other men. You are so beautiful. You are so different from the others. I will look after you and ensure that your happiness is the most important thing. You will not regret a single moment of our time together. I will promise you that.'

I smiled nervously at him and put my hand back on his arm, urging him forward.

'Well, um . . . I want to interview the others first. But I can honestly say I'd probably go out with you even if you weren't paying, Mahut.'

I began to wonder where on earth I'd parked my car.

Mahut just walked along contently, my arm crooked in his, continuing to stare at me. Every now and then he'd shake his head slightly and touch me lightly on the arm with his other hand, as if he didn't quite believe I really existed. He wasn't even watching where we were going. I could have led him up the garden path and he wouldn't have noticed.

It was incredibly flattering. I was lucky to even meet a rocket scientist, let alone infatuate one! Under his gaze I felt like the most desirable woman in the world. It didn't even occur to him that our wandering around the car park was drawing all sorts of amused glances. So much for being discreet. He was probably glad I couldn't find the car – it made our time together longer.

Thank the sweet Goddess for conversational bluffery, I say. At times like these I could maintain a steady stream of it, do the 12 times tables in my head and not even pause for breath.

'I'm so sorry about this,' I said, after our third circuit of the huge interior. 'Maybe it's on another level.'

Mahut just nodded serenely and kept holding my hand in the crook of his arm as we walked. When a little girl pointed us out to her mother he didn't even notice. We must have looked a funny sight – a statuesque, impeccably dressed Indian man in a three-piece suit straight out of a Bollywood movie walking around and around the car park with a straight-backed, trendy Darlinghurst girl with verbal diarrhoea. We didn't even have any shopping bags!

I mentally laughed uproariously at myself and our predicament. Utter absurdity always brought out my humour. I didn't feel annoyed at losing the car. Instead I felt rather fabulous. I was quite literally in the pursuit of pleasure at three o'clock on a Monday afternoon. You couldn't get any better than that.

I looked at Mahut and smiled. 'I'm so sorry about this. You must think I'm an idiot. I'm wasting your precious time. My car's got to be around here somewhere.'

'Do not concern yourself,' he said. 'I am enjoying the

pleasure. That such a person as you exists at all, Holly, is a wonderful thing indeed. Even if you don't choose me, I would like to be always your friend. I have learned a lot with you today. For the fact that such a person as you exists has brought hope to my heart. We shall meet again. I feel we shall be friends for a very long time, Holly.'

As nice as Mahut was, my warning bells were starting to clamour. Surely sugar daddies shouldn't be so enamoured of their charges? Dick seemed like a much safer option.

'Er . . . yes, well . . . remember the exclusivity,' I hastily replied. 'I know it mightn't seem like it, but I'm an old-fashioned girl at heart. One man is more than enough for me. I'm not sure it would be fair to see someone else. Besides, I don't know if I'd like to play with your feelings like that.'

Mahut just nodded happily, as if there was no way I wouldn't choose him.

I looked around in frustration. Bloody hell. Where was my fucking car?

'Maybe it's not on this level either,' Mahut observed after our second circumnavigation.

I shook my head. 'You go, Mahut. Honestly, I'm hopeless at this kind of thing. I'll find it eventually. I think there are only another couple of levels, anyway. Maybe I should try and find the toilets where I came in. It's got to be here somewhere. Please, you've got better things to do than help me find my car. I'll be OK. I promise.'

But Mahut wouldn't hear of such a thing. Instead, he guided me to the middle of the level, holding my hand all the while – I suspect he would have thrown rose petals along my path if he could – and spun me slowly around, asking me to feel which direction I'd parked the car in.

This was not a good thing to do to me. I have as much sense of direction as a circle.

I had to face facts: I had no bloody idea where I'd parked the car. I'd been so distracted when I'd arrived that I couldn't even remember if I'd parked it in the middle or along one of the sides. To make matters worse, it was a very small, dark and very dusty car and it could've been anywhere.

I began to giggle. My hand was getting pins and needles from being in the crook of Mahut's arm for so long. Kev would love this, I thought. Bloody Kev and his brilliant ideas. He got me into this. I wondered what could be more open-minded than getting a sugar daddy. Then I wondered how I was going to goad Kev into doing something similarly stupid.

We finally found my Barina on the next level. Parked next to a sign that said 'Beware of Leaving Valuables Unattended'. Naturally, it was unlocked.

'It has been an honour,' Mahut said, kissing my hand again. 'Until we meet again.'

'Thank you,' I said, meaning it. 'You're an amazing man, Mahut. I won't forget you.'

As I drove away I glanced in the rear-view mirror. Mahut was still standing there, staring at me. I felt a terrible sadness that he was totally unsuitable. I had to keep my heart safe. I had to pay my rent. I was doing this out of necessity, not for love.


On the way home I bought a pack of cigarettes and smoked two in quick succession when I got up to my apartment. Other people have Adjustment Disorder with Depressed Mood; I had Adjustment Disorder with Smoking Mood. Sometimes I'd buy a packet of cigarettes, smoke a couple, then throw them off my balcony into the alley for the derelicts to find. I'd thrown some chocolates down there once. One landed on a car – from seventeen storeys it wasn't pretty. But when the driver got out and saw he'd been hit by a strawberry cream, he just smiled.

Another time, I'd taken a heap of pastries from the Chinese bakery down to the alley. I'd bought them for an afternoon tea that didn't eventuate, and had smoked a joint while I was waiting. Fearing the onset of the munchies and my tendency to over-indulge, I put the buns on a large paper plate, added a couple of paper napkins and some plastic cutlery, and delivered it to the gutter below. Imagine how wonderful that small offering might be to a hungry person staggering by. It might have been eaten by rats, but it might also have been regarded as a gift from the gods.

I smiled as I logged on to my computer. I realised I was genuinely happy again. I had expected to feel so many negative things about this experience; that they hadn't eventuated seemed extraordinary. I almost felt guilty about not feeling guilty. If what I was doing was so wicked, why did I feel so good?

I studied my inbox. Among others, there was a message from Mahut.

Hello Holly, Just a follow-up email from our initial meeting. To be honest with you, I was just blown away by your personality and your intellect. I was very impressed with the way you carried yourself, your experiences, basically everything about you. I hope that didn't sound too tacky and scare you away! :) As I mentioned, I am 29 years old, but as you may have gathered, I have a mature outlook towards life. To me the age difference doesn't mean anything, all that matters is that we understand and respect each other. You are a beautiful person, inside and out, and you deserve the best. Perhaps you've already made up your mind about me, and then perhaps not. I fully understand that you may choose to turn down my offer after reviewing all the options. In which case, I will be more than happy with your friendship, if you wish to extend it. I look forward to hearing from you on Friday, and whether you say yes or no, I will always cherish the hours we spent together. Best wishes, Mahut

I gave a big sigh of regret and smoked another cigarette. If only he wasn't so perfect.

# CHAPTER 7

Hello Hostess with the Mostest . . . With such a classy profile and a great picture you must have been wowed by hundreds of guys. If you have not yet been scared away and are still looking to meet with someone then please email me as ide love to have a chat. I work in the CBD for one of the big international firms and i understand the high stress level you talk about so ide like to see if there may be some arrangement we can come to. I'm also in my 30s and single and i would like to think im normal. Ha ha. Hope to chat soon, Brandon

As I strolled through Hyde Park on the way to meet Brandon I felt like an old hand. I had come to the conclusion that these meetings were the easiest 'interviews' I'd ever done – mostly because it was such a relief to have nothing to hide. When I thought about it, whether I was interviewing for a job, a flatmate, a loan or even first dates, there was always something I needed to disguise. It might only be the small hot-water tank or my fetish for fabric, but I was never completely myself.

It was often my appearance and my social life that I tried to downplay. In the past, for job interviews I'd often deliberately tried to appear less attractive by wearing unflattering spectacles and pulling my hair back in a severe French roll. I'd been on job 'interview panels where the men had been mercilessly teased for preferring highly attractive female candidates. It didn't matter whether a good-looking woman was the best qualified; in several cases, such applicants hadn't been successful merely because of their appearance. 'I couldn't stand rolling into the office feeling like shit on a Monday and having to look at "that" all day,' I remembered one woman saying. 'Let's go with the fat guy, he's just as qualified and at least we won't have to worry about him at the Christmas party.'

(Do I hear you groaning, dear reader? Yes, there are many, many good things about being considered attractive, but there's always a reverse to every coin. But I do admit, it's probably one of those 'hardships' that everyone would like to experience for themselves.)

In the same way, when interviewers asked me what I did in my free time, there was no way I could tell them that I mostly enjoyed sex, spoiling people and dancing till dawn with hundreds of gorgeous unavailable men. Instead I told them I played golf and attended a lot of barbecues on Sunday afternoons.

I also had to disguise the real me on dates. I'd tried internet dating for a while after John, to try to rid myself of the grief. It only made me feel worse. Imagine if I confided to my date that my favourite ex used to hire a float plane and we'd romp naked on a private beach with a gourmet picnic, and that this had (unfortunately) become my new boyfriend benchmark!

Nor could I tell them same boyfriend had broken my heart and I considered myself incapable of love.

I sighed as I crossed the park. If only John's conscience had been as underactive as mine currently was. If only he'd realise that a loveless marriage for the sake of his children wasn't doing them any favours. If only he knew how bad it was to listen to your parents quietly argue night after night, talking to each other in nasty tones they reserved only for each other. I'd been there. For years I'd been there. Listening. Watching. As newcomers to speech, children are better at non-verbal cues than adults. My sister and I were the primary witnesses to the torturous deterioration of my parents' love. It remains one of the ugliest things I've ever witnessed.

I arrived at Starbucks right on time. Once again, it was obvious my date hadn't arrived yet. Even though there were several men sitting by themselves, they were fixated on laptops or mobiles or licking the froth off their cappuccino spoons.

I ordered a medium iced chai tea latte.

The waiter raised his eyebrow at me and asked if that meant the 'grande'.

I raised my eyebrow back and repeated sternly, 'Whatever is the *medium*, please.'

Yeah, maybe I was becoming a grumpy old woman, but I'd boycotted terms such as 'regular', 'grande' and 'family' years ago, on principle. I referred to all of my size requests as small, medium or large and became very annoyed if the person didn't understand what I meant.

The waiter asked if I wanted a loyalty card. I refused. For one thing, I didn't want to be 'loyal' to Starbucks. And imagine if I found my perfect 'gent' on date number five and proudly produced the card in order to pay for our beverages!

I laughed to myself. Maybe wives could introduce their own loyalty cards. Five cunnilingi (surely there must be a plural form of my favourite thing in the world?) and the husband gets a free night in a brothel. I bet that would put the life back into a few marriages . . .

I sat down at a table facing the door and made my body language easy to read. I looked up every time someone new walked in and glanced at my watch often. I smiled at a few false alarms but they just gave me vague smiles back, if at all, and hurried to the counter. Call me old-fashioned, but I have a problem with people you smile at who don't smile back – I mean, how hard is it to turn up the sides of your mouth? You have to feel mighty sorry for people who can't do that.

By now I wasn't nervous, I didn't have excitement butterflies and I wasn't answering pre-prepared questions in my head. The worst thing that could happen would be my time being wasted. Then again, meeting these men would never really be a waste of time, no matter how unsuitable they were. The bad ones would just help me define the good ones.

In the end, Brandon found me. I'd turned my attention from the door and was studying a homeless man who'd set up camp on the busy pavement. He'd spread his blanket and various plastic bags around him and arranged a bottle of orange juice, half a bag of dried apricots and an old newspaper on a milk crate. He was singing the Rolling Stones' 'Satisfaction' and doing a mighty fine job of it too. He seemed amazingly happy.

I was gazing at him with a huge smile on my face when Brandon tapped me on the shoulder.

'Holly?' he asked, sounding stressed. 'I'm so sorry I'm late.'

I jumped.

'Brandon,' I said. 'Great to meet you.'

I rose out of my chair to shake his hand and show him my fabulous outfit. This time I was wearing a pair of beautiful brown fitted pants teamed with my trusty boat-necked pink floral top that showed off my cleavage in a way that didn't scream 'trying too hard!' like a plunging V-neck sometimes did.

Brandon was olive-skinned, slightly overweight, balding prematurely and dressed in a cheap suit with a poorly knotted tie. I'm not good at picking nationalities (and am always afraid to ask) but he seemed to have both Asian and Indian features. He was probably in his late thirties. He looked nervous and seemed glad of the opportunity to go through the rigmarole of ordering his coffee so he could compose himself.

I watched him place his order, then noted the way he fidgeted while he waited, studying everything in the room besides me. I wondered if I would ever meet a person that ordered a coffee and then stood completely still, using the opportunity for some deep thought or imagination time. If I was honest about it, I usually spent the time I was queueing or waiting for service worrying – about silly things like whether the other queue was moving faster or whether we were being served in the right order.

I noticed Brandon wasn't wearing a wedding ring and guessed he was in the young-and-no-time-to-find-a-woman category. I hoped I was wrong. I wanted a man with major family commitments and a wife who liked her husband in her bed every night, albeit on the far side.

A medium coffee in hand, Brandon finally plopped down with an audible sigh and apologised once again for being late, telling me a meeting had run over and he'd been unable to step out to use his mobile phone. He ran his fingers through his hair continuously and looked like he was about to run away at any moment.

I tried to send out soothing vibes. 'Hey, don't worry about it,' I told him. 'I've had a lovely time watching the locals.'

I nodded at the homeless man, who was now using an empty soft drink can as a microphone. Maybe I'd misjudged him and he was really a busker.

Brandon glanced at him and rolled his eyes.

'Poor old codger,' he remarked. 'Probably thinks he's Mick Jagger.'

'How wonderful!' I replied, in all seriousness.

Brandon raised his eyebrows and looked at me sideways. 'Huh?'

I couldn't resist.

'Well, I wouldn't mind being Mick Jagger for a day,' I said. 'Even if it was only in my imagination.'

Brandon turned and studied the homeless man. This time he smiled when he saw how joyful he appeared.

'There are lessons in everyone,' I said, trying to work out

what it was that Brandon held for me and hoping it wasn't merely confirmation that I could no longer work in a job such as his.

'So, what do you do?' I went on, falling back on the age-old question in an attempt to avoid the pallet of soapboxes that seemed to be following me around.

'I'm an economist,' he said. 'But I head up the marketing department.'

The old Holly, networking a cocktail party, would have said, 'How interesting! Did you first become an economist and then move into marketing or was it the other way around?' But I just couldn't do it. It would have been dishonest, for one thing. And listening to this man drone on about his job might sabotage my only opportunity to hear his real stories. So I asked him why a good-looking marketer such as himself needed a woman like me. It was so refreshing to get straight to the point!

'Finding a girlfriend's too hard,' he told me. 'Not one that I like, anyway. I don't usually finish work till late and by then I'm too stuffed to go to a bar, much less pick up a chick. I'm fussy too. But the good ones don't go for me, anyway; I need to lose these kilos first.' He patted his stomach for emphasis.

'I guess I just want a pretty woman for company. You don't have to say much.' He winked at me and continued. 'My friends are mostly married too. It's hard being the only single – you should see some of the trolls they've tried to set me up with!'

He broke into a big grin. 'I know! You could pretend to be my girlfriend!' he exclaimed. 'You're wicked! I could introduce you to everyone. My mates would be so impressed. So would my brother. He'd try and grass cut you for sure. No-one would have to know . . .' He trailed off.

'Know that you were paying me?' I finished for him. 'No, I would prefer that no-one knew that either.'

'It's not that I couldn't get a girlfriend like you,' he said defensively. 'It's just that I don't have the time. I'm a nice guy, really!'

'Have you thought about RSVP?' I couldn't help asking.

'Isn't that the internet dating service?' he asked. 'I couldn't do that. It's like a meat market, everyone trying to make themselves appear better than they really are.'

'Isn't that human nature?' I said. 'With the internet, at least you get to find out all about the person before you have to meet them. I'd much prefer that than the other way around, which is what happens in pubs and clubs. I was on RSVP a few months ago. I met some really nice people. It's like a sales catalogue. It's honest.'

'Maybe,' Brandon said, looking unconvinced. 'But what about the women who just want me for my money?'

I laughed. 'You've just met one. Are we really so bad?'

He studied me closely. It was obvious he didn't think I was half as bad as I probably was. In fact, the poor man probably thought I was very good.

'You could be right,' he mused. 'You could be right.'

I reminded him about the $1000 a week and how I wanted it in advance. It didn't seem to be a problem.

Then I asked what foods and beverages he enjoyed. He liked pasta too. If in doubt, feed the man pasta, not meat.

'How do you stay so skinny?' he asked. 'I've been trying to budge this for yonks.'

I laughed. 'I'd like to say I was like this naturally. But I'm still a fat teenager underneath. I've only got to look at carbs and I put on weight. All my life I've had to exercise. Drag myself there, usually. But I've finally cottoned on to the least amount of huff and puff for the most amount of results – Pilates. Most of it's done lying down, for one thing, and that's gotta be good!'

Brandon looked serious. 'Maybe I should give it a go,' he said, patting his stomach. 'Lying down, eh?'

'All the best things are done lying down,' I joked, winking.

Good heavens. I was starting to sound like a cheap hooker. Somebody stop me!

'Yeah, well, I haven't done much of that lately,' he said

gloomily. 'In fact, these days all I seem to do is go to work and get pissed on weekends.'

He glanced at his watch – the universal signal of business-men. I wondered if watches would become obsolete when they realised their phones kept time as well. Either that or Rolex would start making mobiles.

'I'd better not keep you,' I told him. 'Thanks for the chat. I'll let you know by the end of the week.'

We both stood up and Brandon drained his coffee.

'It'd be so nice to have someone like you on my arm,' he said passionately as we parted, giving me his business card. 'I'd like to get to know you more. Maybe you could change my life for the better.'

I hoped someone would, but I knew it wouldn't be me.

As with Mahut, Brandon's follow-up email was waiting for me by the time I got home.

Hi Holly, Thanks so much for meeting with me . . . it really was a pleasure . . . i may have seemed a little anxious at times and i guess it was because i had the couple behind you constantly staring and smiling at us . . . no big deal! Let me start by saying i think you are fantastic. you have a great personality and fantastic looks. I think i might have to start with Pilates too if it makes you look so good . . . ha ha ha. i would be very excited if you decide to spend the time with me but having seen my calender i have got a couple of minor concerns which i wanted to let you know in case you find this an issue and decide it wont be able to work for you. next week i will be free to meet mon-thur however friday i need to travel to Hobart for a week. im happy to pay for the week in advance and even though im aware that you are waiting to see what happens friday, I was going to suggest maybe we can meet tomorrow night for a drink and check out your apartment too. If you like i can even give u the money then. Please dont think im being pushy, im just trying to make it easier. the second concern i had was that the second week ill be in Hobart so i will be back again on monday 20th . . . would that be a prob for you? I have not been able to concentrate since lunch thinking about what things i really enjoy . . . ha ha ha. chat soon, Brandon

Reading it made me feel sad. Here was yet another lonely man hoping to buy love. What a shame free love wasn't available any more.

# CHAPTER 8

On Wednesday I got another email from Dick.

> Hello Holly, How is your decision-making process going? Need to know soon. Today? For my part, I am looking forward to a mutually rewarding relationship. I think you realise I am quite naïve sexually. I think you can fix that. I also forgot to mention that I am hoping for some outstanding sex outdoors with you. How soon can I start spoiling you? Would you consider allowing me to take you to lunch? Best wishes, Dick

He rang later that morning and asked me to lunch at Bilson's on the harbour.

'I'd be delighted to have lunch with you,' I told him. 'Where would you like to meet?'

After I hung up, I pondered my response. I had two more 'meetings' to go: a man called Alexander, who lived in York Street, was married and searching for someone 'between meetings'; and Roger, the BDSM fetishist who was very keen to take me to lunch. The former had potential but sounded very young and insecure on the phone. I also fostered strong doubts about Roger, but I was trying to be non-judgemental. It seemed to me that seriously considering whether to become a submissive for someone who liked to whip people was surely the ultimate in open-mindedness. Besides, how I would relish telling Kev all about it!

Perhaps foolishly, I had regarded second dates as part of the 'arrangement', but Dick was at the top of my list so far, so it wasn't a 'freebie', it was a second interview. Besides, what girl from Port Stephens could resist a seafood lunch?

As I got ready, I wished I'd asked him if he'd prefer me to dress like a business colleague. He was considerably older than I was and it might seem odd if I appeared in something that looked sexy or beguiling. I was proud of what I was doing, but I couldn't expect Dick to feel that way too.

In the end, I chose a turquoise silk tunic that ended well past my knees, with nearly transparent white silk pantaloons. I had worn the outfit to work on numerous occasions and had received compliments all day. It also matched the only handbag I had ever paid over $200 for and the expensive lingerie set that John had bought me. I felt like a million bucks.

Well, a thousand, anyway.

I walked down to the Rocks and lurked in the shops near the restaurant until 1 p.m. on the dot. One of them was selling beautiful lingerie; checking the prices, I resolved to fake mine. Target had a fabulous selection, and I was yet to meet a man who scrutinised the brand name in my knickers – it would be like being interested in the wrapper after unwrapping a chocolate!

Dick was sitting at the bar looking at his watch (again) when I walked in. He appeared very different in a beautifully tailored navy suit and a neat blue and white striped college tie. He glanced up and saw me and seemed incredibly relieved. I began to wonder if his watch was fast and he thought I was late.

'Hi, how are you?' I said breezily. 'Am I late? What time do you have? My watch has been playing up.' I scowled down at it as if the offending object had deliberately kept this man waiting.

'You're exactly on time,' he assured me, rising to greet me with a kiss on the cheek. 'What would you like to drink?'

'A vodka and soda would be wonderful,' I told him. 'I'm sorry, but I'm a bit phobic about time. Running late is one of the few things that really stresses me out. Keeping someone waiting for you is a power trip, I reckon. Keeping a group waiting is even worse. There's no excuse with mobiles. If you're caught in traffic or on a train, you can just text them and let them know.'

Dick couldn't have looked more pleased. Thank heavens for small soapboxes!

'I couldn't agree with you more,' he told me in his American twang. 'I have a twenty-minute rule myself: no matter who they are, if they're not there in twenty minutes, I'm off. I did that to the Syd-e-ney lord mayor one time – he wasn't impressed! After twenty minutes of waiting, I asked his PA where he was and she told me that he knew I'd arrived, but he was in the middle of something. I told the PA that I was now in the middle of *my* next thing and left.'

I laughed. 'What happened? Was he pissed off?'

Dick shrugged. 'Not really. I even won the portfolio in the end.'

He looked so good sitting there in his blue suit. For the first time I noticed he had lovely blue eyes. Just like John's. With the same laughter lines etched along the sides.

'Are you ready to dine?' Dick drawled. 'I reckon I could consume a side of Texas beef.'

I gazed out onto beautiful Sydney Harbour. Gulls flew around the masts of a tall sailing ship moored at the jetty. Fellow diners sat at tables with large platters heaped with fresh seafood, accompanied by ice buckets of champagne and willing waiters.

'Absolutely,' I replied.

He took my elbow as we walked over to the maitre d'. I smiled to myself. I'd had more contact with elbows this week than ever before in my life! There was something very nice about it, I decided. A polite gesture of caring, directing, watching over someone. It often seemed to belong to this generation of successful businessmen. People of my generation tended to hold hands; sometimes we linked arms, but that was usually when we were full of enhanced confidence and sashaying somewhere. Even then, it was more a statement of 'go around' to the other pedestrians than anything else.

Dick had reserved a table not quite on the waterside and insisted on facing inwards to allow me the magnificent view. I couldn't help wondering if he didn't want to be recognised by passers-by. I wished I'd worn my corporates, after all.

'What kind of wine would you like?' he asked me, perusing the wine list.

'Anything white,' I told him. 'Don't get me wrong, I love a good red, but I'd prefer white at lunch.'

He made a selection and conferred with the hovering waiter about the year. I felt a small twinge of concern and hoped he wouldn't want me to guess the vineyard or something.

The wine came quickly and I wondered about my half-drunk vodka. I was tempted to knock it back. Instead, I reluctantly put it to one side and started on what was an excellent vintage. I made a mental note to make the man at the bottle shop my new best friend.

Dick turned out to be an excellent conversationalist and dining companion. After a brief moment of concern about the crustiness of our bread rolls, he relaxed and spoke openly about his work.

'I'm what you call a money man,' he explained. 'Some people call it investment wanking or financial engineering, but I prefer the word "entrepreneur". I'm not one for the blue chips either – even though share prices have been singing over the past couple of years. Most of our growth is underpinned by the superannuation industry, which has been awash with cash for over a decade now – ever since compulsory employer contributions, in fact. But booming equity markets can only deliver so much; I've spent decades building the business. Most of my rivals have disappeared over the years – tried to grow too fast or borrow too much, the fools. My philosophy is to spread your risk as far as you can. That way, if you get a bad egg, your portfolio's not too narrow.'

I nodded wisely. As confusing as all this was – and please forgive my translation – it seemed that Dick was one of those people who had a paper empire with a posh office and lots of people at computers.

'I read about pollution derivatives in the States once,' I ventured bravely. 'Fancy selling pollution! Something about under-polluting factories being able to sell the difference. Futures, too. If they think they're going to emit a lot of pollution for something specific in the future – maybe an energy company in winter – they can buy emission futures at today's rates, just in case the prices increase. Is that true? It's unbelievable! There are people starving out there and there are numbers sitting in bank accounts for unused pollution. It doesn't seem right somehow. Call me old-fashioned, but I reckon an honest day's work for an honest day's pay.'

Shit. What was I saying? The words were straight from twenty years spent in offices. Was having a sugar daddy putting in an honest day's work? I vaguely wondered if what I was doing was even legal. It had to be. Wives did it, didn't they?

Dick just laughed. 'Those "numbers", as you call them, are what make the world go around,' he said. 'Without them we'd be living from hand to mouth every day.'

'But most of us *are* living hand to mouth,' I told him. 'It's only the people with the numbers who aren't.' I tried not to think about all of the numbers on my unpaid bills.

Dick examined me as he would an earnest child.

'Holly,' he said. 'Look at you. Do you really think you're

living hand to mouth? You told me the other day you've got an investment unit on the coast – that alone counts for some of the numbers in a lot of the banks. Someone had to give your bank the money to lend you. Who do you think that was? Every single person and business in the world has some of the numbers. Just because they don't actually buy anything physical, it doesn't mean the numbers shouldn't exist. They're like a . . . service, I guess – money has to be bought and sold, just like everything else. It would be very naive to assume that it maintains the same value all the time.'

Lesson number one in the sugar daddy gig – never try to argue about money with a numbers man. Oops, make that an 'entrepreneur'. Especially when you have absolutely no idea what they're talking about.

'Well,' I said, mostly to change the topic, 'speaking of money, is there anything in particular you'd like for yours?'

Dick looked thoughtful. 'I hadn't really thought about it, to be honest,' he replied. 'I thought we could make it up as we went along.'

He was going to give me $1000 cash each week and he hadn't even considered what he wanted for his money?

'I guess I'm searching for a sanctuary more than anything. Someone I can talk to. Somewhere I can go to get away. Can't we play it by ear? There is one thing . . .' He trailed off, looking uncomfortable.

Oh no! He was going to confess that he was into fucking Labradors or something.

'Come on, Dick – spit it out,' I prompted, starting to feel anxious for the first time since I'd embarked upon this mad plan of mine. 'I'm a psychologist, remember – you can tell me anything.'

'Well . . . it's just that . . . I haven't had sex with anyone but my wife for thirty years. I don't think I could wear a condom. I've had a vasectomy – you won't get pregnant or anything. Is that OK?'

The original sin. Unprotected sex! My friends wouldn't be shocked about the sugar daddy gig, but they would be about this.

'The trouble is,' I told him, reciting the posters on local toilet doors, 'I'm not just sleeping with you. I'm sleeping with your wife as well. What about her? How do you know that she's not having it off with someone?'

He smiled sadly. 'I doubt that, Holly. She had part of her uterus removed after the birth of our last child – a mistake, I might add – and has used it as an excuse not to sleep with me since Sally was born. And she'll be ten in June.' He laughed bitterly. 'Every time we celebrate her birthday I'm reminded of my own celibacy. Don't worry, I think you're safe in that department,' he concluded.

The poor man. The poor woman. The guilt she must feel. How horrible for them both! I took a very deep breath. The whole sugar daddy thing suddenly didn't seem so naughty any more. This was serious.

'So you haven't been with a woman for that long?' I asked, incredulous that such a thing could happen to anyone, least of all this kind, sweet, blue-eyed man before me.

'No sir-ee,' he drawled, hamming up his American accent and taking a big swig of the excellent wine.

I gave a big sigh and mentally apologised to my friends. 'Well, unprotected sex it is, then,' I said. 'I'm happy to go through any tests you want. I've never had so much as a crab in my life, but I got tested when I broke up with my ex, just in case. It was only a couple of months ago. I've had a bit of a drought since then but I'm happy to do them again. But I need to know you're clear as well. Just in case.'

STD by Immaculate Conception. As if!

Dick just looked relieved.

'The tests you've already had are fine. I'll do anything you want. I'll make an appointment for Monday. I'll have to go to another doctor – the family GP might think it was a bit suspicious . . .'

Call me a sucker, but I decided then and there that Dick was my man. I could help this poor soul like I had helped no other before him.

Our meals arrived and the food looked superb. Dick had ordered Cajun-spiced barramundi with mashed potato and mixed green salad. I vaguely wondered where I'd find barramundi in Darlinghurst. My own slab of salmon with its pink centre and lemongrass seasoning tasted divine, especially washed down with a sip of the wine.

As we ate and chatted, I wondered about Dick's wife. I must admit, I'd tried not to think about the wives very much. Mostly because they were the one flaw in my otherwise fabulous plan – not because I didn't want them around (I still thought them essential to my own free time); rather, it was because they were being deceived. But in Dick's case, his wife might very well be relieved that I was taking over the bedroom duties. I knew I would be in her position.

Finally I couldn't help myself. 'I'm sorry, Dick, but I've got to ask this question. Are you going to tell your wife about this? Maybe she'd like the idea. Maybe she could even meet me. I'm not a bad person – if she knew where I was coming from and that I didn't want to steal you from her, maybe she might give us her approval?'

My mind raced ahead. I could become a fully approved mistress. We could have a contract signed by all parties. Everything else was sub-contractable, why not sex lives as well?

Dick shook his head, looking very grave.

'I can't, Holly. I just can't. Years ago I suggested a prostitute and she practically hit the roof! She's a Catholic. Told me masturbation should be good enough. Masturbate and think of her, she said. She said we'd taken vows to stay together for better and worse and she expected me to stick by them. She said I was a dirty old man,' he whispered the last as if it was a horrible secret, 'and that if I ever got a prostitute she'd divorce me and take everything. She would too. Men like me don't get divorces, Holly; we're caught up in too many family agreements. For one thing, there's no way I could afford the tax if the assets got split up, not to mention what would happen to the trust. Nope, I'm stuck with her. In a way, it's good to have different interests – that way, she lives her life and I live mine.'

I pushed my salmon around my plate. What had started as a desperate attempt to make money was beginning to resemble another counselling job. Dick's wife sounded like a real bitch. But it wasn't her fault, I reminded myself. If she did openly permit Dick to fuck other people, she faced the ridicule of her peers, not to mention excommunication from her church. The poor woman really had little choice but to deny her husband one of his most basic instincts. How awful for them both.

'Well, you've got me now,' I told him cheerfully. 'I'm not even going to bother having the other meetings. Why don't we go back to my place after we finish lunch and I can show you my apartment? Just in case you don't like it. Then we can start the arrangement on Monday.'

Dick's face lit up and his gorgeous blue eyes crinkled at the corners.

'I'd like that very much,' he drawled, beckoning the waiter for the bill. 'Check, please!'


As we walked to the car park I felt tremendously relieved. I wasn't selling myself out. I was helping to right a wrong. For the first time in my entire life, I was going to offer an employer every single skill I had available. I resolved to earn my keep. We had ten years of loving to catch up on.

Dick unlocked his car. I had come to realise there were three main types of car for wealthy men: Mercedes Benz, Smart cars (to appease their consumption guilt while their bored wives re-renovated million-dollar homes) and BMWs. I should have guessed that Dick, being a banker, would fall into the BMW category.

He opened the door for me and got me settled before he went to pay. If I'd been devious I would have looked in the glove compartment, but I really liked this man and I respected his privacy. Instead, I waited and told myself how lucky I was to find him.

He handled the vehicle well as we drove through the city traffic to my apartment. I gave him a running commentary as we went, pointing out my neighbourhood landmarks just like a country girl and forgetting that the Sydney CBD belonged to everyone. Perhaps I was getting nervous. If Dick was going to turn into an axe-wielding maniac, it would probably happen in about fifteen minutes. My first ever John to cross the threshold, I thought. Second, the voice in the back of my head reminded me; and no-one can ever hurt you as much as the first John did.

Dick walked into my unit and went straight to the window, as everyone did. The view was breathtaking (and continued to take mine away every morning when I woke up). It wasn't your standard view, with famous landmarks or tranquil waters; it was mostly rooftops, actually. Sure, there were a couple of iconic buildings if you counted the Horizon Apartments tower or craned your neck to glimpse part of the Sydney Harbour Bridge and most of one of the Opera House's sails, but it was the bird's-eye view of the world in action that so impressed everyone. It was like being in a permanent helicopter over Toy Town. People, buses, cars, planes, helicopters, even birds, all rushing around going about their daily business.

The apartment itself was pretty dodgy. There were a lot of marks on the walls that no amount of scrubbing would remove, and suspicious cracks everywhere, which was a bit of a worry for the top floor of a seventeen-storey building. I'd also inherited some rather hideous furniture, with a very large fake leather recliner chair the chief target of my objections. I'd placed the chair in front of a desk I'd made from pieces of wood I'd found in the car park and perched on the edge of it as I wrote.

But as I'd said numerous times before when a derelict flat

with excellent views had presented itself, you really can make anything look good with the right touches; particularly ones that highlight the pluses and hide the flaws. (A bit like people, really.) One of the positives of this flat was that it had beautiful parquetry flooring throughout – albeit damaged – and a great long sofa that enabled at least eight post-dance party people to lounge comfortably while they admired the sunrise and sipped my good coffee.

I had put my sister's art over most of the worst marks on the walls, and disguised some of the lower cracks with tall pot plants placed directly in front of them. And never underestimate the power of a beautiful ornament – my own included some purple and orange blown Japanese glassware that caught the sun, and a set of three stainless steel Georg Jensen bowls John had given me, telling me they resembled the spoons we so enjoyed at night together.

My entertainment system comprised my computer and two speakers connected to a faulty amp I had inherited with the apartment. One of my high-tech friends had added some software and I ran my television and DVD through the same system. The same friend was also a music angel who delivered great chunks of new songs onto my computer at regular intervals. In such a small space, it all worked remarkably well. The end result was a bright, light, cheap but chic apartment that felt incredibly spacious even though you could barely swing an arm in it, let alone a cat.

'This could be very good,' Dick mused, looking around and smiling.

I wondered if he meant the apartment.

'May I get you a drink?' I asked, as he arranged himself on the couch and gazed outside.

'A bourbon and Coke would be great, thanks, Holly,' he replied.

I made the drinks, thanking my lucky stars for the small flask of Jack Daniel's Jason had left behind months ago. Always the hostess, I also kept small bottles of assorted mixers in the back of the fridge for moments just like these. It gave me a real kick to be out all night with a friend who was drinking vodka and soda with fresh lime and to press the exact same thing into their hand when they arrived at my place. The simple considerations are often the best – and certainly the most remembered.

Then I relaxed on the couch beside Dick and gazed out at the world with him. This afternoon it was putting on a very good show – a giant tanker was negotiating the harbour and a group of sirens were screaming off to some tragedy somewhere to our left. The sky was an endless expanse of cloudless blue occasionally dissected by giant aircraft threading their way north. A helicopter was hovering over a point in East Sydney – probably a traffic accident preventing workers who tried to get home via the Harbour Bridge.

I would have been there a couple of months ago, I thought. Snarling at some poor person who was crushed in their vehicle and had the audacity to hold me up. And yet here I was, mid-week, satiated from a lovely harbourside meal with a charming man, discussing why it would be in his best interests to pay me $1000 a week to fill the gap left by his wife. Pardon another pun.

I kept up a steady stream of chatter, once again grateful for my gift. They should make conversational bluffery a subject in schools, I thought. It would certainly be more useful than algebra and algorithms.

We didn't really talk much about the 'arrangement' itself – mostly because it felt strange to be discussing such things and both of us seemed a tad uncomfortable about it.

Although I was enjoying his company, I was quite relieved when Dick finished his drink and rose to leave.

'Well, I'll see you on Monday,' he drawled. 'I'll bring the money then.'

He hadn't so much as kissed me yet!

'OK,' I said. 'Any special requests?'

'No,' he replied. 'Nothing I can think of. I'm a pretty easy-going sort of chap.'

As he turned to leave, I grabbed his hand. 'Wait,' I told him, leaning forward.

I planted a long, lingering farewell kiss on his lips. It was probably one of the bravest things I'd ever done. But if he didn't show on Monday, it would be my credit rating I'd be kissing goodbye.

It was what he'd been waiting for.

He pulled me against him and kissed me passionately, showing no sign whatsoever of a decade's lack of practice. I was instantly aroused. That in itself was extraordinary. Normally I wouldn't have given this man the time of day, much less been turned on by him!

'I'll see you on Monday,' I said huskily.

Dick was all smiles. 'I'll look forward to it,' he said.

The minute he was out the door I got online and deleted the ad on Persona. It was an enormous relief. I was no longer up for sale. I was now officially undesperate!

I spent the next hour composing a polite email advising all my 'applicants' that a successful candidate had been chosen.

Thank you so much for making this such a wonderful experience. I am sorry, but I have taken the coward's way out and chosen a person who is very much like me, who even works in the same profession and lives close by. I enjoyed our meeting immensely and wish you well in your search. Cheers, Holly

I hoped my words would allow them to save face. I tried to communicate that I hadn't rejected *them* per se; rather, I'd done what society expected and chosen someone who was similar to me. I sent the email to myself and blind-copied them all to maintain their confidentiality. I must admit, I was glad to be finally rid of them. It might sound wonderful having a flock of men panting after you, but a week or so was enough!

Some of them expressed their disappointment immediately, and I wondered once again how these men found the time to hover over anonymous email accounts during their supposedly frantic business hours.

# CHAPTER 9

On Sunday I rang Kev. 'Guess what?' I said excitedly. 'I've taken your advice! I've hired a sugar daddy and it's all your fault!'

'What?' It was the reaction I'd hoped for.

'I advertised on the internet,' I gloated. 'I've been interviewing applicants all week. It's been amaaazing! I've never felt so empowered in all my life. I've been masturbating like crazy! I've got a guy starting on Monday and he's paying me a grand a week. In cash. In advance. I can finally pay my debts! Well, some of them anyway.'

I couldn't wipe the grin off my face. I was positively gleeful.

'Whoa, Holly!' Kev said. 'You've actually gone and done it? I can't believe it. You know I was only joking, don't you? You can't be serious! Only you'd be crazy enough to do this, Holly. You're one mad bitch, you know?'

I could picture Kev shaking his head on the other end of the line.

'Don't feel guilty,' I told him. 'This is one of the best things I've ever done. I can't begin to tell you how good I feel! I thought I might feel like a pervert or something, but it's quite the reverse. It's so weird! I've got to tell you, I have honestly never felt so sexy. The guy I've got starting on Monday is lovely, very debonair. His wife is sick and he hasn't had sex for ten years. Can you believe it? His name's Dick. A John whose name is Dick! How ironic. He's really nice, Kev. He even took me to lunch on Thursday at Bilson's. He's going to be perfect!'

'Dick, eh? Come on,' Kev laughed. 'Admit it. You picked him because of his name! You always were too honest.'

I chuckled. 'No, seriously. He was the best, really. He's American. His name's really Richard but his friends call him Dick. It felt strange calling him that at first, but it suits him. I don't even really notice his accent any more, and he writes just like a normal person.'

Kev snorted. 'I still can't believe it – a John whose name is Dick. You're the bravest woman I know, Holly! If anyone can make this work, you can. But watch out for yourself. What happens if you fall in love again? How are you going to protect yourself from that?'

'That's the beauty of doing it now,' I told him. 'It's like you said – right now, I'm still broken. There's no way I'm capable of love at the moment. Maybe six or twelve months down the track, then I might get hurt. But you said it yourself – you can't hurt a heart that's already broken. I might never be so damaged again. Maybe John did me a favour! Honestly, Kev, if I don't try this thing, I'll always wonder. You know I was mourning him. This way I've found other men just like him. Putting a grand on my head has flushed out the Johns of the world. All those RSVP dates and not a single man like him. Now I'm inundated with them! I've met more men like John in the past week than I have in my entire life. Who'd have guessed that?'

'Well . . . if you think so,' Kev said. 'But remember, I didn't put you up to this – you did it all by yourself.' Now he had his devious tone back.

'No way!' I replied, laughing. 'This was your idea, Kev, and you're going to wear it!'

Kev laughed.

'I'm proud of you, Holly,' he told me quietly. 'You're one of the most incredible people I know.'

As I hung up the phone, I felt proud of me too. I hadn't let my own prejudices cloud what was a logical solution to a dire situation. It felt disturbingly *good*.

On Monday morning, I used my last dollars to buy a bottle of Jack Daniel's, Coke and the most expensive array of cheeses, dips, pâtés and other delicacies I could afford. The *pièce de résistance* was a sliver of Roquefort cheese that had cost me $11. Apparently it had only been allowed back in Australia in the past few months, after being banned by our over-zealous Food Standards Code because it contained unpasteurised milk. It was worth a bit of conversation at the very least.

Then I made good on my mental promise and flirted outrageously with the man at the bottle shop, who ended up recommending a $30 bottle of semillon chardonnay. He promised to refund my money if it wasn't one of the best things I'd ever drunk. Too bad I paid for it with my credit card: the cash would have come in handy.

Five changes of clothing later, I still didn't have a clue what to wear. I was beginning to panic. I rarely take more than a few minutes to put together an outfit, but this was the first day of my second John. Should I wear something sexy? Or would that convey to Dick that I wanted him to fuck me right away even if he might have wanted to get to know me first? But if I appeared 'normally' dressed, would that suggest that I *didn't* want to have sex with him? What outfit was appropriate for both lunch and (possible) sex? Worse still, what shoes did one wear in one's own home at lunchtime while entertaining one's first ever sex-for-money client? High heels seemed ludicrous and slutty. Bare feet didn't go with any of my outfits (except perhaps swimmers and pyjamas). The Birkenstock thongs I normally wore seemed too casual.

In the end, I chose an olive green antique lace mini dress that had been a favourite for at least a decade. Although it was short, it was too classy to be slutty, being of intricate French lace that had cost me a mint at the time. It was also very sightly see-through and perfectly matched the lingerie John had bought me. Luckily, the dress also dictated the footwear. I didn't have a lot of shoes, and the only thing that went with it was a pair of flat gold roman sandals.

Five minutes before Dick was due to arrive, I placed the platter of gourmet treats on the table and the bottle of wine in an ice bucket. It was then I realised that I didn't have any decent wine glasses. I was forced to use a mismatched pair, including one shaped like a cactus.

I lined my lips perfectly in Mostly Mauve and checked myself in each of my mirrors, just in case one opinion differed from the others.

Dick arrived exactly on time, bearing a bunch of roses. Bless his cotton socks.

I invited him to sit and bustled about putting the roses in a vase. Had I been thinking instead of bustling, I would probably have asked him to open the wine at this point, but instead I did it, and was grateful to all the years of waitressing I'd done to put myself through uni.

I sat down beside him and faced a momentary dilemma over which glass to choose. The cactus-shaped one was clearly the biggest but the decorative spines made it difficult to hold.

'I'm so sorry about the glassware,' I said, eventually choosing the cactus. 'All of my good stuff is in my unit on the coast.'

He nodded sympathetically. 'Don't worry,' he said. 'It's the wine that's important.'

I'd never drunk out of my depth before!

'Salute,' I said, toasting him, and careful to look him in the eye.

'Salute,' he repeated.

We both took a sip of my last $30.

'Ohhh, that's a lovely young drop,' Dick said, studying the label. 'What a perfect choice for a Monday afternoon!'

I hoped the man in the bottle shop enjoyed a commission. Then I wondered how much an old drop cost. Darn my bit in the ad about fine wines!

Dick put his glass down and surveyed my platter. 'And what do we have here?' he enquired.

I gave him the tour.

'Roquefort cheese,' I said, pronouncing it as the woman at the shop had. 'King Island double Brie, homemade brandy pâté, smoked salmon, sun-dried tomatoes, smoked oysters, baba ghanouj, rocket leaves, lavosh, crusty bread, and of course . . . me.' I said, trailing off, hoping I didn't sound like something out of a badly scripted film.

'It all looks lovely,' Dick said, leaning forward and giving me a peck on the lips. 'Including you.'

I beamed at him and took a very large sip from my cactus.

'Oh . . . I should give you this,' Dick said, producing an envelope.

I was puzzled for a moment and took the envelope from him. It was unsealed. Good grief. Inside was a wad of $100 bills!

'Oh, thank you,' I said, as if it was the furthest thing from my mind. 'How lovely of you.'

How lovely of you? What a dill. I couldn't believe I'd said that!

I got up and carefully put the envelope on my desk. My heart was pounding. I wondered if skolling the lovely young drop was uncouth. Instead, I solemnly handed Dick my spare set of keys in exchange, explaining how to get into the building and where he could park his car in the secure area. I felt a small flicker of consternation when he casually stuffed them into the pocket of his pants, and resisted the urge to deliver a small lecture about not losing them.

Immediately after passing them over, I realised my first real mistake. I had given him the keys to my unit, as well as the security chip that gave him access to my floor and the car park. He could enter my home at any time he chose. I had met this man twice and had just given him the keys to (most) of my worldly possessions!

So I resorted to what I did best and commenced the best bluster I could muster. I managed to disguise the most pertinent question amidst a raft of soapboxes interspersed with comments about the weather. 'How much time do you have off this afternoon?' Translation: do you only have time for lunch or do you intend to fuck me as well?

'Oh, most of the afternoon, actually,' Dick replied, almost blushing and taking a sip of wine.

Oh my sweet Goddess! I was going to have to fuck him. A stranger. On a full stomach too! I took another sip of wine and wondered whether it would be appropriate to serve bourbon instead of coffee.

My heart pounded. I hoped this wasn't one of those uncrossable boundaries. Dick had just given me $1000 and now I was going to have to earn it. A whole $1000. I didn't know if I was cheap or expensive. Maybe I was a bargain and didn't even know it. The worrying thing was that it didn't feel bad. Dick was married and considerably older than I was, yet I was about to have sex with him. For money. I'm amazed to say it, but I was *glad* that I was about to fuck this man. There was no internal argument about whether or not I was 'in the mood' either. I was pre-paid. No-one ever reneges on pre-paid.

I timed my move perfectly.

'You know,' I said, tipping my cactus up and draining the last bit out of the stem, 'you have the most incredible, sexy blue eyes.'

It was true. I reluctantly put the cactus down then stroked a finger over his face. I wondered if it was a coincidence that my first John had sexy blue eyes as well.

'And you have beautiful deep brown ones,' Dick returned, cupping my chin in his hands.

I took the cue and leaned forward and kissed him on the mouth. At first gently, then more passionately as he responded. He was a darn good kisser. He didn't use his tongue too much and he had sensitive lips. He had shaved off every last skerrick of his beard and left me with a smooth palette that even a drag queen would be proud of. I also liked the smell of his after-shave. What a bonus. This was looking better all the time!

No matter how easy teenagers make it look, any kind of intimacy beyond kissing between two tall adults on any lounge is difficult. But somehow I managed it. I'd been worried about his erection – what if he didn't get one? What if our first fuck was a dud? But no problems so far. Lying sideways and craning my neck at a very unnatural angle, I somehow managed to squash my torso against him and grind my pussy into his crotch at the same time as kissing him passionately on the lips and neck. I continued to feel incredibly, amazingly, weirdly aroused.

When Dick started rubbing my breasts and nibbling at my neck, I suggested we go into the bedroom. I was hot for it.

Midway we paused for an embrace and he tried to undo the bra beneath my shirt. The $350 one. Without even seeing it first! It was the only really good underwear I owned. I couldn't wear it again so soon. So I removed his hands from around me and lifted off my dress in one motion. Then I stood back and gave him the full view. He was going to notice my fabulous lingerie even if I had to stick it under his nose and make him sniff it.

I don't think Dick even really saw it. Maybe he needed his glasses at this distance too. Instead, he ran his hands wonder-ingly up and down the curves of my waist. 'Oh, Holly,' was all he could say, shaking his head. 'I can't believe it. You don't know how long . . .'

I undid the buttons of his shirt and took it off while we were still standing in the lounge room. He was built remarkably well for an older man. Leaner and with less of a beer belly than many of the younger men I'd dated. His skin was whiter and older and redder than I was accustomed to, but my own wasn't exactly olive and glowing either.

I kissed his nipples and his chest while I grappled with his belt and the fly of his trousers. I could feel his erect penis beneath my hands.

I finally managed both belt and buttons and gently kissed his penis beneath his underpants while I swept his trousers down. Dick groaned gently.

Dammit. I'd forgotten his shoes! Shiny black Italian lace-ups with red socks. I vaguely wondered what he used to get them so clean. Maybe they were new.

Luckily, the hideous blue recliner that I loathed so much was right beside us. Dick sat down on the arm while I undid the laces and took off his shoes. Then I wondered about his socks. Should I take them off too? What if he had hideous, gnarled feet? I left his socks on and gently kissed the soles of his feet instead. They smelt OK. Prada socks. I didn't even know Prada made socks, let alone red ones.

I finished removing his trousers, kissing his hard penis again as I did so. I was glad to see he was a jocks rather than boxer shorts man – they're the unsexiest things I've ever had to negotiate in my life, not to mention the terrible things they do to the line of the thigh.

I led him into the bedroom and lay beside him on the bed, rubbing his crotch all the while and hoping he wouldn't lose his hard-on.

Dick groped for my bra again and this time I helped him, knowing full well that my nipples were erect by now and I was completely aroused.

'Beautiful,' he exclaimed, taking one nipple gently in his mouth and playing with the other between softly caressing fingers. I found myself watching the top of his balding head and being relieved that he didn't have a comb-over.

When he came up for air, I kissed his chest and moved down to his groin, kissing his penis again before taking off his underwear. Lucky me, it was a beauty! Perfectly formed, medium thickness and long. With a pair of nice clipped testicles lying underneath it. Maybe I should have bought a lottery ticket.

I gently kissed him everywhere except his cock – on the soft skin between his thighs, on his balls, little tiny nips on his hips and pelvis – all the while exploring his body and learning where his tickly bits were. It was an amazingly good body. Firm. The hair nicely trimmed. The fingernails manicured and clean. Whenever I got near his penis I gave it a soft little lick. Dick gasped with pleasure every time.

Finally I took it in my mouth suddenly and firmly, driving the full shaft down my throat in one swift motion. Dick just about had a heart attack. He gasped loudly and jumped about a foot in the air. I couldn't help giving a little giggle, but with his cock in my mouth it probably felt quite good. Dick seemed to think so, anyway. I hummed a bit to try to disguise the laugh that had escaped me.

He continued to moan as I deep-throated him, ignoring my gag reflex and sucking for all I was worth. I rolled my tongue over the head every time it came out of my throat and into the cavity of my mouth. Then I changed the tempo completely and took it gently and delicately, holding it ever-so-lightly in my fingertips. It was a tad confusing: he seemed to enjoy both techniques equally. Most men I'd fucked went for one or the other.

I continued to alternate between hard and fast and soft and slow. When my mouth got tired I used my hands and rubbed the tip of his cock gently over my wet lips. I must say, the effect it all had on Dick was very rewarding.

'Enough,' he eventually moaned, pulling my head up and towards his face. 'I can't wait any longer.'

Here goes, I thought. Deep breath. It's just another fuck. He's less than a boyfriend but more than a one-night stand. Fucking doesn't mean anything.

Does it?

I rubbed my pussy up and down his cock, ensuring that I was wet. I was. Very. How bizarre!

Then, mentally apologising to sex educators for what I was about to do, I lowered myself onto him, condomless and very horny.

Goddess forgive me, for I have sinned and am enjoying it!

Dick practically shrieked with pleasure. Three years of Pilates made for a very tight pelvic floor.

I moved myself up and down him, grabbing him with my muscles on each upward thrust. Every now and then I changed the tempo, moving between slow and lingering, hard and fast.

Dick moaned away, fondling my breasts distractedly with his eyes tightly shut. I vaguely wondered if he was pretending I was his wife. It sounds strange, but I hoped so. Maybe she'd get flowers too.

I continued to move up and down the length of his penis, seizing it over and over again with my pussy muscles. Sometimes I stopped and rested my thighs, still clenching him on and off inside me.

I checked his face. His breath was labouring. He looked a bit blue. I wondered if I should take his pulse.

His groans got louder so I started moving faster and harder, squeezing as tight as I could. 'Slow down,' Dick managed to stutter and I all but stopped, taking forever to slide his cock the full length of my pussy, nearly letting him fall out at the end of each movement, but grabbing him again with my pelvic floor just in the nick of time.

'My turn,' he whispered, pulling me off him and depositing me on the bed beside him. Yikes. Maybe this was where I found out he was kinky, after all.

Dick knelt beside the bed (lucky I had a fluffy white rug there) and spread my legs wide, exclaiming with delight at what he saw. He gently pulled apart the flaps and tentatively touched my clitoris. Then he leaned over and started licking it softly.

It was my turn to groan with pleasure. What an unexpected surprise. And I was the one getting paid!

Dick continued to lick and suck my clit, inserting his fingers in my pussy as he did so. Sometimes he rubbed his whole face in it or licked me like an ice-cream. I continued to groan and move beneath him, using my pelvic floor muscles to prop up the whole area to grant him better access.

I was approaching orgasm. Getting licked out by my second John. This couldn't be happening!

But I'd seen too many movies where the best lovers always orgasm spontaneously.

'Fuck me,' I whispered as my orgasm drew near. 'Fuck me hard.'

Dick gave me a look of great disappointment, his face still half buried in my pussy. Mistake number two, I thought momentarily. Always let the customer do what he wants, not what you'd expect him to want.

Dick rolled me over and entered me from behind. For a brief second I thought he was going for my anus and was grateful when he found my pussy easily and in one fluid movement. I put my hands up on the wall at the base of the bed and rocked against him for all I was worth.

'Oh Holly, oh Holly,' he kept saying. 'Thank you. Thank you.'

His thrusts got more urgent and all I could hear were the sounds of my own groans and heavy breathing. I've got to tell you – it felt good. Bloody good. Mindblowingly, distressingly good!

'Holly, Holly, Holly,' Dick eventually cried.

I forgot my own orgasm so great was my relief. But I didn't care. I had given Dick something denied him for ten years. A whole decade of no sex! I felt almost honoured that he had wanted me to fill the hole. No pun intended. But when was *I* going to start feeling bad about this? He was married. I was fucking him to pay my rent. Surely I had reached new heights of wickedness!

Dick collapsed on the bed beside me and I curled up against him, putting my head on his chest and stroking him. The strange feeling of exhilaration continued unabated. It must be me, I decided. Maybe I'd unconsciously been a pervert all this time. Or perhaps Darlinghurst did that to a person. Maybe I had some kind of mental illness and I just didn't know it. Lack of insight was a common enough symptom. Perhaps my over-active conscience was sick or something.

Harder still to believe was the possibility that I was merely doing a wonderful thing for a really nice man. Yet that was the impression I was left with.

'Oh Holly, thank you,' Dick kept saying over and over again, stroking my hair as his panting (and my own) gradually subsided.

It was the most satisfying orgasm I'd never had!

'That was extraordinary,' Dick finally managed to say. 'Thank you so much. You are a wonderful person, Holly. That was the greatest gift you could have given me. It's been such a long time – you've got no idea. I sometimes thought I'd never have sex again. I'm not sure if I could've lived with that. You've made me look at the rest of my life in such a different way.'

If Dick was telling the truth, he'd practically been revirgined. I felt incredibly privileged. Not only was he a fine and generous lover, but he was also paying me. It was inconceivable! I was actually doing the right thing. Everything would turn out for the best, after all.

I brought in the dregs of our wine and we drank to the relationship amidst the rumpled bedclothes.

'May this be long and happy,' Dick said, to my immense satisfaction.

And you know what? I wholeheartedly agreed with him. That in itself was weird, weird, weird!

He finished the wine and got up to shower. I happily pottered around the apartment naked, making the bed, nibbling at the leftovers and wishing I'd been able to afford something sweet for dessert. Next time, perhaps.

Dick emerged from the bathroom and realised with a shock that it was 5 p.m. 'I've got to dash!' he exclaimed, dressing quickly.

I must admit, I was glad he was going. I found his keys for him. Then I wondered where he kept mine.

'I can't make it tomorrow – maybe Wednesday?' Dick asked as he hurried out the door.

'Sure,' I said. 'I'm flexible.'

I gave him a wink, then watched as he rushed down the corridor towards the elevators without giving me a backward glance.

I stepped back into my dishevelled apartment, filled with relief about so many things. The absence of guilt was foremost amongst them, but so too was the fact that I enjoyed Dick's company, and that having sex with him wasn't nearly as hard as I'd thought it would be. Most importantly, I would be able to pay my rent and some of the outstanding bills. I finally had a job again.

But there were a lot of unanswered questions too – for instance, why I'd found sleeping with someone else's husband so rewarding. It wasn't for love this time. Surely it couldn't just be the money?

There had to be more to it than that.

# CHAPTER 10

Dick couldn't make it on Wednesday – he texted me early, saying he had meetings, and suggested a rendezvous on Thursday instead. So I spent the entire day revising the novel I had commenced all those months ago with John. At 10 a.m. Thursday Dick texted me again, saying not to worry about lunch and he'd see me about 3 o'clock.

This time I got a wonderful assortment of little cakes from the famous patisserie down the road and had a pot of coffee waiting for him. I had decided that I would wear my 'normal' clothes from now on, which were always smart casual, in case he wanted me to meet him somewhere or only wanted to talk.

He knocked on the door at 3 p.m. sharp and gave me a slightly distracted kiss as he walked in. He was beautifully dressed in another immaculate navy suit with his American college tie.

'I've only got half an hour between meetings,' he said, collapsing on the couch. 'This next one's a doozy – an investor wants to pull out of a $5 million portfolio we've just cranked up for him. Fool. Worried about one of the speculative stocks. Not a big position, either. Doesn't believe he'll get his 10 per cent – silly bugger will probably get 15, maybe even 20! Always was a soft cock. Oh Holly, sometimes I feel like taking my bat and just walking out on it all. I'm getting too tired for all of this.'

I made sympathetic noises and poured the coffee, trying not to wish *I* had an investment portfolio to pull out of.

Dick reached for a chocolate tart.

'You're going to make me fat,' he grumbled. 'The wife's had me on Pritikin for years.'

'Nah,' I told him. 'I'll work it off you.'

He gave me a sideways look, a tad shocked. I had to remind myself that he wasn't one of my horny nightclub suitors. He was, in fact, a man reasonably near retirement who'd only had sex once in the past ten years.

'Not today, unfortunately,' he said morosely, his thoughts clearly on the meeting ahead.

So I decided to don another of my hats instead.

'So why shouldn't this man pull out of the portfolio?' I asked, wondering if a 'portfolio' was a group of those numbers he'd talked about at Bilson's. 'What's wrong with it?'

'There's nothing wrong with it! While one or two of the investments might be speculative, the majority are all in com-panies whose stock we've carefully checked over and over again. It's a bull market, for Christ's sake! If value gets bashed down, ultimately it will recover. All we need to do is to keep dripping money into the portfolio and he'll come out a very rich man.'

I refrained from saying that, to my way of thinking, he already was a very rich man. 'You've convinced me,' I said instead. 'Now tell him the same thing.'

Dick stared at me and laughed.

'You're a treasure,' he exclaimed, leaning forward and kissing me on the forehead. He gulped down the rest of his tart and his coffee and rushed out the door. Once again, he didn't look back.

The entire visit had lasted about fifteen minutes. I thought of the money he'd given me earlier in the week and hoped

I could somehow make it up to him. Call me old-fashioned, but I liked to earn my keep.

Sugarbabes have strong work ethics too.


I spent a very quiet weekend devising ways to spoil Dick. I bought a set of excellent wine glasses, an expensive aroma-therapy candle and a couple of extra cushions for the couch. I fingered sheets with high thread counts that I couldn't afford yet and bought a couple of trays that I could use to bring him culinary delights in bed. I staked out gourmet delis and cake shops and flirted with sales staff in bottle shops. I decided that if Dick only wanted to see me a couple of times a week, I would make it up to him with treats. It seemed almost criminal that I would partake in them too.

He texted me at about nine on Monday morning. *Lunch again at 1?*

I texted back: *That would be delightful. C u then. H.*

I briefly wondered if he meant lunch at my place and then assumed that would be the case. It didn't seem right to text him back asking if he'd meant a restaurant or my apartment. Remembering his concerns about his weight, I walked down to World Square and bought the best prawns the rest of Dick's money could buy and some tropical fruits.

I took my time, meandering around the shops and rejoicing in the fact that shopping was now part of my job description. It felt incredibly liberating and free-spirited. I could move slowly like the jobless people did. I wasn't even dressed in a business suit. I was wearing thongs!

For the past twenty years I'd spent Monday mornings bemoaning the fact that the weekend was over and that I had to get through five days before it came around again. I was often hungover or feeling depressed from the fading echoes of parties with my friends. I couldn't tell my work colleagues the truth of what I'd been doing either. I was a freak in their world of children and family barbecues. I often cried on Monday mornings, no reason needed. I ended up going to a naturopath and getting a prescription for it, but gave up when I found myself pounding on her door at eight o'clock one Monday morning because I'd run out of the herbs.

But now the smile that John had put on my face so many months ago was back. Sometimes I'd even give a little giggle when I thought about how wonderful my new job was and how good it made me feel.

People smiled back at me. Men stared at me with lust in their eyes. If they didn't look twice I wondered if they were gay. The female components of couples put their arms protectively around their partners. Single women looked me up and down then touched their hair or adjusted their clothes. It was almost like being an attractive mannequin. I confidently returned the stares of my admirers instead of ducking my head down and feeling slightly defiled as I had before. I can't really describe the feeling. It was like: you can't afford me. It felt so darned sexy! No-one could have me unless I said so. Unless they paid the price I'd set. The ultimate empowerment. It didn't matter that they wanted me because they were lonely, or to make up for their wife or their business or their ego or their battered childhood. It was because they were prepared to pay for me. The ultimate in unpolitical sex.

Unpolitical sex. I was an unpolitical sex worker. Maybe it would catch on? I laughed aloud.

For the first time since the break-up, I hardly thought about John. Instead I thought about how to make Dick happy. I decided it really was a nice way to earn my money.


I trundled my groceries home and peeled and salted the prawns. Then I took a long, leisurely bath – at eleven o'clock on a Monday morning. How deliciously decadent!

By the time Dick arrived (exactly on time again) I had twin

plates of prawns, mangoes, avocados and organic peaches drizzled with a homemade dill mayonnaise sitting on the beautifully laid table. Beside them was a bottle of Bridgewater Mill riesling. This time, the wine had cost me $52. It was more than I had ever paid for alcohol in my life! My pair of new, freshly polished wine glasses stood there too, as well as a corkscrew and an ice bucket.

Today Dick was dressed in smart casuals – Ralph Lauren polo shirt, business trousers and expensive-looking brown loafers. I wondered if they were Gucci to match his Prada socks.

'You can do the honours,' I told Dick grandly, passing him the bottle of wine and fussing about, putting my new pillows behind his back and making sure he was comfortable.

Dick opened the wine like a pro and made suitably impressed noises about the vintage and the lovely presentation of my food.

'Sorry, gorgeous, but I can't stop long today – I'm supposed to be taking my wife out shopping for the grandkids' birthday presents.'

I felt a tiny twinge of disappointment. Was I jealous? I pushed the thought aside. Kev would probably think these sexless meetings were a bonus.

He took out an envelope and handed it to me. Inside was another bundle of hundreds. Once again I placed it on my desk.

We toasted each other and consumed my fabulous lunch. The prawns were as good as the man in the shop had promised and they went beautifully with the tropical fruits. We chatted about the investment market (thanks to Google, I now knew the difference between public and private companies) and Dick told me about his grandchildren and some of the problems his eldest daughter was having with them. He also told me he felt happier than he had in years, just knowing I was there for him.

He was gone within the hour, leaving behind an empty plate, most of the bottle of wine and his $1000. I resisted the impulse to ask when I'd see him again.

I sat down, consumed the rest of the wine and tried not to feel guilty about taking his money.

Thankfully, alcohol can do that for a person. Temporarily, anyway.


On Thursday Dick texted me again. *I need your urgent advice about something – can I come around about 3?*

Had we been discovered? Had I made him too happy? Maybe his wife had become suspicious. Perhaps his STD test results were in and he had a hideous disease – his cock had developed sores and he needed me to look at them.

I texted him back: *Of course. C u then. H.*

I walked down to World Square and visited the Asian bakery for some cakes, then went home and sweated it out, wondering what on earth a man such as Dick needed my advice about and becoming certain it was about to lead to my financial doom.

He swept in the door right on time, collapsed on the couch and put his head in his hands, completely ignoring the Chinese pineapple custard buns I'd placed before him.

'Good heavens, Dick. What's wrong?' I asked him, wondering what could possibly cause such despair.

'I think I want to leave my wife,' he said.

'Can I get you a drink?' was all I could say.

'Bourbon would be great, thanks.'

I poured stiff drinks for both of us. Oh shit. I hoped he didn't mean to leave her for me. I'd been through that one too many times before. Please don't let my second John become like my first.

I took a deep breath and donned my counsellor's hat. Then I took a very big swig of my bourbon and Coke. Wow. I was counselling a client and drinking alcohol at the same time!

'Well, er . . . that's understandable,' I said, wishing the bourbon was vodka. 'You've just realised what you're missing out on, that's all. And you said you've got nothing in common. But maybe I'm the wrong person to talk to. It mightn't be ethical. You know my opinion of troubled marriages isn't the best. I'm an animal lover – I hate to see a carcass being flogged, especially in front of the kids! But that's only my own experience; yours is probably completely different. Maybe you could live together on paper. Most of your kids have left home, for one thing. Plus you've got a big house; Sally doesn't have to know when you argue.'

Uncalled-for memories of my childhood flooded back to me. 'Argue,' I mused quietly. 'That's what my dad used to call it when we'd plead with them to stop fighting. "We're not fighting," he'd say. "We're just arguing." '

I made a face at Dick, who was shaking his head.

'We don't talk enough to argue!' he said. 'We just don't have anything in common. I don't think I can stand it much longer. You're right, of course – we'd stay married on paper, for the sake of the taxman, but we could sell the house. If we split it fifty–fifty she'd have enough for the rest of her life! I guess it's the kiddies I'm worried about – I couldn't stand it if I lost them too. Plus the trust would be vulnerable if we all started squabbling. But I just can't do it any more, Holly. The fight's gone out of me. I've lost my dazzle. And the love is gone – way gone – I realise that now. It's not fair to the kiddies either. We're living a lie for them. Every family get-together is like acting in a play! You've shown me what I'm missing, Holly. You've given me a baseline. I want to enjoy the rest of my life, not wait around to die in a strange country with someone I don't even like any more.' He put his head in his hands again.

I took another deep breath. Oh shit oh shit oh shit. I wanted to help marriages, not break them up!

But maybe she'd like the millions, a little voice said in the back of my head. Maybe she'd be relieved that he was finally leaving her. Perhaps neither of them had wanted to hurt the other.

I decided to act like the gutless psychologist I was and remain absolutely neutral.

'Well, you're a business man – why don't you approach the whole thing like a business partnership? Study the bottom line – can you afford to split? Suss out your champions – your own family – what do they think of the idea? Talk to the people that might walk with her, like your friends and children – would they take sides? I don't mean do it out in the open, just lay the groundwork; that way you're not committed if you change your mind. Apply the things that you do well. Do exactly as you would if it were a business partner you were contemplating splitting with. You're always fair to your partners, aren't you? Leave on good terms and all of that. And talk to *her* about it. Maybe she'd like to have her life back too. Have you ever tried to reignite things? She might have some good ideas! Besides, you know my theory about penis kilometres. Maybe it isn't dead; maybe it's just tired. And if it does all go pear-shaped, at least everyone will know you've tried and you haven't gone into the decision lightly.'

Somehow it was the right thing to say. Dick gazed at me with wonder in his eyes. 'Holly, you're a genius!' he said. 'I've broken business partnerships before – I can do this!'

I took another deep breath. I had to say the next words, even if they sounded my own death knell.

'You're an incredibly attractive man, Dick. You're an accomplished lover. You've got money. I don't think you'd have any trouble finding someone else. Talk to your wife. Even try relaxing the relationship for a while. It might sound drastic, but it's better than separating for the rest of your lives. You could even start a legitimate affair with someone suitable while you're laying the groundwork. Not me, I'm afraid. I'm too young; people would think you're having a mid-life crisis. But that way, if you meet someone nice, you wouldn't have to be alone for very long. Please, don't rush into anything. At least try all your options first. You're both intelligent adults. Surely you can negotiate your relationship into something you can live with.'

Dick continued to stare at me, mouth agape.

Now, I must digress briefly here. These were very unethical words for a person with my training. Psychologists were supposed to standardise behaviour, not redefine it!

'Er . . . I'd better let you know,' I warned, 'that's not professional advice. It's er . . . mistress advice, I guess. It's only my opinion. Not what a proper marriage counsellor would recommend at all.'

Dick merely nodded enthusiastically, as if musing upon all of the unattached females closer to his own age.

I felt a gloomy sense of déjà vu. Once again, it seemed I was providing the confidence to change a life. Once again, someone's new-found self-esteem would enable them to live without me. It was like John all over again. And my regular day job. I was just wearing the same spots in a different jungle.

'Holly, you're a treasure! You're absolutely right! Why can't we treat our personal relationships like our businesses? We should be negotiating, not compromising! We can't expect a marriage to stay the same, just like we can't expect a business to. How incredibly naive I've been! Needs change. *We* change! I loved my wife when I married her but we're both different people now. We have to be! You know, I was feeling incredibly guilty about all of this. I felt like I was betraying her because I didn't love her any more. But that's poppycock! It's natural when you think about it. She's had a different set of experiences than I have, become interested in different things. I haven't failed her – I've just grown in another direction! Holly, thank you so much. You're my treasure – you know that, don't you? I'll talk to my wife. Properly this time. See what she thinks. Maybe it's not too late to meet someone else – someone who I don't have to sneak around on. Maybe we could even be happy for a change!'

I couldn't help wondering about all of the men just like him who'd responded to my advertisement.

'Is that why you answered my ad, Dick? To find happiness?'

He gazed at his hands. 'To be honest, I don't think I really realised just how unhappy I was. I suppose it was a cry for help, in a way. People with happy marriages don't read personals! We were like that, once. But somewhere along the line, the fun stopped and we didn't even notice. Our marriage became a habit – a bad one, at that. It's hard to break habits. It's hard to even notice them! People like you are important, Holly. You remind us of how our marriages used to be. Should be still.'

Disquiet stole upon me like the poison from a sting. I thought of the 11,000 hits. Was it just me or was I on to a theme here?

I said nothing as Dick drained the rest of his drink.

'Don't look so worried, Holly-girl!' he said, noticing my concern. 'You might not have saved my marriage, but you sure have saved me!'

He left shortly after, hugging me to him and thanking me profusely for talking to him.

I poured myself another very large glass of Dick's bourbon and ate both of the untouched pineapple buns. Then I yearned for a cigarette. Dick wasn't the only one with unhealthy habits.

# CHAPTER 11

I spent yet another quiet weekend, some of it trying to write my tale about the old ladies. But I couldn't stop thinking about Dick. It was hard to tell whether I'd made things better or worse for him. In the end, I clung to the memory of the relief on his face when he realised the end of his marriage could be the start of a new life. I reminded myself that stories about couples who lived 'happily ever after' either left out the details or encountered problems in the sequel.

On Monday, Dick popped in for five minutes on the way to work, gave me my $1000 and left, telling me he was incredibly busy. 'I probably won't be able to get around until Friday,' he said as he rushed out the door. 'Thank you for being here. I couldn't do this without you.'

That made me feel worse!

I rang Kev at work.

'I can't believe he's paid you three grand and you've only fucked him once!' he said. 'You must be on the best wicket in the world.'

I wished I had his enthusiasm. I still felt amazingly good about myself and the sheer audacity of what I was doing, but

I couldn't shake the unsettling feeling that something was wrong.

Finally I decided it was guilt, and resolved to appease it when I saw Dick on Friday.

I didn't spend the week worrying; instead, I put aside my novel and wrote down my thoughts about the whole sugar daddy experience. Just bullet points in no particular order. Possible lessons for the future. It was tremendously cathartic. It seemed to make it more real somehow. It was almost hard to believe the woman I was writing about was me. The old Holly would have sat on the couch and worried and analysed and re-run all of the conversations in her head (this time with better replies). But the new Holly couldn't stop writing it all down. Recalling the sense of empowerment, remembering the conversations, reliving the feelings, tasting the emotions, examining the conclusions. Sometimes you need to describe undescribable things – writing helped me do this.

Above all, I continued to think that if the whole thing failed – even now – I was further along the chain of human experience than I'd been before. I'd done something I was incredibly proud of: I had moved beyond my boundaries and into the realm of the truly open-minded. The words flowed from my fingers onto the screen almost joyously as I recorded the details.

Maybe I'll write a book about this one day, I thought. I could help other women, just like me. Show them that their options aren't as limited as they think; that courage is an ideal travelling companion when pursuing happiness. But then I pushed the idea of publication away. I told myself that writing about these experiences would be unethical. Unprofessional. All of the things I didn't want to be. In the end, I saved the file as 'Possible Future Non-Fiction' and idly wondered if one of my geriatric heroines could suddenly develop a cheating husband.

\* \* \*

I filled in time by buying the *Australian Financial Review* and made myself read every word. Then I started reading back copies on the net.

I placed a bourbon in Dick's hand as soon as he walked in the door. A chunk of very soft Camembert and a sliver of Roquefort sat with crisp bagel chips and strawberry slices on the table. A platter of peeled prawns and lobster medallions drizzled in homemade seafood sauce were beside them.

I'd bought an $80 bottle of red wine this time. I wasn't sure if it went with the food, but Dick had told me red was his favourite. I couldn't even pronounce the name. How strange that there was an inverse ratio between the time we spent together and the cost of our food and beverages.

I wore my transparent silk pantaloons with a short green top and made sure he had a good view of my arse as I bent over to access the fridge. Once again, I wore John's fabulous under-wear.

Dick had barely finished his drink and sampled my canapés before he took me in his arms and kissed me, pulling me against a penis that was already hard. He pulled off both our clothes, leaving them in a heap on the living room floor. Like before, I was incredibly turned on. This time I tried not to question my luck.

He threw me down on the bed and parted my legs and went down on me, aggressively licking and sucking and making me groan in ecstasy. Every now and then he would look up at me, never stopping, but ensuring I was enjoying it. I met his eye each and every time, not saying anything, just writhing beneath him and using my pelvic floor muscles to prop myself up and spreading my legs as far apart as I could make them.

This time when I felt the beginnings of an orgasm I went with it, calling to him not to stop, thrusting beneath his tongue, feeling his fingers at my G-spot, moaning loudly, not caring what the neighbours might think. Finally it came and I could keep my eyes open no longer. The waves of pleasure rode over me and I don't know what I yelled, only that it was loud and intense and very, very welcome. Dick came up grinning broadly with my juices all over his face. He continued to probe at me with his fingers. I had to close my legs on my throbbing clit and roll away from him in a foetal position, gasping with pleasure.

'I thought it was supposed to be the other way around,' I finally croaked. 'You're the one who's supposed to be having all the fun!'

Dick just grinned. 'That *is* my fun,' he confessed.

He then made love to me like a man possessed, driving his cock into me harder and harder until he came too. Then we curled up into each other's arms and lay there smiling for hours, not saying a word.

Perhaps sin was in heaven, after all.

I spent the weekend in bliss, boasting to Kev about my 'gent' and telling him that I had accidentally discovered the best job in the world. All of my previous reservations had vanished. I'd made Dick happy! That was how it was supposed to be. I had a permanent grin from ear to ear and strolled about Darlinghurst and Paddington delightedly, believing my courageous new occupation was the most satisfying thing I'd ever done.

I bought some new clothes in the trendy boutiques along Crown Street: 'lounge room attire' with just the right amount of sex appeal. I got pedicured and manicured and waxed and bought some expensive cosmetics, joking to myself that I could claim them on my tax. I rationalised that spending money on my appearance was helping Dick too. Selfish, I know – but wonderful.

By Monday, there was just enough money left over from my shopping binge to prepare a fantastic lunch for Dick. I waited for his phone call all morning. At midday I checked my email. There was a message from him.

Hi Holly, I have spent most of the weekend thinking about our arrangement going forward. I've come to the pragmatic realisation that I simply don't have the time needed to devote to/and cherish the relationship. You deserve better than that. I sincerely regret being unable to continue. I hope you can find a replacement without too many hassles. So sorry, Holly. I feel really bad about this. Call you later. Dick

I couldn't believe it. It was just like John all over again. Dumped by email with no right of reply. Twice in one year and it was only March.

But unlike John, this time all I could think about was the money I was expecting to receive this week. My rent was due. And my mortgage. Once again I was flat broke.

I hit the reply button.

Hi Dick, It's your decision but you've left me in a terrible spot financially – this is not good :( Holly xxx

His response was immediate. He'd sent the original message at 9 a.m. He must have been waiting for my reaction all morning.

Holly, I know and I'm sorry for that. I do acknowledge my responsibility, however, and will pay you another $1000. I hope that helps a bit. Dick

I sweated over his words all day. It was the lack of feedback that was the most difficult. I was pre-paid; I wasn't entitled to feedback. That was one of the reasons why men had wanted to employ me. They could end it at any time and not endure a hissy fit. But not knowing the 'why' drove me crazy. With the exception of John, I'd always discussed the reasons when a relationship failed. Admittedly, half of them had been shouted at the time, but they were reasons all the same. I always had a *why*, even if it was a cliché. But Dick was different. I thought

I'd pampered him so very well. I couldn't understand where I'd failed. It was awful not being able to talk about it. Especially a second time.

I couldn't help myself. I had to know. At 3 p.m. I emailed him, with 'One question' as my subject line:

Hi Dick, I'm sorry but it's been bugging me all day – did I do anything wrong? Holly xxx

Once again, his response was almost instantaneous:

Hi Holly, No, not at all. You have been just sensational. The issues are all mine. Dick

It was about as clear as mud.

In the end, I guessed he was probably off seeking a legitimate mistress, just as I'd suggested – one who would be an easy transition from his wife if he decided to leave her, after all. That was why he hired me, I continued to remind myself – he wanted the break-up to be clean. Paying someone for a service meant there was no fear of stalking bunny-boilers, messy break-ups, retribution.

The trouble was, it brought up all of my issues about John again. Even though we'd declared our undying love for each other, I'd allowed that break-up to be clean as well. For the same reasons: I hadn't wanted to hurt his wife and children. Now I wondered whether I should have fought John's decision; confronted his wife and told her that their marriage was an illusion and he didn't love her any more. It wasn't my style, but perhaps I shouldn't have given up so easily. Maybe I had needed to learn about relationships with Dick before I attempted a long-term one with John. Surely his marriage was still as unhappy as he'd led me to believe. He said he'd been unhappy for ten long years. He'd even contemplated hanging himself! He was probably still depressed, even now. Surely our affair couldn't have improved things between them. Maybe they'd given the marriage their last best shot and failed. Maybe it wasn't too late to try and win him back. I could rescue him all over again.

Once again, I turned to my writing. This time I wrote a poem.

It took me ages. I called it 'Hidden Pride' and emailed it to John late that night. It was my first communication with him since I'd learnt about Charlene's threat to kill herself and murder the kids.

I checked my inbox first thing in the morning. There was no reply. No knight in shining armour come to rescue me. Maybe I was suffering some kind of princess complex, I thought. I was alone and very nearly penniless once again.

But I didn't mope. I had bills to pay and a rewarding new means of making money. I put John and Dick out of my mind and told myself to stop mourning the closed doors behind me. I would open one in front of me instead. I thought about Brandon and Mahut and wished I'd still conducted the meetings with Alexander and Roger. Out of the four of them, I considered the unknown Alexander as the only real possibility; I wasn't ready to become a submissive quite yet, and Brandon and Mahut had far too much boyfriend potential.

Curses. I was going to have to readvertise.

I put the very same ad back up on Persona. This time I resolved to let it run the full week and to establish a back-up list if I could. I even paid an extra $20 for a 'premium' placement and put it in both the 'escorts' and the 'men seeking women' sections. If you're going to do something, you may as well do it properly, I told myself.

In the afternoon I went to an internet café to read my responses, catering to my paranoia that somehow my respondents could find me if I downloaded their messages to my computer at home. The café was reasonably full and I cringed when I saw SUGAR DADDY in big capital letters in some of the subject lines. Two people were using the computer beside me, one looking over his friend's shoulder. I had a sneaking suspicion he could see my screen too. My inbox was already half full. I felt incredibly guilty at seeing one from Mahut.

Dear Holly, Hope you are well. The reason for this email is that I saw your ad again on Persona and was wondering if you are free again. If so please let me know if you'd like to meet with me. Cheers, Mahut

I'd only placed the ad a couple of hours ago! Maybe rocket scientists were good with software and he'd somehow put an alert on me. I answered his message first.

Dear Mahut, You are indeed a very lovely man. I am so sorry, but I don't think you are suitable. I'll be honest – I want someone with whom there is no risk of love. I have kept your contact details, and if things don't work out I will certainly get in touch. Once again I am promising exclusivity and I am a woman of my word, so we cannot meet again. Good luck in all that you do. Cheers, Holly

I'm ashamed to say the 'we cannot meet again' gave me a little rush of pleasure. It seemed so decadent to be using those words! I sent off the email with a sigh of regret. He was indeed a lovely man.

Then I turned to some of the other 'applicants'.

Hi, I am very interested in your proposal. I have assisted women in return for favours several times before. Please send your full proposal with an outline of your financial requirements. I look forward to discussing it further. Sincerely, Kevin hi little lady, what are you doing tonight? I'm hot for you. Bill

Hello there, I am 17 years old and looking for a ldy. How much are you? Adam

Hi, I am a businessman searching for someone to spoil. Please call me on ——. Tony

Like before, the various respondents seemed to fall into three main groups: young men who had no time to find a girlfriend; men with children whose wives were probably too exhausted to have sex; and older businessmen who had grown out of their marriages.

I answered them all with the same blurb I had used before, once again inserting the fact that I cost '$1000 to live' at the end. I also inserted a line telling them I was using an internet café because of problems with my ISP and that I would only be checking my email once a day.

Like last time, there were a lot of men proposing part-time or one-off arrangements. Some of them sounded like really nice people. I politely refused most of them immediately. To me, having part-time sugar daddies bordered on prostitution. Maybe that was why I was so obsessed with being faithful to just one man, even if he was being unfaithful himself.

But I also wanted to help these men. If the number of responses was any indication, there were an awful lot of sexless marriages and cheating husbands. In the end, there were so many requests for casual or part-time arrangements from married men that I cut and pasted some advice about communicating with their wives more and tried to tell myself I was somehow helping them anyway.

On Wednesday there was another email from Roger, this time with a different username:

Holly, I see you advertised again on Persona. Let me once again say I am intrigued and would like to invite you to lunch. Please accept. Roger

Hi Roger, Thank you for your lovely invitation. Glad to see you are consistent! As before, I have received a lot of responses and am hoping to start someone on Monday. If this does not eventuate, I would be delighted to have lunch with you. However, if it does, I will in effect be breaking my word re exclusivity and I do not think that is the right thing to do. I'll let you know early next week. Cheers, Holly

Holly, the businessman in me says this: you start the exclusive Monday week; you meet me before. I am a gentleman, and would never white-ant another gentleman where a lady is concerned. Cheers, Roger

Roger, LOL! OK, since you asked so nicely I would be pleased to have lunch with you. This is as much about personal growth for me as it is for you (no pun intended). You have knowledge in areas that I didn't know existed. Cheers, Holly

Then I forgot about Roger and spent the next two days arranging meetings. This time I wasn't going to rush it. Thanks to Dick's generosity, most of my bills were paid and my money situation wasn't too dire. I resolved to start my new 'gent' in ten days' time.

# CHAPTER 12

Hi Holly, I have raed your description in detail and I really liked your sincerity . . . Let me give you a brief about my self . . . I am 41/m/married . . . well educated with enginnering as my base degree and then MBA . . . I am software professional and is involved in execution of large projects I enjoy lot of sports like cricket, tenis, AFL . . . and most of all is stimulating conversation . . . Yes we all have physical needs and when these needs are coupled with inner beauty then it becomes enjoyable experience . . . I really liked your idea of trying this out for a wek and see where it leads to . . . I would like to meet you soon and have a chat to ensure that we are on the same page. Cheers Alfred

Dear Alfred, I would be delighted to meet you and discuss the proposed arrangement further. Where do you suggest? Cheers, Holly

Dear Holly, I work with an enginnering company in netral bay. I have very buse week so can we met at the Oaks which is nearby? Alfred

The misspellings seemed to be a combination of rapid typing, little proofing and English being his second language. I couldn't help wondering if Alfred was frightened of being caught by his boss or his wife. Then I wondered which was worse.

Ignoring my previous reservations about meeting my potential applicants in pubs, I walked into The Oaks feeling very glamorous. The North Sydney 'suits' apparently thought so too, and I received a lot of appreciative glances from men who had probably had far too much to drink. Once again, it was obvious there were no Alfreds hovering, even though it was a big pub and the bars were very crowded. I wished I'd had the guts to ask him what nationality I was looking for – but it seemed so politically incorrect.

I texted him: *I'm here in the room with the big TV screen. H*

Then I went to the bar and got myself a vodka and soda. The room I'd chosen was mostly occupied by post-work groups and I was the only single person there. I kept glancing at my watch and gazing around so that no-one would try to pick me up.

Alfred texted me a couple of minutes later: *Still in meeting – can't talk now.*

I decided to investigate the tavern while I was waiting and wandered through the various rooms with my drink in hand. Everywhere I walked, men gave me admiring glances and their girlfriends or work colleagues glared at me. I wondered what they would think if they knew why I was really there.

I had just settled myself down in the outside area when Alfred texted me again: *Here now in the bar with the TV screen. Where are you?*

I texted him back: *Stay there. I'm coming. H*

I walked quickly back to the first room and scanned it. There he was, an Indian man looking around expectantly and holding two glasses of champagne. I walked over.

'Alfred?' I asked needlessly.

'Holly,' he said.

I gave him a quick peck on the lips.

He saw my vodka and seemed a trifle embarrassed about the champagne.

'Ohhh, that's much better!' I declared. I placed the remains of my vodka to one side and took the proffered flute though I couldn't help a twinge of regret for the waste of good Stoli.

Alfred was very overweight and it was difficult not to compare him unfavourably with the elegance of Mahut. His hair was very greasy and his teeth were crooked. His breath smelt of garlic. He also looked stressed and over-worked. I knew immediately that this wasn't my man. I wished I could leave.

Worse still were the looks from the men who'd given me the eye earlier. They were staring at Alfred as if they were thinking, 'What's that guy got that we haven't?' It probably saved the day. I felt immediately defensive of Alfred and resolved to make the experience as pleasant as possible for him. I launched into my bluffery and even bought a second round of champagne, mostly for the benefit of the men who were watching us. I touched Alfred's arm as often as I could and laughed merrily at his jokes. I knew he wasn't for me, but there was no way I was going to let him lose face in front of all the men around us.

He cited the same old story – a wife who'd lost interest in sex and a disinclination to divorce. He wanted to see me in the evenings and I found myself wondering – yet again – about the wives who were left home alone.

After the second glass of bubbly, he asked me if he could take me to dinner and then looked very disappointed when I regretfully declined, citing a 'previous engagement'.

'I must travel into the city. May I extend you a lift in my taxi cab?' Alfred asked me.

It seemed petty to refuse. Besides, it would be good 'face' for us to be seen leaving together.

'Sure,' I said. 'That would be lovely.'

In the end, we couldn't find a taxi and we both took the

train to Town Hall station. It was difficult to talk with commuters on either side of us. I was glad for the break.

'I'm interviewing people all next week,' I told him. 'I'll let you know by Friday.'

I gave him a kiss on the lips, knowing it would be the last time I saw him. I hoped he had enjoyed the experience and the looks of envy he'd received. He was a nice man. He deserved better.

I spent yet another quiet weekend adding to my 'Possible Future Non-Fiction' file. I'd realised that it was better to keep writing down what I was feeling, rather than go over and over the same thoughts and self-doubts in my head. I also tried to ignore the themes that were emerging.

On Monday I checked my messages at the internet café.

Hello Holly, Your profile sounds very similar to me, as I appreciate the quality things in life. I will be upfront with you as I dont want to waste your time. I am married and am 40 years of age, live in an executive apartment at Erskinville my wife is a professional and I am a business owner. I require a PA to assist me within my business and would also appreciate a long-term arrangement to en-corporate your finer qualities and enjoyment of life. I can offer you a job as my personal assistant with the added arrangement as per your advertisement , I am very interested to meet you and hopefully get aquatinted. Below are my contact details for your perusal, and hope to hear from you soon! Regards, Henry

It was an interesting proposal. Being a PA would be less stressful than counselling, but the sex component would provide a comparative income. Maybe this was a way to fuse both occupations.

I met Henry at Taylor Square and we walked down Victoria Street in search of a café. I liked the look of him right away;

he was what I'd describe as a 'man's man' – you could imagine him driving a ute and drinking VB with his mates. He was probably in his mid-forties with straight blond shoulder-length hair and one of those little goatees I dubbed 'clit-ticklers'. His eyes squinted with the look of someone who'd spent a lot of years in the outdoors. He was probably just under six foot tall and his body was tough and wiry with barely a hint of a beer belly.

Henry confessed a love of cakes and desserts so we selected a café with a windowful of French pastries. He chose a chocolate fudge brownie with double cream. I asked for a flat white coffee without the froth.

'Have a taste,' he urged me, cutting off a great slab of the brownie and proffering it to me on his fork.

'No, no, I'm fine, thank you,' I replied, recoiling from the giant mouthful that would've surely finished up in my lap.

'Beautiful,' Henry concluded, his mouth full of chocolate. 'Not better than sex but on a par, eh?' He winked at me.

'That depends if you're on a diet or not,' I replied, smiling.

'Bah!' Henry declared. 'Show me a woman with a good appetite any day! There's no bigger turn-off than women who only eat salad. I like my babes with handles.' He eyed my chest. 'Jugs too, eh?'

I laughed.

'So why are you interested in buying jugs?' I asked him.

Henry chuckled – the easy laughter of a man with a blokey sense of humour.

'Well,' he replied, 'I've gone and won more work than I can bloody handle. Never thought I'd see the day! Got myself a multi-million-dollar contract building a display village in western Sydney. Impressive, eh? Trouble is, the work's snow-balled – more trucks, more sites, more equipment and more blokes. I'm looking for someone to help me. Someone with a brain or two. Figured you might be interested. I realise admin ain't your thing, but it's a lot of other stuff too. When I saw your ad, I thought, here's the girl for me – a genuine all-rounder. Nothing like a pretty offsider to win respect from the blokes, I reckon.'

'So you want to combine the job with sex?'

'Bit different, eh?' Henry said. 'To be honest, I can't afford to pay you a grand a week – not yet anyway. But I could if you'd do some work for me as well. That way, I'd be rolling two jobs into one and the paperwork still looks good for the wife. Not a bad idea, eh? Was pretty pleased with it myself.'

'What would the work involve?' I asked.

'It's mostly PA stuff – answering the phones, typing up correspondence, organising my diary – there's a lot of work to get through. Builders are an ornery bunch – before I go onto a site I try and know everything about them first. That way, there's no nasty surprises. You'll be able to help with that too – do the research while I do the hard yards. But it won't all be hard work – there'll be lots of play too. Sometimes we might have to fly interstate together or do a round of golf with a client. Or we might just give ourselves the afternoon off and spend it under the doona.' He gave me another wink.

'Where are your offices?' I asked. 'Where are you proposing to base me?'

'I work from home,' Henry replied. 'We've got a lovely place in Erskineville, plenty of parking – you'll be going against the traffic so it won't take you long in the a.m. The job'll be full-time, but you could do it in four days if you wanted. Besides, you'll probably make up for it when we go away on trips.'

'What about your wife? Where does she work?'

'She works in town – she's not home a lot. But it's important to me that you like her and she likes you. I'd lay down my life for that woman! But the trouble is, she ain't as highly sexed as I am. Don't get me wrong, she's a real spunk-bucket; all the blokes think so. I'm just hoping that she'll grow to like you in the same way I do. Then we could have some real fun together – come out of the closet, so to speak.'

He grinned. He'd obviously thought about this a lot.

'But is she . . . er . . . that way inclined?' I asked. 'Have you had threesomes before?'

'Once we did but the other babe wasn't really into her,' Henry replied. 'She's got the potential, I reckon. Always checking other women out. Keeps herself nice too. Nothing worse than a woman who lets herself go. But she'd like you, I reckon. She'll come around, I know she will. Nothing like a good-looking sheila to add a bit of spice, eh?'

In a way, it was incredibly appealing. He was the first man to suggest being honest about me to his wife. Well, eventually.

'So at first we'd be having sex in your wife's own bed under her very nose,' I clarified. 'This woman I'm supposed to meet and be friends with first?'

'Er . . . yeah. But that's OK, ain't it? Sex with you has got nothing to do with my love for her. She's not stupid by a long shot – she'll realise that, especially if we play our cards properly. Ease her into it, like. Even let her think she came up with the idea. Lead her on a bit. You're good at romancin', aren't you?'

That was half the trouble – he was probably right. My work made it easy for me to establish a rapport with people. I wasn't especially likeable, merely well-trained! Poor Mrs Henry would have no chance. She'd probably never guess that Henry and I had been 'practising' in the meantime. I couldn't become friends with a person that I was knowingly betraying. It was wrong. I wasn't exactly travelling the moral high road these days but I wasn't going to stoop that low.

'I've got to be honest, Henry. You've pressed a lot of buttons for me, but unless you're prepared to tell her right from the start, I just couldn't do it. It's hard enough as it is. Besides, I'm not very good at lying; especially to someone's face. I'm sorry. I don't think I can help you. Thanks, I'm really flattered, but I don't think I'm your girl.'

Henry appeared dumbfounded.

'But surely this must be your best offer! No-one could afford to have you sittin' about every week! It's a good plan of yours, but just not practical. Better to work for me, eh? That way, everyone wins.'

I laughed. 'You'd be surprised, Henry. To be honest, you're the only person that's suggested I do other stuff for them. Most of them would probably be horrified if I got involved in their work! They want to keep me at arm's length from their lives. I'm sorry you can't afford me, but there's no way I'm going to work a 40-hour week *and* have sex with you.'

The audacity of my words! 'You can't afford me.' You don't get to say that too often.

'Bloody hell,' Henry said, shaking his head. 'Some blokes have got it all. They must be earning a fortune!'

'You will soon be too,' I told him encouragingly. 'If this deal comes through, you'll be in the top hundred companies before you know it.'

He laughed. 'I hope you're right. Is it OK if I keep in touch? Maybe catch a beer one day?'

'No problem,' I replied.

I walked him back to his car – naturally it was a Ford V8 ute. Unusually pristine for a builder. Maybe he didn't like getting his hands dirty either.

Walking home, I hoped things would never get so desperate that I ended up sitting beside him in that ute. Betraying a wife was bad enough; betraying a friend was unforgivable. Henry was suggesting I do both.

# CHAPTER 13

Hello, I may not fit your profile as I am only 31, but I am married with four small children and looking for a woman very much like yourself. I am the assistant general manager at a major chemical engineering plant and have considerable time 'between meetings' ;0 May I take you to an obligation-free lunch? I adore Japanese – are there any restaurants near your place? Andre

Dear Andre, I too love sushi so I would be delighted to have lunch with you. There is a sushi train around the corner that is both popular and tasty. Cheers, Holly

Andre was late. I texted him after fifteen minutes asking if we were still on. He rang me from his cab, telling me the driver had driven him to the wrong area by mistake and he was on his way.

While I waited, I watched the trade pass in and out of the sushi bar. There were an awful lot of diners, packed in shoulder to shoulder – I wondered what they would think of the conversation Andre and I were about to embark on.

A guy I vaguely knew was having lunch with a woman. They

were both in suits; probably work colleagues. I sighed with relief when people took the chairs on either side of them. I couldn't for the life of me remember how old Andre was – what if he was elderly and pawed me in full view of my acquaintance? Running into friends with an older man on my arm wasn't something I'd considered before. Most of them would think the worst right away, and in this case it was the truth.

When Andre finally got out of his taxi, I was incredibly relieved. He was young, tall, dark and very, very sexy. He spotted me immediately.

'Holly, I'm so sorry I'm late,' he said, rushing over and kissing me on the lips as if he'd known me all my life. 'The taxi driver thought I meant Oxford Street at the Junction!' He looked at his watch. 'Pfft!' he said, with an elegant shrug of his shoulders and a toss of his head. 'It doesn't really matter, I've got all afternoon.'

I bristled a tad at his assumption that *I* had all afternoon, but then reminded myself that such afternoons were, after all, what this was all about. As we walked into the restaurant it struck me that life as a sugarbabe was a lot easier than being a wife or a girlfriend. I had a clear job description for one thing.

Andre ordered us a Sapporo beer each. I told him I didn't need a glass. 'Salute,' I said and we touched bottles, drinking whilst holding each other's gaze.

The restaurant was still packed and we sat shoulder to shoulder, thigh to thigh.

'So,' Andre said, smiling. 'Tell me about yourself.'

I prattled on with the usual story about leaving my counselling job to work on my novel. I told him my savings had run out mid-project and I was trialling the whole sugar daddy thing as a means to work from home. I gave him my spiel about the cooking and the pampering and the sex. I made it sound like I had chosen to be a sugarbabe rather than being forced to try it out of desperation. I certainly didn't mention the failed relationships with John and Dick.

He looked sheepish. 'I've got to be truthful with you, Holly. It sounds like a fine plan but unfortunately I'm not your man. Although I'm married and I love my wife and children, I already have a wide circle of women friends who I entertain regularly. I think I love women too much – I'm Latino, you know.'

As if that explained everything!

'I must admit, I wanted to meet you,' he continued, 'to meet a woman who proposes such things. But I can't afford $1000 every week. I'm sorry I got you here under false pretences. I was wondering if you'd be interested in going out on the occasional date. I want to get to know you better. You're incredibly beautiful – I'd like to be seen with you, if I could.'

I felt a surge of disappointment. Andre was a very attractive man and easily one of the sexiest I'd ever met. He had brown intelligent eyes and a lovely clean-shaven mouth, and his teeth were very white and perfectly straight. That didn't explain why I was so attracted to him though. Surely it wasn't because he was a 'ladies man' – I hated those guys!

I laughed to myself. It was probably a good thing anyway. I'd never feel happy as part of a 'harem', and what had happened to choosing someone I wouldn't fall in love with? Andre was a danger man – in so many ways.

'I'm sorry, Andre,' I replied. 'I'm not sure if we could. This is business for me, not pleasure. Besides, I'm going to be exclusive, remember? I'd never be able to have sex with you – I'd just be a . . . tease.' I would like to say I blushed, but I was far from it!

Andre laughed and leaned back on his stool to study me.

'Men tease themselves all the time with women like you – don't you realise that? Half the men you know probably think about you when they have a wank. That's what men do! Hell, why do you think we keep our eyes closed when we make love? So don't stress – you'd never be able to tease us half as much as we tease ourselves!'

I was unconvinced. For one thing, half the men I knew were gay and definitely *not* fantasising about me, and the other half were long-time friends who probably wouldn't even notice if I grew an extra set of tits! But there was something compelling about Andre. I'd regretted letting that something slip away with Mahut. Perhaps it was time to ignore my misgivings.

'Well,' I said reluctantly, brushing aside everything I'd resolved so far, 'as long as we don't have sex, I guess it would be OK to see you.'

'There!' he said. 'That wasn't so hard, was it? I'm not proposing to molest you or anything – just a long lunch every now and then, fine food and wines, good conversation. Is there anything wrong with that?'

If there was, I couldn't think of it. In fact, all I could think about was the hole this man's thigh was burning in my own. The sexual tension between us was extraordinary. I hadn't met anyone like him before. It certainly wasn't love; it was pure and simple get-down-and-dirty lust.

He ordered us another beer and I wondered how I was going to keep my hands off him. Maybe that was Andre's gimmick – he tortured women with lust to see how long we could last under the pretence of *us* teasing *him*! I hadn't realised there were so many games to play. The trouble with naivety is that you need to lose it in order to realise you had it in the first place.

I debated whether to have another dish of sushi or not. I'd gobbled down four already, including three California rolls. Andre had eaten three, his fourth sat untouched in front of him. He put one hand on my thigh, cupped my chin with the other and kissed me.

So much for not molesting me! Darn those Sapporo beers!

Phew. What a kiss. It was as if all my erogenous zones became joined together by lengths of string. There were no in-between bits, just horny parts of my anatomy screaming for attention. Andre's hand brushed my neck as it came down from my face and ever-so-slightly brushed against my chest. Right on the nipple. Funny that.

I almost led him out of the restaurant and up to my apartment. I was prepared to shatter my promises and break all my boundaries. But only for a moment. Even with all of my buttons on fire and being temporarily single and available, I still turned him down. With great reluctance. He was a tad too practised; too smooth; too confident. I couldn't help observing behaviours he probably wasn't even aware of – the way his tongue flicked over his teeth, or the way an accidental touch was always a trifle too long and bang on target.

Perhaps I was rejecting those aspects of myself that I feared would develop along my new career path. I didn't want to become a predator; I just wanted to pay my bills and help people at the same time. So I excused myself, rushed home and masturbated like crazy.

I texted Andre afterwards: *Thanks for a wonderful lunch. Sorry I fled. Went home to have a play. H*

*Oh darling*, he replied. *I could have helped you with that.*

An email followed later that afternoon:

Hi Holly, Today was brilliant, really enjoyed looking deep into your eyes . . . it's a real pity you had to take care of yourself . . . I would have luved to watch you while I did the same . . . I think the excitement of not being able to touch each other would really set my juices rushing!!! I will have a think of your proposal. As I said, I have a very sexy circle of girlfriends I regularly indulge in dinners drinks . . . cook for them and so on . . . the cost of 3-4 dinners or lunches a week is enough to be realistic. i don't think I can allocate more funds without raising suspicion. I am still happy to entertain you purely as friends as I understand your commitment. However I really do not want to stop communicating with you as you are one very Sexy individual which I am happy to speak to and go home to masturbate . . . Andre

Hi Andre, I agree, I think our meeting was the most enjoyable one of all so far – albeit probably the most dangerous, because I am tempted to join your circle for pleasure rather than business. Alas, I am a woman of my word and as from Monday, I will no longer be a free woman. There are several likely prospects and if it makes it any easier for you, I will probably choose someone who is 'safe' rather than someone who is 'dangerous'. I enjoy playing and my own fantasies immensely, so this will certainly not be the last time you are in my thoughts . . . Ciao, Holly

# CHAPTER 14

I was reading your post today on Persona and I am interested in learning more about you, who wouldnt be :) I am a successful businessman aged 39 . . . so not too old :) . . . married but looking for some extra fun. I travel a lot and would love to have a companion for those trips away both interstate and internationally. So hopefully you would be available to this . . . of course happy to cover these costs. I suppose my first question is how much allowance are you looking for ?? Not wanting to waste each others time. The next step is to meet up and have a chat to see if we click, because thats an important part for me. Hope to hear from you soon. Philip

I had sent my usual response and waited several days for his reply.

Holly, I finally got some spare time so thought I would take the time to respond further so you know a little bit more about me, my motivation and my likes . . . as opposed to my quick response before. Only fair since you took the time to put it all down. I mostly own media interests, plus a few investments. But often get described as 'too normal' for media, which I take as a compliment. I am 6'1", about 110 kgs so I am carrying a few extra kilos which is a result of my busy life and no time for exercise. So maybe your motivation skills can come in handy and get me exercising :) Having weekday meetings is fine and fits with me as well, as I can always sneak out for an 'important meeting'. The trial concept seems like a good place to start as well. My motivation is purely sexual . . . the idea of having somebody who enjoys my company and me is a great desire. I enjoy the company of a woman who likes to control and is confident in what she wants . . . I can see you meet this point. I love to be teased . . . a woman dressed in lingerie just close enough to allow my fingertips to brush but not enough to grab is ultimate, watching a woman satisfying herself putting her desires above mine and a woman confident enough of her body to enjoy playing dress-ups in a costume is another sexual desire. I love buying my lovers lingerie so if we make a connection then I can see me taking you shopping. I look forward to meeting you on Friday if you can make it, some additional photos of you would be an excellent treat as well. Philip

Dear Philip, My goodness! How can I resist an offer like that? Would you like to meet on Friday for a coffee? H

I hung around the entrance to Starbucks for about fifteen minutes before going to the counter and ordering an iced chai latte. The waitress asked me if I wanted a loyalty card again. I really had to find somewhere else to meet my gents.

Philip walked in just as I was approaching the seated area out the front. Once again, he was easy to spot – a man by himself, running late, nervously scanning the patrons for someone who might look like the whore of Babylon but wrote a halfway decent email.

'Philip,' I said, noticing the question mark had gone from my voice.

'Holly.' He looked relieved. 'I'll just get a coffee. Where do you want to sit?'

I eyed the staff eyeing me.

'Outside in the sunshine would be nice.'

'I'll meet you out there.'

I selected the table with the fewest neighbours, sat down, crossed my legs, uncrossed them again, put my bag on the chair beside me, took it off again, put it on the ground and then ended up putting it between my feet. Somehow Philip had managed to pass his nervousness onto me.

He sat down at the table, bearing a large hot chocolate. He was somewhere in his late thirties with dark wavy hair and clear brown skin. He sounded like he was suffering from a bad bout of sinusitis and his nose was very snuffly. He was considerably overweight, but as someone whose own weight had fluctuated enormously over the years, extra kilos had never been a problem for me.

'I'm sorry I was delayed,' he said. 'My meeting ran over. The chair was a pansy. Don't you just hate it when they fart around?'

'Absolutely,' I said, as if farting chairpeople were the bane of my everyday existence.

'It's the industry,' he went on. 'Never stops. Geez, I'm glad we got into IT when we did, otherwise we'd be screwed by now.'

'What do you do again?' I asked (as opposed to 'who do you work for?', which was too prying under the circumstances).

'I've got a lot of media holdings,' he replied. 'Mostly private. I started out as a journo and now hire the plebs to do that. Not just conventional media either: I was lucky enough to get into technology just when the dot-com boom was taking hold. Commonality of interest and all that. Thank Christ I did – wouldn't like to be in just print right now! But I like a challenge. That's why I'm the first at work every morning and the last to leave. Not much goes on without my knowing it. That way, people respect me. They come to me first if there's a problem. That's how things should be.'

He gave me a wink. I laughed dutifully.

'So, apart from filling in time between meetings, why are you interested in me?' I asked. 'You're young and attractive – you could get yourself someone easily. Why would you want to pay?'

How refreshing that I got to ask all of the most important questions upfront! In a single meeting, I got to know these men better than most of my clients and all my first dates.

'Compromise,' Philip declared. 'You're halfway between a wife and a hooker. Tried to get myself a mistress once – we had sex a few times but then she got all serious on me. It was completely one-sided. She even wanted me to leave my wife! Rang the house a couple of times – during dinner too! It was terrible. My wife found out all about it. I was a nervous wreck; nearly lost the business. I don't want that again. She'd leave me next time. My wife, I mean.'

'So I'm a . . . compromise?' I prodded, trying hard not to be offended.

'Don't let it worry you,' he replied. 'Today everything's a compromise. Take my wife, for instance – she's a compromise. Shouldn't have married her really, never was much good in the sack. But I knew she'd be a great mother and she's a brilliant cook. But the goddess part – well, I have to outsource that. Can't expect her to be good at everything, I suppose. Don't get me wrong – I love her dearly, but she's so involved with the kids. When I get home she's too exhausted for sex and she's up feeding the baby half the night. I feel guilty every time I get a hard-on! These days we're lucky if we do it once a month.'

He looked gloomy. It was hard not to smack him.

'I guess that's the key to people these days. We're specialists. No single person has everything you want. Certainly not staff anyway; or wives, for that matter. Not enough time, for one thing. That's why I want you on the payroll – to ease the workload, so to speak.' He studied me carefully. I gave him what I hoped was my most reassuring smile. 'This is just easier. No chance of people who want to perform outside their job description,' he concluded. 'What about you? You don't seem the . . . er . . . type.'

I told him my usual story. Once again, I tried to convey that I had voluntarily chosen to become a sugarbabe out of my commitment to the novel, rather than being forced to do it out of financial necessity. It just sounded better that way.

'Dreams, eh?' he said. 'I'm really into what motivates people – usually I can figure it out within moments of meeting them. You can tell a lot about a person over coffee or lunch. Normally it's money or power. But people who are motivated by their dreams have the most passion. They're the ones who stay late after work or come in on the weekends. It's a pity there isn't a job test for it.'

I laughed.

'I think you might have dreams mixed up with attitude,' I told him. 'A lot of people don't do anything about their dreams. It's attitude that makes a person exceed expectations. Big companies have cottoned on – they're recruiting for attitude, not skills, these days. You can always teach someone how to use a computer or how to run a company, but you can't teach them high motivation or a desire to succeed. They can measure it now – it's called behavioural interviewing. It's incredibly interesting. I could give you some tests for it, if you like.'

Philip looked impressed.

'So what motivates you?' he asked.

'It changes,' I said. 'If I haven't got enough, it's money. But when I do have enough, I'd like to think it's the desire to help people. I've always believed that you should leave people in a better condition than you found them. Trouble is, that's very subjective. I've lost a lot of friends over the years because of my meddling. The trick is to get their permission first!' I smiled.

'So what's your novel about?' he asked. 'How's it going to help people?'

I didn't tell him that I had just converted the 'Possible

Non-Fiction' file into a diary and it now had its very own icon on my desktop. Nor did I tell him it was raising issues I hadn't known existed. And I certainly didn't confess I'd probably be jotting down today's conversation.

'It's about the adventures of four little old ladies,' I told him. He didn't have to know that I hadn't touched it for days. 'They're very unpolitically correct – they make me laugh even as I write. I guess they're all of the things I'm too frightened to be. They're controversial because they're supposedly too old to be doing the things they're doing. Little old ladies being reckless is shocking! It's written on several levels – a bit like *The Simpsons*. Elderly people will laugh at very different things to people our age. Hopefully, anyway.'

Philip nodded. 'Have you got a publisher?'

'I haven't even thought about it,' I told him truthfully. 'I want to get it finished first.'

I thought back to my previous manuscripts. Most of them were propping up my bookcase.

'Well, I'm in the media,' he said. 'Maybe I could help you. You scratch my back and I'll scratch yours. I tell my staff that all the time. I've got to admit, this is an excellent proposition of yours. I don't usually read Persona. It's lucky I saw you.'

'To be honest, I'm quite amazed how many people have seen it. I didn't even know Persona existed before this. They don't even advertise! It's incredible.'

'Well, a lot of us have more time on our hands than you'd think. Just because we're sitting at our computer doesn't mean we're working. Someone told me the other day that RSVP gets more hits on a work day than any other website. Geez, I believe them!' He winked at me again.

'But surely most men aren't in your position,' I protested. 'Most people are too busy at their jobs to scour internet sites. You're just one of the lucky ones.'

'You'd be surprised, Holly,' he said. 'I'd be willing to bet that ad of yours has had hundreds of responses and thousands of hits. Let's call it a gap in society that's not being filled. Men are men. We'll never change. We need sex and people like you in our lives. It doesn't mean we don't love our spouses; they just learn to turn a blind eye for the sake of the finances. Look at the Rich 200 list – how many of them are divorced? Not many. But they all name mistresses when they're divvying up the estate. When have you ever heard an outcry about that, huh? Never, that's when! That's because mistresses are *expected*.'

I was wrong – this wasn't a theme, it was a three-part saga! In my urgent attempt to feed myself, I had somehow stumbled upon a secret kept by half the world. What a pity the other half weren't in on it.

Or were they?

Philip looked at his watch. 'Speaking about expectations, I've only got a few minutes left. I'm very sorry, but I've got to go soon. I'm still very interested. I've also got a trip overseas coming up. To Europe. You could come with me. How would you feel about that?'

I'm glad to say I was still naive enough to wonder whether he was trying to lure me into some kind of white slave trade. Then I scolded myself. As if!

'I'd love to travel,' I said coolly, pushing up my excitement and down my misgivings. 'My passport is current. You're definitely the best so far. For lots of reasons. I like the fact that you're interested in motivation too. I tell you what – let's make an executive decision right now. Let's do it. I've spoken to enough people already. I know what I want. Would you be prepared to start on Monday?'

'Sure,' he replied. 'That's what I'm here for, isn't it? A Monday start it is.'

I gave him a peck on the lips and he picked up his briefcase and walked back down the busy street.

It wasn't until after he'd left that I realised I hadn't even got his phone number.

# CHAPTER 15

Hi, Am very intersting in your ad – you look erotically elegant I was in similar position for about six months and ended when her visa expired. Please send your proposal with financial expectation and we discuss. Cheers, Tom

I sent him back my standard $1000 reply.

Hi Holly, Thanks for reply. Your proposal sound reasonable. Would you like to meet for coffee – somewhere you feel safe and comfortable to discuss detailed arrangement, since anticpate that you would do screening process. Lot of questions in mind, from you? A home cooked dinner for all visit is appetising and indulgent, any desert? No need for Moet and lobster – we can dine at restaurant heeeeeheeee. Pardon, I do have wicked sense of humour. Let me know a suitable time. Cheers, Tom

Call me what you will, I ended up meeting Tom on Saturday, mainly because I'm a sucker for a wicked sense of humour. It couldn't do any harm. Another meeting or two before Monday would hopefully just confirm the decision I'd made about Philip.

Was I becoming addicted to these meetings? I had to admit, they were awfully flattering. But it was much more than that. I was starting to think there was something terribly amiss with traditional marriage. Maybe I just wanted to find someone who could prove me wrong.

Naturally, I was five minutes early. I was hovering in the shop next to Starbucks when I got a text from Tom: *Here early*.

I smiled and looked around. There he was, coming towards me, just as he'd described – tall, thin and elegant in an immaculate suit and looking every inch Chinese new money with heaps of designer bling. He saw me immediately and we gave each other a smile.

'How are you, Hollee?' Tom asked, hugging me. 'Let's go here.' He nodded to a French patisserie.

'Sure,' I replied, following him in. I hoped they didn't have loyalty cards.

Tom went rather haughtily up to the counter and ordered us two coffees, plus a pastry for himself. I declined. It's very hard to look elegant eating a flaky pastry. Believe me, I know. I studied his back. I had finally found a man with John's walk! That authoritative swagger of a man who has spent much of his life telling other people what to do.

We sat down at a small table along one of the walls and I tried not to speculate how good the proprietor's hearing was, given we were the only people in the tiny shop.

When our order arrived, he'd given me a mini chocolate tart alongside my coffee. Gratis. Maybe he recognised Tom's walk too. Or maybe he just knew a tart when he saw one.

Tom eyed my treat and confessed a terrible love for desserts. I couldn't help thinking that perhaps I should introduce him to Henry.

'You got that as a child?' I asked. 'I'm a bit the same. My mother used to cook us beautiful homemade desserts like steamed jam pudding with custard from scratch or golden syrup dumplings and ice-cream. It's good in a way, because shop-bought cakes just don't do it for me. But if we go to a café and there's home-made old-fashioned stuff, I'm a goner!'

I smiled at him and hoped he knew what 'goner' meant.

'Not for me,' Tom said with a graceful wave of his hand. He had extraordinarily long fingers. 'When we grew up we had servants. We just tell them what we wanted and they cook for us. Even dessert. Everything. They do special for me though. I'm favourite.'

He laughed.

'You were the youngest?' I said, eating the tart in a single bite and hopefully leaving my lipstick intact.

'Not youngest. Smartest,' he said, with a wink and a giggle. 'I very lucky. Most of my brothers and sisters gone early. The servants missed them. I was spoilt.' He giggled again.

I couldn't help wondering if he would treat me like a servant. For that matter, how *did* one treat a servant?

'Ahhh, the favoured child then,' I said, watching him expertly dissect his vanilla slice with a cake fork.

Tom waved his elegant fingers in the air and dismissed the notion with a shrug. 'Not so favoured. Just shrewdest. Most opportunistic. My father died owning many, many properties in China. They all still in my name. He died ten years ago and they still in probate waiting for me. The whole family, they look to me now. I look after everyone. I am the most important son.'

'But what about your older siblings? Why did your father choose you?' I couldn't help asking. Maybe it was a Chinese thing.

'I am the most trained,' he replied, not offended at all. 'I have people everywhere. All of them loyal to me. Whoever I need, I take.'

'And is that what Chinese people do?' I asked him. 'Take mistresses?'

He laughed. 'Chinese people more civilised,' he said. 'When wife is unable to make love, I mean. For instance, when wife has baby, we lock her up for six weeks. We lock her up!'

'Lock her up?' I said incredulously. 'A new mother and her baby?'

He giggled again and I couldn't help noticing the really long fingernails on his pinkies. I wondered what they were for. They were obviously long on purpose; his other nails were beautifully manicured. I put my own well-bitten fingernails in my lap.

'We hire woman,' he explained. 'Even poor families find the money or they get an aunt to come. She take over the role of housekeeper and mother. She take on all the roles. The new mother, she just rest. She not allowed to go out at all.'

It sounded like a formalised arrangement of visits by the grandparents shortly after Australian births. But I wondered what he meant by 'all' the roles – did that include lovemaking as well? I was tempted to ask, but I didn't want to offend him. Not yet, anyway.

'Well,' I said, desperately wishing for a bona fide Australian mother beside me to inform me whether I should be outraged or pleased by this arrangement, 'that could be a good idea, I guess. Most of the new mothers I've known always seem exhausted in the first month. They're always complaining about lack of sleep anyway. Poor things look shattered! Maybe it would be good to just rest for a month or so after the birth. But what about feeding the baby? Doesn't that take up a lot of her time?'

'Ahhh,' said Tom, waving his hands around again. 'Sometimes she just do that or sometimes we get wet nurse. Poor woman, usually. Need money. Same thing. Same thing.'

'And the baby?' I asked, trying to ignore the concept of an Australian baby sucking on some other mother's tit. 'Is it allowed to go out or is it locked up too?'

'Oh no!' said Tom, as if I had blasphemed. 'Child stay in house also. Birth very traumatic. Baby sometimes bright red. Sometimes yellow. Sometimes they have bruises. Many babies ugly at first. Cry a lot too. World different from womb. They need to recover. They need to adjust. That way, both rested and happy by the time they come out of house.'

Call me a traitor to western ways, but it sounded like a bloody good idea to me. I wouldn't have minded being quarantined when I was hormonal. A lot of my friends would probably agree.

'So Chinese people are used to having other women? What about your wife? How would she feel about it?' I asked.

He looked sad. 'No . . . we separate now. Marriage no good. I have two sons, age ten and eleven. I only see them weekend. That why I need woman. To replace wife's duties.'

He took another bite of his vanilla slice.

'How long have you been separated for?' I asked, wary of so-called 'separations' and envisaging someone like John's wife coming at me with a pitchfork.

'She no want me for eight years,' he replied. 'Eight years long time to wait.' He shook his head and looked gloomy.

A beautiful young man appeared and asked us if we would like some more coffee. I did a double-take – where had he come from? He was absolutely gorgeous – dark-haired, olive complexion, tall and lean. The proprietor was still standing at the counter. We were still the only customers in the shop. Surely we didn't warrant being served by two staff! I couldn't help being paranoid. Even I would have liked to eavesdrop on our conversation and I was in it!

Tom squinted at the waiter, having taken off his glasses. I gave a mental chuckle when I realised Dick wasn't the only man who didn't want to appear with 'four eyes'.

'Where you from?' he demanded.

The handsome young man looked taken back. 'Er . . . Chatswood,' he said.

I shifted uncomfortably in my seat but Tom just laughed.

'No. Where you *really* come from?' he demanded.

'Oh,' said the gorgeous young thing. 'I come from Malta – a small place, no-one has ever heard of it.'

'Near Cyprus?' Tom prompted.

'Yeah,' said the young man, looking impressed. 'You've been there?'

'Not there,' Tom replied, with one of his graceful shrugs. 'But near there.'

'It's not a very big country,' the man said. 'You wouldn't want to stay there for very long.'

'A weekender,' I quipped.

Tom laughed uproariously. 'A weekender!' he said. 'She just call your whole country a weekender!'

I was embarrassed but the young man just laughed nervously. I don't think he realised I had just insulted his country. Tom saw he didn't get it either and gave me a mischievous wink.

'She say your country only good for two days,' he explained to the man.

Don't you love that? I could get on well with this man. He reminded me of my friends!

To my relief, the waiter turned to me and smiled. 'Yeah, two days would be good,' he said in all seriousness.

I gave him a big smile back. 'I was only joking,' I explained, sheepishly.

As the waiter moved away, Tom took my hand and we gazed at each other over the table.

'You'll do,' Tom said with a wink.

'I'll do?' I said, laughing. 'But will you? Do you have any other interviews?'

Tom shook his head theatrically, looking doleful.

'Well, I do,' I replied playfully. '*I'm* the one picking *you*, you know – not the other way around.'

'Where do I come on list?' he asked.

'Don't worry. You're up there near the top.'

'Near top is best,' Tom said. 'Not good to be number one. Number one always get shafted. Number two better.'

He looked at his watch. 'Must go now,' he said. 'No time.'

He swallowed the last of his coffee and paid our bill.

'Thanks for the tart. I'm quite partial to a tart,' I told the proprietor, setting it up for Tom with a wink.

But Tom put his head down and kept walking. The proprietor, on the other hand, looked me up and down suggestively and gave me a very big smile. I was now enjoying the sexist glances of strange men who ran patisseries. My wallflower had finally bloomed.

Tom had unknowingly parked his car in my street and pointed it out to me. A black new model Mercedes Benz. Not being into cars, I barely gave it a glance. I pointed out my building.

'Ahhh,' he said, scrutinising it closely. 'Remember, the East is best. You tell me soon? Where I come on list?'

'Soon,' I said, wondering vaguely how Philip would feel if I gazumped him for a giggling Chinese man with a playful disposition.

Tom insisted on walking me to my door and solemnly shook my hand goodbye. Unlike the others, he glanced back several times.

As I took the lift up to my apartment, there was something about him that I couldn't put my finger on. I was tremendously attracted to him, but it was hard to know if it was merely his air of mystery and intrigue. I could learn a lot from this man, I thought. But curiosity killed the cat too.

I puzzled about him all afternoon. I'd never met anyone like him before. In the end, I emailed him for more information.

Hi Tom, I hate to do this, but I am having problems choosing between yourself and one other. I am about to delete my advertisement. You are very different people, but he is 'safer' and less mysterious. I say 'safer' because it might be easier to make him happy because he is quite easy to read (and therefore easy for me to deliver what he wants). However, I keep coming back to the East. There is something about you that intrigues me. I am incredibly drawn to you. I think you have more lessons for me and

I really like your sense of humour. So I need to ask you a few questions that I didn't cover earlier so I can decide . . .

The first (and most important) is are you still interested? The second (and I'm sorry for being so direct) is what kind of sex do you enjoy? Is there anything in particular that you like or dislike? The final one (and I guess this is what I am a tad worried about because I do not know a lot about your culture) is how will you treat me? Will I be just another 'servant' to you? I'm sorry to ask these questions – I hope they're not too rude. Cheers, Holly

I didn't receive his reply until almost midnight.

My dear Holy, I was waiting for your call all afternoon – disappointed that you did not called quickly not realizing that you send email. The afternoon was low time for me and had dinner date tonight. Feeling unwell now. Nevermind, will try to answer question. I must be 'watching' an episode of The Apprentice – only that all applicants were eliminated with the last two. My most desirable friend, I am not that complex but suppose it can be difficult with just one meeting of one hour duration. We did discuss the ranking as a joke, yet it eventuate that you are faced with a decision only you can make yourself. I wll try to make it easier. I am surprised that you are still not sure of my committment and interest. One word YES. The attraction are mutual and you are very warm, compassionate and sensous lady – sex with you will be most pleasurable. My imagination are running wild . . . I am easy to please when it come to sex, my past experiences had been the vanilla type of sex, supposed it is the Eastern culture – would love to experiment with you. How about some kinky sex-toys fetishes etc and have this fantasy of watching group sex, 3some MFF only is fine with me. I like sex and find it arousing – remember do not like routine as I been restrained in the past. To pleasure and be pleasured!!!!!! Emotional satisfaction with personal and physical. Do not be overly concerned about my culture, I am called a 'banana' in our eastern social group. A banana person is with yellow on the outside and white inside – does it make sense to you? You would be treated with most respect I would with any person – I am down to earth person and easy to get along with. I am 'true blue aussie' and adapted to the australian (western) way of life. I love to be pampered and 'spoilted' but not in the manner as master, would never subjected you to a servant status, you can be assured. You did mentioned you enjoyed cooking and entertaining. That is the key to my heart. I am struggling to express my sexual needs in words. Hope this had enlighten you to make your decison. Whatever decision you make, I am sure we can remain as friend in future. Thinking of you. Lot of kisses and hugs. Tom

Tom was right when he said number one always got shafted. I went to bed wondering if Philip checked his email on Sundays.

# CHAPTER 16

Hi Holly, I am very interested in your advertisement on Persona. I will be back in Sydney this weekend and would like to meet with you. Jacques

I sent him my usual response and he quickly wrote back.

Thanks for replying, Holly. I am most certainly still interested. I am actually in Boston right now and will be for the next couple of days, but would love to catch up for a coffee on my return to Sydney – maybe on Monday. I imagine that your delightfully worded personal will attract no shortage of attention and loads of replies, so I'll make my own case briefly. I'm a postgrad educated corporate type; usually operating under significant stress and so the idea of a sanctuary has an obvious attraction. At the risk of blowing too loud on my own trumpet, I am youthful, highly intelligent and have lived in several countries. I'm civilised, love to be spoiled and have no difficulty spending money. As you describe it, the arrangement sounds remarkably good. I cannot help but think what's the catch? (Natural cynicism.) Whilst I am a realist, the idea of exclusivity is so mentally appealing that this is likely to be a far better type of arrangement for me than other situations that I can imagine. I'm sure the exclusivity appeal relates to something in the murky past of evolutionary biology. I have some concerns about discretion, and of course there is the issue of compatibility. I have lots of questions in my mind, but for all this I think the best way forward is to meet up as you suggest and we can both see how well we relate. Let me know if Monday or Tuesday sometime is good. For now, Jacques

Hi Jacques, I can promise you there is no 'catch' per se, I merely want to meet my living expenses and lavish attention upon a lover whilst I finish a novel. I am an extremely honest person and I daresay I could find someone to support me by the usual means, but I would prefer to be upfront about why I want a relationship. Interestingly enough, I feel incredibly mature to be doing such a thing – it is a first for me and it is good to know my lateral thinking is backed up by a mind that is truly open, rather than some of the minds that pretend to be. The ad has received an extraordinary amount of attention, but it has been relatively easy to sort the wheat from the chaff (so to speak!). There have been several late replies from people OS such as yourself and I am almost tempted to delay my choice another week, especially as Easter may interfere. LOL! You are absolutely right about 'evolutionary biology' – I am beginning to realise the Darwinian survival of the fittest is very much alive and well, no matter how progressed we think we are . . . As for discretion, it is both part of my professional ethics and reputation ;0 Ideally, the arrangement would last several months as that is the minimum time I judge my novel will take to finish. At this stage, I am really hoping to have someone start next week, however I will get in touch if arrangements fall through. Cheers, Holly

It was with deep regret that I had pushed the 'send' key – Jacques had somehow managed to tick boxes I didn't even know I had!

Holly, Sad that it seems I have missed the opportunity to . . . audition. I'm back in sydney tomorrow, Saturday, if that information helps my cause. Btw I'm 40 and half african-american with a cappucino complexion. (oh the downside of a competitive nature!) Let me know if you are still looking for an arrangement at some stage. Jacques

Hi Jacques, you got me on the competitive nature ;0 How about meeting on Sunday? I am available all day and am open to suggestions. My telephone number is ——. Perhaps you might like to call me on Saturday. Cheers, Holly

OK, I'll confess – it was his last email that got me. How could the daughter of Mrs South Port Stephens resist an invitation from an inward-bound, cappuccino-coloured man?

The last one, I promised myself. No more.

And so once again I found myself loitering outside Starbucks. Trouble was, I was running out of suitable outfits. I hoped the staff wouldn't remember I'd been wearing this yesterday.

Jacques was late. I hovered out the front. An olive-skinned, South American-looking man was sitting on the lounge near the door. He was watching me intently. He looked more like a drug dealer than a sugar daddy. His skin wasn't exactly what I'd call cappuccino, but then again, I was no expert.

'Are you Jacques?' I asked him, frowning.

'I could be, if you wanted me to be,' he replied.

'No . . . that's OK,' I said, backing away.

At 12.15, I started to worry that Jacques might not turn up and I didn't have his number, just his email address. I resolved to wait another half an hour and then go back and email him, telling him that I had already found someone I was interested in.

At twenty past, I got a chai latte.

The man out the front kept staring at me and I hoped this wasn't some weird test of Jacques's to see how I'd react. So I chose a table out of his line of sight and became engrossed in one of the café's street rags. I was getting very blasé – no more regular glances at the door or at my watch. Let him find me.

'Holly?'

I looked up.

A very large man with an incredibly hard face stood before me. He was dressed in a very dark, beautifully tailored double-breasted suit with a mobile phone apparently glued to his ear.

I nodded. Despite his bulk, he was strangely appealing. Tall, black beady eyes, mostly bald and very, very cappuccino. I wondered if only cappuccino-coloured people got to call themselves that. I hoped not – it was an apt description for a truly beautiful skin tone.

'I'll get a drink,' he mouthed at me, going over to the counter, still talking on his mobile phone.

We studied each other from across the room. How he managed to do so at the same time as talking on his phone and ordering his coffee I had no idea, but it certainly felt as if I was under intense and undistracted scrutiny. Maybe men could multi-task, after all.

By the time he got back, I'm ashamed to say I knew I wanted to fuck this man. There was something about him, something totally forbidden – a tad evil perhaps. It wasn't the colour of his skin; it was something animalistic. He seemed like a man for whom sex was a way of life rather than a pastime.

Jacques sat down, placing his coffee on the table and his mobile in his pocket. 'I'm sorry I'm late,' he said in a slight French accent, patting his pocket. 'Business. Always.'

'That's OK,' I told him. 'It's Sunday. I haven't got anything better to do.'

Duh! What happened to my 'being late is a power trip' speech? It had gone down well with Dick. But somehow I didn't think it would with this man.

'You are very beautiful,' he observed clinically.

'Er . . . thank you. I'd like to say it was good living, but it's probably more a case of lots of artificial preservatives and colourings. I'm probably also a bit pickled in vodka,' I joked.

I smiled my most winning smile. He didn't smile back.

'I must tell you, this conversation must remain very confidential. I have a family. Connections. It cannot be repeated to anyone,' he said sternly.

'Don't worry,' I reassured him. 'I hold more people's secrets than you could possibly imagine. It's part of my professional oath.'

He nodded.

'I have another secret. I'm not really African–American. I just look that way. I'm French–Algerian. I find it easier to describe myself in terms people can understand.'

I just nodded dumbly.

'I also have a dark past,' he continued. 'I have seen wars, death – I have seen things you would not believe. They were not pretty and they have scarred me ever since I was a small child.'

I continued to grin like an idiot. Admitting a bad childhood to a psychologist was like waving candy in front of a baby.

'Er . . . maybe I could help you with that,' I replied. 'I'm good at childhoods. That's part of the service I'm offering – counselling, I mean. If you have any problems, maybe we could work on them at the same time.'

Jacques nodded again, still studying me intensely with those black eyes. It made me feel like a cheap hooker. The really weird thing was, it was turning me on. Sure, I'd been studied in this very way many times before, but it was always by someone who wanted to pick me up; never by someone who wanted to *buy* me. I felt like a traitor to all of the years of feminist training by my wonderful mother.

'What else can you offer me?' he demanded roughly, casually sweeping his glance down to my breasts and up again.

Sweet Goddess. Those eyes. They were positively evil. But I wanted them to sweep me again. I took a deep breath.

'I can offer you fabulous cooking, a great apartment with 24/7 parking . . . and I really like sex,' I ended, almost shyly.

What was happening to me? This very unattractive man was turning me into jelly!

'What kind of sex?' he asked.

'Well . . . I'll give almost anything a go. The first time, I mean. But if I don't like it, I won't try it again. Mostly "plain vanilla", I guess . . . plus I like the occasional threesome.'

'Do you like women?'

'Sometimes. If I like their boyfriends,' I joked.

I smiled again. Jacques just nodded.

'Why are you doing this?' he demanded.

I told him about my old job and my increasing sense of alienation in offices. I told him about the novel and Kev's idea. Somehow I managed to keep the diary to myself, but it was hard not to tell this man everything.

'Kev?' he said abruptly. 'Who is Kev?'

'Kev is one of my best friends. We went to uni together. He has one of the best relationships I know. They've been together for over ten years now. He's gay,' I concluded, as if that explained everything.

'Ahhh,' said Jacques. 'Gay men make good partners for beautiful women. What about your family? Where are they? Do they know what you're doing?'

'As if,' I replied, beginning to relax a little. 'My mother would kill me. She wants me to work in an office and accumulate long-service leave. She'd be horrified! No-one knows – except Kev, that is. I guess I don't want anyone to know. They'd all worry about me, for one thing. This is something I need to do by myself. It's *personal*.'

Jacques nodded again, still studying me intently with those wicked eyes. Now I knew why vermin froze when snakes observed them!

'What about you?' I asked tentatively. 'What do you want out of this?'

Jacques looked at me sharply.

'I want a woman,' he said. 'You might do nicely. When do we start?'

'Er . . . well . . . I was thinking of starting tomorrow, actually. Trouble is, I've already . . . er . . . . I've already told someone that . . . er . . .' I trailed off when I saw the expression on Jacques' face.

He was scowling ominously. All he needed to complete the picture of a hard-bitten commando was one of those bullet belts strung across his chest and over his shoulder. It didn't matter that he was wearing a three-piece suit. It was his presence. There was something about him.

'Maybe you'd like to come and see my apartment first?' I said meekly.

Now 'meek' is not normally a word in my vocabulary. The effect this man was having on me was bizarre. I had dealt with mass murderers more assertively than I was behaving now.

'OK,' he said, getting up immediately. 'Let's go.'

Thank goodness I'd cleaned up before I left.

Jacques didn't offer to take my arm like the others did. But he did glare at every man who perved at me. I could see it in their eyes. They would look at me and then they would look at him. Normally, they gave my companion a glance of casual envy. Today they gave a little start and turned away.

My heart pounded as we walked. Jacques exuded an extraordinary aura of everything I'd never wanted. I could easily picture him as a rebel soldier leading a group of toughened mercenaries. The closest I'd ever been to a seasoned fighter was on Anzac Day.

I snuck a sideways glance at him as he walked silently beside me. I have to confess, I wanted to be this man's chattel! Where had this come from? Why was I attracted to this horrible person? Could it be that all women felt like this or was I a freak?

Maybe I'd overdosed on my own pollen, or something. Please Goddess, I prayed. Don't let the chauvinists be right.

When we got to my floor, I swept my door open with a flourish, mentally checking my underwear and sternly telling myself I was not going to let this man fuck me.

I needn't have worried. Jacques took one look at the room, gazed out at my view a moment, then casually threw a large bundle of hundred-dollar bills on my coffee table. 'I'll see you tomorrow,' he said bluntly, kissing me on the lips.

I'm reluctant to report that I didn't even hesitate. Instead, I responded in kind, kissing those cruel lips underneath those cold, dark eyes. It was a long, lingering kiss, as sensual as I could possibly make it.

'I'll come tonight,' Jacques amended.

'OK,' I said timidly and showed him out.

I collapsed on the couch and tried to analyse my reactions. My personality was exhibiting adjectives it had never known before. I didn't care. Even the money didn't matter any more. Or my bills. I just wanted to bathe in Jacques' presence again.

I know, dear reader, you are probably considering me quite a fool by now – a nymphomaniac bimbo with some kind of perverse childhood that led me to this life of sin and debauchery, despite all of the advantages of my upbringing. But I swear to you, not a single sleazy uncle or randy school teacher ever crossed my path: in a way, I almost feel ashamed that I have taken so long to explore the most important frontier in my life – me.

I had time on my hands, so I went into the bedroom and masturbated, imagining that Jacques was fucking me. If it were possible to masturbate from behind, I would have done that too. Somehow I imagined doggy-style would be his favourite.

That night, I got onto the internet and told everyone I'd made my choice. This time, I kept it open-ended, saying it was only on a trial basis. I didn't actually say I wanted them as spares but I implied it. I told Philip I'd met a publisher. I hoped it would fit with his assessment of what motivated me.

I sat up for hours, waiting for Jacques to call. I woke up on the couch with my hand between my legs. I suspected it was the first time ever my instinct had completely overruled my intellect.

The next morning, I got up early and typed up everything I could remember about Jacques in my diary. It wasn't because I needed to understand him: I needed to understand myself.

I think up until that point in my life, I had always felt some kind of intellectual attraction for the people I'd had sex with. Some of them were funny, others were mysterious, and I knew I had a fetish for intelligence. But I didn't even *like* Jacques. In fact, he stood for everything I despised. Yet I couldn't get him out of my mind. All I could think about was fucking him.

Then I realised my mistake. Up until meeting Jacques, I had always confused my physical need for sex with some kind of emotion. It sounds weird now, but I needed to *love* the penises I was using. But that was almost like saying I couldn't be massaged by hands I didn't feel an emotional attachment to, or I couldn't exchange conversation with a tongue I didn't find attractive. I finally understood that I had attributed an emotion to what was, in effect, just another working part of someone else's body. I had confused nouns with adjectives; instinct with intellect; function with process; sex with love.

The really disturbing thing was that I realised men already knew this. When women joke that men think with their penises or will fuck anything that moves, we're actually ridiculing our own confusion, not theirs. Of course, this doesn't mean that emotions can't improve (or worsen) sex, they just aren't mandatory. That had been my mistake, and my reaction to Jacques had proved it.

Once again, I found myself spending my precious money on a wax and 'treats' for the fridge. These were my priorities now. That in itself felt good; it sure beat paying the phone bill.

Jacques had said he liked vodka, so I bought a bottle of that too. Maybe he had some good qualities, after all.

He wasn't coming around until 9 p.m. so I bought some little cakes for 'dessert'. I couldn't help wondering if he'd want to smear them all over me. So I went out and bought a couple of custard tarts, just in case.

Then I took a long bath and hand-washed John's underwear.

John. What would he think of me now? Would he still love me? He'd once described himself as a doormat – they tended to wear thin; would he be damaged beyond repair? Do human beings love the very essence of a person, or just their particular mind-set? Maybe that's why the divorce rate is so high, I mused. Mind-sets change. People don't grow in different directions – their needs and wants do.

By the time Jacques arrived, I had put a password on my diary and was looking my radiant best in the turquoise silk number with the matching cream silk pants. I had also consumed a very large vodka and soda.

'Drink?' I asked him, as he walked in. 'I'm having vodka myself.' I nodded at the untouched drink on the table. In a small glass, this time.

'Vodka would be nice,' he said, sweeping into the room and over to the magnificent view.

I made his drink and joined him on the balcony.

'Cheers,' I said, chinking his glass.

'Cheers,' he replied, holding my eye and taking a swig of his drink.

Then came the moment I'd been waiting for. He roughly pulled me into the lounge room and put down his drink. He took my own out of my hand and put that down too. Then he enveloped me in his arms and kissed me.

It was a powerful kiss. Not a kiss that you'd want to spend hours doing; not a sensual explore-each-other's-mouth kiss. It wasn't even a hard kiss. But it was a hungry kiss. A pre-fuck kiss. A kiss meant to convey another need.

A large need that was pressing into my cream silk trousers right at that very moment!

'Take them off,' Jacques commanded, noticing my interest in his trousers and kicking off his shoes.

I hate to use the word 'meek' again but that's what I did. *I meekly obeyed.* Goddess strike me down, I bent over and undid his belt and took off his trousers. Followed by his underpants. Then I got down on my knees before him and sucked his cock. It was black. Almost blue-black, medium to large. And very erect.

He cradled my head in his hands and did what I'd always hated; he pushed his penis down my throat. Using me like a whore. Like a slave. I loved it. I sucked in my tummy, ignored my gag reflex and waggled his head across the back of my throat.

'Ahhh . . .' Jacques said. 'Very good. Very good indeed.'

After a few minutes, he pulled me up. 'Take off your clothes,' he demanded. 'I want to see you naked.'

I held his eye as I undressed. It wasn't exactly a striptease, but I wasn't blithely throwing them off either.

'You'll serve,' he declared rudely.

He drew me over to a chair. The same one that Dick had used so long ago. He sat down on the arm. I hoped it would sustain his massive weight.

'Suck me again,' he commanded.

I squatted before him and took his balls in my hands, slipping his cock into my mouth. Jacques reached around and grabbed me on the butt, hard. When I slid my mouth up and down his cock, rubbing my tongue over the vein at the front and around the head, he began to moan loudly and started to slap my arse.

Then he grabbed my head and held it there while he came. In my mouth.

'Aaaahhhh . . .' he said. 'You are good. Very good.'

He released his hands and I came up for air, wiping my mouth with my hand. I still had an ounce of self-preservation left – I didn't swallow. Thank goodness I didn't have any mouth ulcers – I tended to get them a lot.

'One day you will suck, the next I will spank, then we will fuck,' he said. 'And that is the way it's going to be.'

I shivered with anticipation. His words turned me on like no others ever had. What was happening to me? If someone had said anything like that when I was a twenty-something – or even a low thirty-something – I probably would have slapped them. Yet here I was, being treated like a whore and loving it.

'Er . . . I've got dessert,' I said, coming up off my knees and hoping the cum I had surreptitiously wiped over my neck and chest wasn't too obvious.

'That would be good,' said Jacques, showing no sign whatsoever of the orgasm he'd just had. 'I've got to go soon though. You give good head. I've been thinking about it all afternoon. I'm glad I came.'

Pardon yet another pun, I thought. They seemed to come up a lot, these days.

Still naked, I served dessert and coffee. I ignored the cakes and went straight for the custard tarts, placing them on plates with some King Island double cream. Jacques watched me like a hawk from the couch.

'I won't be able to see you again until towards the end of the week,' he said, taking a sip of his coffee and leaning forward to tweak one of my nipples.

'Whenever,' I said blithely. 'I don't need much notice. I'm usually around. Just text me.'

As he left, I gave him the security pass and told him how to use the car park entrance. He didn't look back as he marched up the hall.

I hoped the neighbours didn't use their peepholes much.

Still naked, I plopped myself on the couch and ate both of the cakes I'd rejected earlier. It soon became apparent that I was trying to satisfy the wrong hunger. I went into the bedroom and masturbated all over again.

# CHAPTER 17

I spent the next couple of days walking around Darlinghurst in a state of near nirvana. At last I had found the perfect man. I felt like the sexiest woman alive. I couldn't wait until I saw him again. Hell, I was even looking forward to the spanking!

Above all, I couldn't stop thinking about his words, 'And that's the way it's going to be.' Every time I replayed them a shiver of lust ran through me. It was as if I'd taken another step towards total disinhibition. It was extraordinarily liberating. I held my head high and dressed in my sexiest clothes. I wore the Mona Lisa's secret smile.

I was crossing Oxford Street when a man on a bike stopped beside me.

'Do I know you?' he asked.

'Take off your helmet and sunglasses,' I said rudely.

He did so immediately. He was gorgeous. Young. Muscular.

'Not likely,' I replied, giving him the secret smile and crossing the road.

When I glanced back he was still where I had left him, mouth open, gazing after me.

I masturbated again that afternoon. I couldn't stop thinking about Jacques entering me from behind, driving his black bulk into me like an animal.

I paid my bills and even had enough left over to get me through the Easter weekend. I assumed I wouldn't be paid again until Tuesday. My mortgage was due on Tuesdays. I was cutting it close, but I didn't care. I was literally and metaphorically living on the edge. It felt exhilarating!

Jacques texted me in the late afternoon: *Will be there about 8. Would you like dinner? H*

*Not required. Just you.*

Just me.

I could hardly contain my lust. He was all I could think about.

Dressing that night was a problem. I had already worn the turquoise number and the sexy white pants. So I chose a chocolate-coloured, off-the-shoulder cashmere jumper that showed off my only other decent bra – a little green and brown spotted lace one with matching green underpants. I wore the same transparent cream pants I'd worn before. Once again, I ensured that my bum wasn't covered by my shirt.

I had walked down to Victoria Street earlier and bought dessert – chocolate mousse this time.

Jacques arrived exactly on time, knocking quietly at my door. I placed a vodka in his hand immediately and then curled up on the couch beside him with my own.

'I've been thinking about you,' he said. 'I can't stop thinking about you. I want you.'

He kissed me on the mouth. The same hungry kiss.

'You are not allowed to kiss other men,' he said sternly after I'd reciprocated. 'A man could be satisfied with that kiss.'

I laughed. I wasn't quite sure if I was willing to part with the pash and dash. 'I doubt it,' I said lightly, kissing him again.

'You will not kiss other people,' he declared loudly.

I stared at him. He was deadly serious.

'Sure,' I replied. 'Whatever you say. I'm yours, remember?'

'You will not forget,' he replied matter-of-factly.

I reached for my drink. There was such a lot I would not forget. Would I ever be 'normal' again?

'I won't forget,' I told him quietly. 'We have a deal. I am a woman of my word.'

Jacques smiled and ran a finger down my cheek. 'You are so beautiful; it is good to know that you are mine.'

'What else is yours?' I couldn't help asking. 'What else do you like to play with? Besides women, I mean.'

'I don't play,' he said. 'I just work. And on the weekends I think about work.'

'But you must do something,' I said. 'Surely you must have some passions, some interests.'

'My interests *are* my work,' he declared. 'I can never escape it.'

'Well, you have me to play with now,' I told him.

Jacques just smiled and looked at me. 'I do not want to think about you when I am working,' he said gravely.

'Well, you'd better start playing more!' I quipped.

'Indeed,' he said, reaching for me.

We went into the bedroom and took our clothes off. Jacques had a large, powerful body with a huge stomach covered in ripples of fat. He lay back on the bed, already erect.

'OK, baby. Let's see what you've got for me,' he whispered.

So much for foreplay! But to be honest, I didn't need it. I was already very, very horny. It was wrong, I tell you! But I couldn't help it. It was like being betrayed by my own pussy.

Jacques put the condom on quickly and expertly. I squatted over him and lowered myself onto his erect penis. All the way.

'Aaaahh,' he said. 'You'll do very nicely.'

I moved up and down him. He reached forward and roughly grabbed my breasts in his hands. 'Such beautiful nipples,' he said.

'And real too,' I replied.

'Fake are good to look at but not to touch.'

I changed my momentum and began to move along him ever so slowly. Gripping him tightly inside me. Watching the reactions on his face.

'Ahhh, Holly,' he said. 'I have thought about you too much this week. You are indeed an excellent find. Eager to please. Willing to explore. You are dangerous.'

'But that's good, isn't it?' I protested, lying down on him and bringing my legs in together, squeezing him within me even more. He groaned while I found my rhythm.

'Now I fuck you,' he said suddenly, sitting up.

He turned me over and stood beside the bed. My fantasy. At last.

I stuck my arse in the air and watched him enter me in the mirror. I hate to say it, but he looked like a giant hippo. His large stomach appeared even bigger side-on and his powerful, chiselled thighs rippled as he moved.

But I didn't care what he looked like. Nor did it occur to me that I scarcely knew anything about him. All I wanted him to do was fuck me.

He drove all of his bulk into my wet pussy and I let my breath out with a whoosh. Then I watched in the mirror as he took me. Like a beast. Our eyes met. He must have seen the look in mine.

'I like it this way,' he commented. 'It makes me feel like an animal. It is a good way to take a woman.'

I hadn't come yet. I wasn't even close. He hadn't even mentioned cunnilingus. Yet here I was, panting with lust and comparing my lover to a creature mostly found in zoos.

When he had finished, he collapsed on the bed beside me. It was the most satisfying unsatisfaction I'd ever experienced!

'I can't stop thinking about you, Holly,' Jacques said angrily. 'You are haunting my thoughts. That should not be. Next time I punish you. Next time I will spank you. Hard.'

I didn't have the heart to tell him I was a spanking virgin and self-conscious about the cellulite on the backs of my thighs.

'Oohhh . . . I love a good spanking!' I quipped in my best camp accent.

I sensed him stiffen in anger beside me. Somehow it was the wrong thing to say. Maybe I wasn't supposed to enjoy it. Maybe he really did want to punish me. I hated myself for thinking it, but I *wanted* to be punished – perhaps desire really did over-ride fear, after all.

He left not long after that. He didn't mention when we would meet again and I didn't ask. Mostly because I was too busy thinking about that spanking.


I didn't hear from Jacques again until Friday afternoon. But I continued to think about him. Mostly with a vibrator in my hand.

*Coming around in half an hour for a quick visit*, his text said. *Just a coffee.*

He arrived at about 4 p.m. He looked wrung-out. Once again he was dressed in an immaculate double-breasted suit with a beautifully knotted silk tie.

'Would you like a coffee?' I asked him.

'That would be great,' he said with a big sigh, his black eyes looking mournful.

'Hard day?'

'The worst,' he replied. 'Everything is turning to shit today. I'm looking forward to the weekend – I'm going away with some of my friends.'

'Ah, that'll be fun,' I said, wishing I was going too. I wondered what his friends would be like. I was willing to bet they were nothing like mine. Somehow I couldn't imagine Jacques letting his hair down. Not that he had much.

'When will you be back?' I asked casually, thinking about my mortgage payment on Tuesday.

'Monday,' he said gloomily. 'Then work again.'

Phew, I thought.

I placed the coffee and some yummy almond and toffee biscuits before him. 'What did you say you did again?' I asked, hoping that I hadn't asked it before or got him confused with any of the others.

He looked vague. 'Shipping, mostly. I set up the deals. I'm nearly through for this week. Just in time for the weekend.' He ran his fingers over his scalp. 'I'll be glad when it's over,' he said.

'The work or the week?' I asked flippantly.

He smiled tiredly at me. It occurred to me that I hadn't seen much of his teeth. They were big and straight and very white.

'Both,' he said, sipping his coffee. 'What about you? What are you going to be doing for the weekend?'

I was probably going out dancing till dawn. Then we might go to a day club and get shit-faced.

'Oh, I'll probably just have a quiet one,' I replied. 'You know, lots of chocolate on Sunday and all that.'

'But what about your friends?' he said. 'Won't they want to see you?'

'Oh well, I'll probably see Kev,' I lied.

'Kev?' He frowned. 'Oh. The gay one. And he's your only friend?'

Somehow, telling this solemn man who had seen wars in Algeria that I enjoyed partying with flamboyant friends who treated me like a princess just didn't seem right.

'Er . . . I have lots of friends in Port Stephens,' I replied. 'I just don't get to see them much. But Kev is my best friend. I tell him everything. He's my confidant. He knows everything about me.'

'What about me?' Jacques said sharply. 'Does he know about me?'

'Of course,' I said. 'I told you, this was Kev's idea. Someone has to know what I'm doing. What if I was cut into a million pieces? Kev has all the details. The phone numbers. The email

165

addresses. Everything. Don't worry. He won't tell anyone about you. Your secret is safe.'

Jacques just frowned. I'd said the wrong thing again. I seemed to be making a habit of it.

His phone rang. He answered it curtly and then listened to the person on the other end. 'Work again,' he mouthed, rolling his eyes.

He made a charade of leaving and shrugged an apology. Then he grabbed a couple of the biscuits and gulped down his coffee, all the while talking on his phone.

'That's all right,' I replied, mostly to myself. 'Someone's got to pay the bills.'

That night, I went to play 'Bingay' in Newtown with some of my friends. It was Susan's birthday and we were all in a jolly mood. She'd asked us to bring along a plate of 'retro' food and we had an assortment of fairy bread, 'little boys' and cubes of cheese on Jatz. Someone had even made one of those pineapples with candied fruit on toothpicks sticking out of it.

Everyone was very amused when I confessed it was the first time I'd ever played bingo, let alone its gay derivative. Our host for the evening was a tall, glamorous drag queen called Mitzi Macintosh. She threatened to place a giant fluffy penis on the head of anyone who yelled 'Bingay' before they were entitled to. I was terrified. I wasn't very good with numbers and the giant penis looked most unflattering on my friend Benedict. I kept double-checking my numbers and falling behind.

When certain numbers came up, Mitzi's accomplice would sing a song or Mitzi would skol an entire Bacardi Breezer. That in itself was a feat. It's hard to skol carbonated drinks straight from the bottle without a straw. Believe me, I know.

During the final game (called 'Fast and Furious'), the number '33' came up and, to my amazement, a hundred or so well-inebriated Bingay non-virgins gleefully recited a poem in unison:

*Tie me to the bed*
*Slap me like a bitch*
*Whip me, beat me*
*Fuck me like you hate me*
*Plough me like the dirt that I am!*

Maybe I wasn't such a freak, after all. I wrote down the words and when '33' came up again, I joyously yelled them at the top of my voice along with everyone else. It was one of the most unsettling public declarations I'd ever made.

# CHAPTER 18

On Easter Saturday I'd invited a select group of friends over for drinks. I'd given Jason and Susan and a couple of others a sketchy account of my new life. They'd been strangely impressed. That was the weird thing about having a sugar daddy – for some reason, it was perceived differently to prostitution. By men, anyway. It was almost prestigious. Who'd have thought? My very own, long-time male friends gazed at me with new admiration in their eyes. It was the exact opposite of what I'd anticipated. I'd thought they'd be ashamed of me. Maybe I just had good friends.

However, I stopped short of disclosing the finer details. Up until recently, my life had been an open book. Even my most embarrassing moments or biggest mistakes had made amusing anecdotes. I was good at laughing at myself; I'd certainly had enough practice. But now, even though I told some of them most of what was going on, none of them had the whole truth. For one thing, I didn't want to hog the limelight. Although I knew what I was doing was daring, some of my friends seemed to think I was some kind of hero. I wasn't a hero at all; I was just a woman with a mortgage trying to pay her bills. I didn't want people treating my life like a soapbox – I carried enough of them around already. Nor did I want to sound like a drama queen as I tried to find my permanent gent. It just seemed easier to keep calling them 'Dick' and be spared all the amazed reactions.

'So how's Dick going?' Jason asked me shortly after they arrived.

His arm was draped over his new girlfriend's knee. Her name was Ivy. She was a babe – blonde and curvy with big breasts, just like the women Jason always dated. That was another good thing about long-term friends – we all knew each other's 'type'. It certainly made things easier when we were perving at the pub.

I pictured Jacques as I answered Jason's question. 'I'm the most incredibly lucky woman in the world!' I gushed. 'Dick is *hot*. I can't stop thinking about him. I feel sexier than I've ever felt before in my life. I thought this whole thing would be disempowering, but it's the exact opposite. I've hardly thought about John at all. I'm finally getting to use all of my skills to make a person happy. And I'm even getting paid for it. I should have done this years ago!'

Jason and Susan grinned delightedly at me. To be honest, I would have expected nothing less from them. But Ivy looked sceptical. She was new to our group and I wished Jason hadn't said anything in front of her.

'But you're getting paid for sex,' she said rudely. 'How can that *not* be disempowering?'

I pushed down my annoyance. *I* was the only person who could raise my doubts! 'My power lies in the fact that *I* choose *them*,' I told her. 'They have to apply for the privilege. If anything, it's monogamy that's disempowering because it removes choice! I know it's hard to believe, Ivy – it goes against everything we've been taught. But you've got to take my word for it – it's one of the most enlightening things I've ever done!'

'But it's *wrong*,' Ivy said. 'How can you have sex with someone you don't love?'

'What's love got to do with it?' I snapped back irritably. 'I've come to realise that comparing an emotion – love – to an instinct like sex is like comparing apples and oranges. These men all love their wives. Women have got it the wrong way around. They think if their husband fucks someone else, he doesn't love them any more. But it's got nothing to do with love! You wouldn't ask a woman to stop nesting, so why would you ask a man to stop fucking? Fucking is an instinct. It's not an emotion! How can an instinct be an emotion? Is breathing an emotion? Is eating an emotion? Why does sex have to be an emotion? I've finally discovered Germaine Greer was right – women have given too much power to the penis. It's just a flap of skin and cartilage! Why on earth should we love it before we can play with it? You don't have to love his arm or his leg. Why should you have to love his penis? It's just another part of his body! Men have been right all along: they'll fuck anything. So they should. It's women that need someone to be good-looking or rich or young or marriageable. It's penile discrimination! Why on earth are we attaching so much importance to a dangling bit of flesh on the male body?'

Jason and Susan laughed.

'Hey!' Jason scolded playfully. 'That's my brain you're talking about!'

Ivy looked unconvinced. 'Well, the whole world can't be wrong.'

'*Some* of the world,' I corrected. 'Mistresses and multiple wives are common in lots of countries. My proof is the divorce rate in the west. I read that five out of seven men cheat. That's a big majority! *And* I'll bet it's under-reported. I know it goes against everything we believe, but I'm starting to think lifelong monogamy is an urban myth.'

'Can you honestly tell me that you don't want to settle down with one person?' Ivy argued. 'What about if you fall in love?'

'I'd love to get married! I'm a hopeless romantic, for one thing. I'm not saying lifetime partnerships are wrong: I'm just saying sexual exclusivity is. It's logical when you really start to think about it. I mean, what's the average age people get married these days? Thirty? Plus, we're living longer. Scientists reckon our generation might live to be a hundred. That's seventy years of faithfulness! I might not want to have sex with the same person for seventy years. That's my right. So why should I deny my husband his rights? Our love has nothing to do with his ejaculating. That's stupid!'

Ivy just scowled. She didn't seem to be getting the point. It was very disconcerting. She was a psychologist as well; she was meant to be open-minded and non-judgemental. If I couldn't convince her, what chance did I have with other women?

'But what about your heart, Holly? What are you going to do with that? What if you fall in love with this man?'

I took a deep breath. Ivy was using the exact same psychologist's voice I'd used. I suddenly realised how annoying mine must have been. I resisted the urge to flick her and rolled my eyes at Jason instead. He just gave one of those mental shrugs that you can recognise in good friends.

'Look, Ivy, haven't I just been telling you that this has nothing to do with my heart? This is about sex, not love. I don't know what I can say to persuade you that I'm flourishing. My bills are up to date. My rent's paid in advance. This might be the only time in my life that I can undo my own ignorance.'

'But are you really happy?' she said, in that irritating voice.

I held my anger in check. Honest questions and answers were important. At least Ivy was *trying* to understand, even though I suspected she didn't want to. I had to realise that I was, in effect, the bearer of very bad news.

'Please don't shoot the messenger,' I said with a sigh. 'I'm not responsible for Mother Nature. I'm just saying that if we can't change our genetic make-up, we should accept it instead of trying to fight against it all the time. Darwin was right! Men don't give women a hard time for wanting to have children and make a nest, so why should we give men a hard time for wanting to spread their seed? Cheating is natural; it's monogamy that's unnatural – for men, anyway. And every statistic in the world proves it! I'm sorry if I've somehow upset you. But I suspect that, deep down, you know what I'm saying is true. Men know it already. They've been telling us so for centuries!'

'Well,' Ivy declared with a huff, 'I'm certainly going to expect *my* husband to be monogamous.'

She gave Jason a sideways glance. He patted her hand reassuringly, trying not to look horrified. I couldn't help grinning at his discomfort. Jason wasn't the monogamous type. I made a mental note to tease him later when Ivy wasn't around.

'Well, go ahead and expect him to be monogamous. But know this,' I said ominously, 'if you shut your legs for any reason, the statistics say he is far more likely to cheat than not. Do you really want to be paranoid for the rest of your natural life? Your choice, Ivy.'

Ivy's eyes filled with tears. Darn the bursting of bubbles. Especially my own. It seemed I'd officially crossed the floor.

Living with it would be the hard part.


I hadn't heard from Jacques by Tuesday morning, so I decided to have the long-awaited lunch with Roger instead. I tried not to think too much about the $35 penalty my late mortgage payment would incur. Roger responded quickly to my email.

Holly, I would be delighted if you would have lunch with me today. I live and work in a competitive world, but where matters of a sugar daddy nature are concerned, I am shy, retiring and definitely not pushy. That you now have another daddy is too scary for me. One day I will find you with an empty dance card. On a personal level, I love the non-vanilla world, as I have told you (to my cost) briefly in previous emails. I know we will get along fine. And good friendships are made only on the basis of common bonds. I'm on holidays at the moment so the choices are: Bill's Café in Woollahra, where the lunch menu is light and the ambience of passing people is pleasant; OR YOUR PLACE where, naked, we dine on each other's body fluids until, exhausted, we desist from further frivolities. It's up you – sorry, up to you. Cheers, Roger

Roger <rueful smile>, I shall take you up on the first offer with a raincheck for the second; albeit I want the real you and not just the vanilla icing atop the cake . . . I daresay we shall enjoy discussing it regardless. Would you like to meet out the front or within? Cheers, Holly

Holly, I find I have so much more to say than ooo and aaah. A good choice. And the food is good, maybe not better, but good. Perhaps in the interests of slightly stripping the vanilla, I will come *en chastité*. Maybe you could consider cocking your snook at vanilla in your own way. I will be sitting at a table outside if the weather permits, otherwise inside – I will get there earlier than 1. I look forward to the disappointment I know I will feel as a result of your unavailability. Cheers, Roger

Naturally I got there far too early. So I wandered the boutiques of Woollahra for a while, and realised that money can't buy good taste, after all.

'So, we finally meet,' I said to the only man sitting on his own outside Bill's.

'Holly! Thank you for coming!' Roger said. He rose out of his chair and ensured that mine had an adequate view of the pavement.

A pot of tea sat on the table in front of him. He saw me glance at it and shrugged. 'Drink it all day long,' he said apologetically. 'What would you like?'

'A mineral water would be fine,' I replied, cursing myself for expecting a liquid lunch. I couldn't help feeling disappointed.

I was meeting a fetishist for this? At the very least I had antici-pated a nice bottle of chardy!

'So you're the woman I can't buy outright,' Roger said as soon as I had ordered a salad and got myself settled.

I laughed. So much for small talk!

'I thought we were here to exchange ideas, not body fluids,' I replied.

'OK,' he said. 'Ideas it is. My first questions to any aspiring BDSM submissives are: Would you be prepared to shave your head? and What would you do if I asked you to drink out of a dog's bowl?'

I remained nonchalant. You might have guessed I had had a psychology client who liked fucking black Labradors. Nothing was shocking any more.

'Well, I like my hair and I certainly wouldn't permit it to be shaved off,' I answered with a grin. 'As for the dog's bowl, I guess it'd depend on whether or not it was clean and if it was on the table. I'm not very good on my hands and knees these days, not to mention what it does to the skin.'

Roger snorted contemptuously. 'A lot of women have shaved heads,' he said, gesturing at the large numbers of immaculately dressed women passing us by.

'I'm sorry, but I find that a little bit hard to believe.'

'Look around you! All the women here are Jewish and most of them wear wigs. Look at that one!' he said rather loudly, pointing.

The woman in question looked fabulous and I'd never have picked the wig. But once Roger pointed it out, I could see he was absolutely right. There did indeed seem to be an extra-ordinary number of wigged women going about their business. I was too polite to point out that Orthodox Jewish women simply cover their hair rather than shaving it.

'Next question,' Roger said smugly. 'They've invented a wonderful new padlock that undoes itself after a preset number of hours. How would you cope if I rang and said I was going to be there in an hour and I'd like you to immediately padlock yourself up and wait for me?'

'I'd probably keep a watch for your car then do it just before you got in the door,' I told him, laughing. 'I've got to admit it, Roger, I suspect I'd have much more fun thwarting my master's plans than following them.'

He didn't laugh.

'Women want to be dominated,' he declared. 'You can't argue with evolution – men want to plant their seed in as many places as possible, and women want to be captured by them and locked up in safety so they can care for themselves and their children.'

'To a certain extent, I kind of agree with you,' I said. 'Although I wouldn't have a month ago. I've got to admit, I'm acting very submissive with my current "gent" and it's turning me on enormously, but it's probably restricted to occasionally being tied up with silk scarves and some hot candle wax. It's the degradation bit that I can't understand – when there's so much horror and suffering going on in the world, why would someone want to go out of their way to create it on purpose? It's like going to see sad movies. I can't see the point!'

Roger chuckled and poured himself another tea. 'Actually, that's rather a good analogy. Why *do* people want to make themselves feel sad during movies? It's a minor form of sado-masochism. Maybe I could pick up slaves outside tear-jerkers!'

He laughed and continued, 'There are lots of reasons, Holly. I only know some of them. But don't think we tie someone up and immediately start flaying them – we usually start very slowly and gradually build up the intensity. If it's done right, most people can feel enormous pleasure from pain and often end up begging for more. Don't ask me why – maybe if people's lives are mostly painful and they can't change things, a good way to cope is by making the pain pleasurable.'

'So does that mean your life has been mostly painful?' I asked curiously. 'How did you develop the association?'

'I enjoy administering pain, not receiving it,' he reminded me. 'Maybe I'm just like you – I like giving non-judgemental pleasure to people.' He smiled and looked at the pavement traffic.

I studied him. He was very distinguished-looking with thinning salt-and-pepper-hair and a matching beard and moustache. His appearance vaguely reminded me of my stepfather. But I couldn't help noticing the predatory look in his eyes. They were the eyes of a hawk. They missed nothing.

I turned my gaze to the passers-by who so captured his attention.

The women were mostly very thin, fake-tanned and botoxed to within an inch of their hairlines. They had long, celluliteless legs and wore short skirts, flashy Italian jackets and oversized designer sunglasses with things like DIOR printed in big letters along the sides.

Roger pointed out a chubby Filipino woman with a hard face who was negotiating the pavers in stiletto heels. 'Whoa,' he said, 'that's hot.'

'Ick,' I replied, grimacing.

'Don't knock the entertainment! There are gorgeous women walking up and down here all the time.'

All I could see were the socialites and their wigs. If what Philip had said about the Rich 200 was true, they probably had cheating husbands as well. I'd never envy them again.

Roger's eyes didn't leave the pavement once. Every single woman who passed us was assessed and categorised. He had a curious technique: his steely blue eyes didn't seem to move up and down their bodies like the eyes of my friends did. Rather, he remained fixated on the women's heads, as if trying to assess the brain beneath.

I quashed a small spark of irrational resentment. I was apparently beautiful, but here I was, sitting opposite a predator who had eyes for everyone but me.

'I advertised a couple of months back for a slave,' confided

Roger. 'I wanted her for a full week. I only got two responses – the first was a hooker who said it would cost $2000 an hour, and I asked the second to coffee. Do you know what she said to me?'

He paused for emphasis. I shrugged, obviously not even able to hazard a guess.

'She said, "I couldn't have coffee with my master. That wouldn't be appropriate. But just to show that you're genuine, could you pick up a gold necklace that I've had my eye on?"'

He grimaced, still not missing a single woman with those predatory eyes.

'Would you mind if I asked you a very personal question?' I said.

'Sure. That's what we're here to do, isn't it?'

'Would you prefer your "slave" to be saying, "No, stop, don't hit me any more!" or would you prefer them to be saying, "Harder, whip me harder!"? I've always wondered. I suspect I'd just grit my teeth and endure it. I probably wouldn't say much at all. Even when I've been badly injured I've scarcely let out a whimper.'

Roger just smiled. 'We'd probably get along then. I'd prefer them not to say anything at all. Nothing worse than a chatty slave.'

I was puzzled. 'But how do you get any satisfaction if you don't get a reaction? Isn't that half the fun?'

He thought about it for a moment, his eyes still scanning the busy pavement. He'd probably looked me in the eye twice during our entire conversation.

'Ideally, I would get them to keep a diary, detailing what they thought,' he finally decided. 'Then I would read it every night after I'd put them to bed.'

He focused his full attention on me, this time meeting my gaze directly.

'You ought to keep a diary, you know. You'll probably go through a honeymoon period with your new daddy and he'll want to see you all the time. You'll cherish the experiences.

Why not preserve them? Your very own words could become like a personal porno.'

I laughed nervously. It was a bit like having lunch with Hannibal Lecter, only Roger could read minds as well.

'I'm writing a diary already,' I confessed. 'Too many issues are being raised. It helps me to understand them. The trouble is, I'm getting very dependent on it. I should really be writing my novel. But I can't help myself; I can't seem to stop writing after each new experience. I'm even tempted to publish it. If I don't, I'm just perpetuating secrets. It's hard to know what's the right thing to do.'

'Your daddies wouldn't be able to do anything about it,' Roger mused. 'They wouldn't want to be exposed. You could tell all and even if they recognised themselves they wouldn't want to make a fuss. They'd be helpless.'

Roger's attention returned to the pavement as a young, leggy blonde walked past. Once again, he didn't even glance at her spectacular legs. He just looked at her head. Her face. Her hair. As he turned his gaze back to me, I deliberately let my eyes wander up and down her body, almost as if to show him what perving was really about.

'Noiice,' I drawled, in the tradition of my gay friends. 'Did you know I like threeways?'

I wasn't sure why I'd thrown that one in, but he seemed strangely excited by my demonstration of the usual manner of perving. He was watching me keenly for the first time all afternoon.

'With women or men?' he asked.

'Both.'

He suddenly looked dismissive. Bored, even. 'Too many details,' he said, his eyes losing interest in me again and going back to the parade of women with too much time on their hands.

I resisted the urge to ask him *what* details. I changed the subject instead, telling him my theory about failing marriages and penis kilometres. Like everyone else, he laughed.

'You know, we are really quite alike,' he said. 'Our juices just require different spices.'

He chuckled again.

I'd like to say it was with horror that I realised he was probably right, but it wasn't at all. Here was a man as contro-versial as I was and I felt affinity more than repulsion. In fact, it was kind of nice to hear a successful CEO with excellent taste in suits verify some of my issues. I rather admired him. By being non-judgemental, I realised it was possible to enjoy a conversa-tion simply for the taking on of new information. A penny dropped in my brain.

'We're all at different points on the same line!' I told Roger excitedly. 'No one is right or wrong or good or bad. We're just coming from different perspectives!' I demonstrated with my hands. 'Mrs South Port Stephens would be here,' I said, pointing to the far right of an imaginary line. 'And you would be here.' I pointed to the far left. 'I'd probably be somewhere near the middle. So Mrs South Port Stephens would regard me in much the same way as I regard you.'

'That's right,' said Roger, unimpressed. 'I've become the person my parents warned me about. It's an old saying. Everyone knows it.'

A chill ran through me. The button I had worn at school had come true, after all.

'So doesn't that mean no-one can judge anyone else? That the truth can't really exist because it's always subjective? This has huge implications for the world! People should know about this.'

Roger smiled. I had his full attention now. I wondered if he'd ever had a conversation like this with a woman like me before.

'Sorry, girl – that particular theory has already been discov-ered.'

'Who stole my idea?' I said indignantly. 'I've been struggling with it for months.'

Roger started laughing. He laughed so hard he had to cover his mouth. I was reminded of when Kev suggested I become a sugarbabe. It's hard to be laughed at when you don't know why.

'Philosophy,' he finally managed between splutters. 'It's called moral relativism.'

'Well, the philosophers didn't advertise it very well,' I retorted. 'If they had, we'd probably be one big, happy family by now.'

Roger sobered. 'Actually, a lot of people are starting to rule their lives by philosophy. It's the only truly non-discriminatory way we can cope with our ever-expanding horizons.'

'But it's so hard to get your head around! The concepts swim about and it's difficult to grab hold of them. This may sound brain-ist, but I wonder if people with an IQ above a certain level use philosophy as a life tool, and people below a certain level use psychology?'

He laughed again. 'You could be right. But it does sound "brain-ist", as you put it. It would be nice if everyone could incorporate some philosophy into their lives. It helps us look beyond our boundaries.'

There was that word again. *Boundaries*. It seemed to be coming up often lately.

Roger leaned forward and looked me in the eye. 'Look, put me on the reserve bench, would you? I'm still very interested. I can do plain vanilla as well, you know. Maybe your current gent would like to share – I could do the daytime shift and he could have you in the evenings. I could ring him up and we could swap if we needed to.'

I laughed with him, and finished the remnants of my salad. I wasn't offended. It felt so 'grown-up' to be talking about such things. Here I was, sitting in the middle of Woollahra, surrounded by women with wigs and no facial expressions, talking to a BDSM master in the same tones we would use to discuss the weather. I was proud of myself for seeing past the fetish. I appreciated Roger's frankness and his humour. He really was a very nice man.

I decided I would definitely have lunch with Roger again – albeit with alcohol. But there was no way I was going to take up his offer of placement on my 'reserve bench' if what he said was true; his 'vanilla' could quite possibly be my 'dark chocolate'!

# CHAPTER 19

By the following morning, I still hadn't heard from Jacques. I began to feel concerned. I hadn't been 'paid' for this week yet, and my mortgage and rent were both due. Jacques had seemed so happy with me; surely he wouldn't change his mind . . .

So when Andre texted and invited me to lunch, I gladly accepted, thinking that he might change his mind about employing me. We arranged to meet outside the sushi restaurant where we'd been before. I dressed carefully for the occasion in my tight-fitting brown trousers and the matching tunic that showed off my breasts perfectly. I was careful to wear the same perfume as last time.

I was running a little early, so I took the long way down Oxford Street. A large black man in a suit stood talking animatedly into his phone on the pavement. I tried not to stare at him and compare him to Jacques. I looked twice. It *was* Jacques! I was glad I was wearing a nice outfit. I slowed down and hoped Andre couldn't see me from down the street.

Jacques spotted me and waved me to a halt, still talking animatedly on his phone. 'I was coming to see you,' he mouthed. He groped in his suit and pulled out an envelope. Something was written on the front. My heart sank. I was being fired. Again.

I hovered as Jacques moved over to the nearby ATM and made a withdrawal, all the while talking on the mobile. Then he put the wad of fifties in the envelope and handed it to me. On the front it said: 'Do not wish to continue the trial. Here's something for your trouble.' Inside was my security pass and the bundle of notes.

'Are you OK?' Jacques mouthed at me, still on the phone.

I nodded, trying to look as if this was an everyday occurrence.

He gave me the thumbs up and hailed a cab. I stood there dumbly with the envelope in my hand. As he got in the car, Jacques gave me the strangest look. I can still picture it – deep regret tinged with fear. As if I were a winning racehorse that might turn feral. He left without a backward glance.

I tucked the envelope into my handbag and resolved to get drunk with Andre.

When I was settled into my chair in a Thai restaurant with a good glass of chardy in my hand, I began telling him the whole story. Well, some of it anyway. All that seemed to register with Andre was that I was 'between gents' and theoretically available.

'You know I want you,' he whispered, rubbing my thigh.

That was the problem. Everyone wanted me. But no-one wanted to keep me! Pardon another bloody pun. I repressed a sigh.

'Well, you can't have me,' I declared grumpily. 'This is business. Besides, you only want me because you can't have me. I'll bet if I ever fucked you, I wouldn't hear from you again.'

Andre looked wounded. 'That's not true,' he said. 'I want to be friends for the rest of our lives. I know this is only our second date, but I feel as if I've known you forever! I've already told you things that no-one else knows. I don't just want to bed you, Holly, I want to be your friend. I can help you through this.'

'Be my pimp, you mean,' I said, only half-jokingly.

Andre stroked his chin and looked offended. 'I just want what's best for you. I want to see you succeed at this. Men's lives are resting on your shoulders. We want you to make this work!' I raised an eyebrow; he was just so over-the-top. 'It's in our best interests,' he continued. 'You're trying to legitimise what we've been doing since the dawn of time. If someone like you can't succeed, then no-one can.'

'What about *my* best interests?' I said. 'What about them?'

He laughed. 'Your best interests will always be men,' he replied. 'And the occasional woman.' He winked.

'But what about when I'm old and ugly?' I pushed, not laughing at his joke. 'I can't do this forever. I'm certainly not going to look like this for the rest of my life. I'm bloody lucky it's lasted this long!'

He stroked my face. 'You'll never be ugly, Holly. As for old – well, older men need sex too.'

He mollycoddled me through three glasses of wine and I began to feel better.

'There's something you don't know,' I told him. 'It's got to be our secret.'

Don't tell him about the diary, I warned myself.

'I've started writing it all down. The conversations. The interviews. Why they want me. I think I might write a book about it someday. Maybe tell the world what's really going on.'

Curse that third glass of wine!

To my surprise, Andre looked absolutely delighted.

'But what about your gents?' he asked. 'What will they say?'

I grinned at him evilly. 'Not a lot, I suspect.'

Andre grinned back. 'Of course they won't. But it doesn't matter anyway. They'll be pleased.'

'Why?' I said, puzzled.

'Because you'll be providing the reasons why they cheated

in the first place. No-one has done that before. Not a woman, anyway. No man has ever dared to, not openly. You'll be the first, Holly.'

He raised his glass. 'To your diary,' he said, meeting my gaze.

'To my diary,' I repeated, thinking that surely Andre was wrong and my catharsis was merely struggling with the blatantly obvious. Philosophers thought so, anyway.

We finished our lunch in silence. Neither of us ate very much. When Andre suggested we get a second bottle of wine and go back to my place, I didn't hesitate. Unsurprisingly, I fought him off for most of the afternoon. I think he enjoyed it. In the end, I succumbed and let him go down on me.

He left in a hurry when he realised he had to be home early for dinner. I was relieved to get my space back.

When he had gone, I counted the money Jacques had given me earlier: $250. It didn't cover my rent, let alone my mortgage. Still half-drunk, I left a message on Tom's voicemail: *You were right. Number 1 just got shafted. Are you still interested?*

He replied about an hour later: *Let me take you out to dinner and spoil you tomorrow night. Tom*

It was exactly what I needed to hear. I'd always known good daddies were hard to find, but this was getting ridiculous.


My date with Tom. Tom who would hopefully pay me immediately as a gesture of good faith. The first night of Tom in my life of Dicks.

Once again, it was difficult to decide what to wear. In the end, I decided to go with my gorgeous chocolate and green silk number and skinny green trousers. It looked very formal, so I teamed it with my Birkenstocks to dress it down.

Tom was exactly on time, picking me up in the Merc. I noticed they'd finally sunk the car's insignia – for a prestige car company it sure took them a long time to learn that lesson!

He opened the door for me. 'You look dress up,' he commented, pecking me on the cheek.

I hoped it was a compliment. It was difficult to tell. Maybe he'd planned something really casual. Like sex.

'Thank you,' I replied, settling myself into the roomy interior.

'I've made a reservation at the Icebergs. It that OK for you?' Tom asked as we drove off.

The Icebergs was probably one of Australia's finest restaurants. I hadn't been there before. 'Lovely,' I said coolly. 'My favourite.'

'Mine too,' said Tom wolfishly.

We were shown straight to our table and I managed to sit down gracefully when the maitre d' pulled out my chair for me. It's quite an art, that of sitting gracefully, especially since you have to hover in mid-air while they shove the seat into the back of your knees. Then it's equally hard not to sit down suddenly with your legs knocked out from beneath you.

'What would you like to drink?' the waiter asked us.

'A Crown lager for me, please,' Tom said. 'What would you like, Hollee?'

I liked the way he pronounced my name, with the emphasis on the 'ee' instead of the 'oll' like most people did.

'My usual,' I said. 'A vodka and soda in a tall glass, please.'

We chatted while we waited for our drinks. Tom appeared supremely confident and slightly amused. He sat back in his chair and flicked his long fingers for emphasis as he talked. I noticed again how the little fingernail on both of his hands was very long. I wondered if it was for cocaine. It would explain the way he acted.

The waitress came to take our orders and we both flirted with her good-naturedly. There was something about him that brought out the devil in me.

'She likes me best,' I whispered when she'd left.

'No! Me!' Tom replied.

'Nah, she doesn't know how to take your humour,' I told him. 'She's just being nice to you because she wants a big tip.'

'Let's ask her,' he said, gesturing her over.

Yep. I was willing to bet the fingernails were for coke all right. Surely he wasn't this uninhibited all the time.

'Do you like her best or me?' he asked when the waitress approached.

She gave me an apologetic look and hedged. 'I like both of you,' she replied nervously.

I laughed.

'Don't worry about Tom,' I told her. 'I can't take him anywhere.'

When she'd left, I turned to tease him. 'You're incorrigible,' I said. 'You remind me of my friends.'

Tom giggled merrily and looked at me over the top of his glasses. Then he must have realised he still had them on after reading the menu and took them off, carefully putting them in his top pocket.

'You naughty. Just like me,' he said.

'So what do you do when you're not stirring up waiters?' I asked him. 'Besides work, I mean.'

'Well . . . not lot, really. Life very boring without wife. I miss her. That's why I want you. I need person to do things with – go to restaurant, outing, that kind of thing. My life empty without woman.'

He waved his hands again for emphasis and then handed me the wine list. 'I'm not drinker,' he said. 'You choose.'

I selected a middle-of-the-price-range semillon sauvignon blanc that was to be a disappointment. Luckily, Tom didn't seem to notice.

I was relieved when our meals arrived. Tom's accent was very strong. He was difficult to understand at times and I kept having to ask him to repeat himself. He probably thought I had a hearing deficiency. He also seemed to become progressively quieter and less sure of himself as the meal wore on.

I had ordered a salt-encrusted rib eye and Tom had the fish of the day. There were some very strange choices on the menu. Our selections proved superb, but I noticed Tom didn't touch his salad and ate very little of his fish. I drank most of the wine.

'Save yourself room for dessert,' Tom advised me. 'They have chocolate pudding!'

He sounded like a small child. I needed chocolate pudding like I needed an extra ten kilos on my stomach.

'I'll have a bite of yours,' I told him.

He gave me a look of mock outrage. 'What if I don't want to share?'

'I was wondering about that,' I said, giving him a wink.

Tom laughed.

'Are you calling me selfish?' he asked jokingly.

'I guess we'll just have to find out.' I grinned devilishly at him.

He poured the last of the wine and looked around for the waitress to order dessert.

'While you're doing that, I'll go to the ladies,' I said.

When I returned, he wasn't sitting at the table. For one dreadful moment I thought he might have done a runner and left me with the bill. Our friendly waitress must have seen my look of horror and gestured to a door.

'He's out having a cigarette,' she said.

I joined Tom on the balcony and regretfully declined his offer of a Marlborough. There was a stunning panorama of ocean stretched out before us. All the way to China.

Another smoker stood nearby, a well-dressed woman with mousy blonde hair.

'You're a dying race,' I told them both jokingly.

'More like a slave,' she said, ignoring the ashtray beside her and flicking her cigarette butt over the handrail. It probably fell into the pool below.

'Charming,' I commented, when she'd left.

'Did you notice her shoes?' Tom said.

I frowned. 'No. Why?'

'Shoes very dirty,' he replied. 'Many Asian people judge her badly. Always wear clean shoes. Take good care of feet.'

I was glad I was wearing my trusty thongs. It's hard to tell if brown leather is dirty.

Tom's face lit up. 'Dessert!' he declared, putting out his cigarette.

He held the door open for me and we walked back into the dining area. Tom's dessert had indeed arrived and he gave me the smallest mouthful imaginable.

'Mmmmm . . . delicious,' I told him anyway.

He grinned. 'Sweets always better than main course,' he said, taking careful spoonfuls of chocolate with equal quantities of cream. 'They also mark of privilege. Poor people no have sweet.'

So *that's* what I was doing wrong!

I thanked him profusely when he paid the bill. 'I really appreciate you spoiling me like this,' I said, wishing I hadn't had so much of the wine.

Tom didn't seem to notice. He'd become quite morose since the last mouthful of chocolate pudding. I couldn't help thinking I'd been upstaged by the pastry chef.

'Let's go home,' he said.

As we walked along the beach to the car he took me in his arms and kissed me gently on the mouth. A nice kiss with big, fat lips. I suspected he'd be very playful in bed. I hoped so.

There was no discussion about whether he was 'coming up for coffee' on the way home. I directed him straight into my underground car park and gave him instructions about its future use. Tom seemed to take it as a given.

He was suitably impressed by my apartment, always especially beautiful at night.

'May I get you something to drink?' I asked him.

'Water fine,' he said. 'Not cold – just tepid out of tap.'

He went to the toilet while I made myself coffee.

Barely had we both sat down before he was all over me – burying his face in my cleavage with exclamations of delight, rubbing his hands up and down my long legs, kissing my neck and my ears. Once again, he reminded me of a child. It wasn't so much innocence as enthusiasm – he seemed to be full of curiosity and wonder. I couldn't help wondering if he'd had a snort in my bathroom.

By the time we got into the bedroom all of my clothes were strewn over the lounge room and he was still fully dressed. He had unwrapped me like a present, exclaiming at particular delights – such as my small pink nipples and my rounded little tummy, which he cupped in both his hands and kissed.

When he'd arranged me (artfully) on the bed, I jokingly protested, 'What about your clothes? Aren't you going to take them off?'

He looked down at himself and only then seemed to realise he was fully clothed. 'Oh,' he said, ripping them off swiftly and throwing them carelessly on the floor.

I admired his body as he stood for a moment above me. His penis was small but beautifully formed. It was uncircumcised. I'd never had an uncircumcised man before. His body was hairless and sleek. Even his balls didn't seem to have much hair. He'd taken off his glasses and looked like he was going on eighteen instead of about fifty.

Tom then proceeded to kiss me all over my entire body. Over my stomach, my thighs and right down my legs to my toes, which he sucked. No wonder he liked clean feet.

A quick digression on the matter of toe-sucking. To be honest, I have never truly appreciated this art, although I realise a lot of people do. It's not that I don't find it erotic, rather it's because I find it very ticklish. It's hard to enjoy something when your face is screwed up and you're trying desperately to master your reflexes and not kick someone in the nose.

I stole a quick glance at Tom's toes – they were immaculate!

I made a mental note to suck them one day; doing unto lovers as they do unto you is often a very good starting point.

Tom moved his kisses back up my legs and then spread them wide. He pulled my flaps aside and carefully examined my pussy. 'Beautiful,' he exclaimed, making a dive for it.

I very nearly said, 'Everyone says that', then realised how slutty it would sound. I'm embarrassed to report I had absolutely no idea what made a pussy attractive. I wondered if it was the kind of thing I could ask Andre, who had also commented positively on its appearance.

What followed was fifteen minutes of some of the best oral sex I'd ever had. Tom was a master at it and insisted on making me come. 'I want to watch orgasm,' he told me when I protested that I was having all the fun. And so he licked and sucked and nibbled at my clit while his long fingers probed my insides. I hoped he wasn't using his pinkies.

The orgasm mounted quickly.

'I'm coming,' I managed to say between gasps and wiggles.

He drew his face away and continued to hold my flaps apart, watching me.

I closed my eyes and gave into it, gasping out loud and then rolling into a foetal position until the quivering stopped. Tom followed my clit like a kid who'd been deprived of a small toy.

I batted him away. 'Sorry,' I croaked. 'It becomes very sensitive – you can't touch it for a while.'

He lay down beside me, his hard-on beginning to wilt. Stifling an inward groan, I rose up and returned his favours, kissing my way down his chest and stomach, slowly working my way towards his cock, which was by now semi-flaccid.

I took it in my mouth and worked my way up and down the length of it like I usually did, rolling my tongue around the head and cupping his balls with my other hand. I delicately flicked the glans and ever-so-gently kissed it with my lips. Instead of getting harder, it seemed to wilt even more. It was the strangest thing: the more I sucked, the softer it got. For the first time in my life, I was at a loss as to what to do. In the end, Tom saved me by taking it in his hand and playing with it his way.

When his penis was fully erect again, he became very business-like. He sat up quickly and carefully arranged me on my side on the bed, putting my top leg over his shoulder. I mentally thanked my Pilates instructor yet again when Tom discovered just how easily the position enabled me to move my pelvic floor muscles. His eyes opened wide as I squeezed him and then released him, all without him having to move a muscle.

'You do Tantric?' he asked, looking surprised.

I wondered what Tantric was. I knew it was something to do with sexual positions. I was reasonably sure it was good.

'Er . . . I can make you come without you moving,' I told him. 'But I'm not sure it would work the other way around.'

'We could learn,' he whispered excitedly.

He moved against me, gradually getting faster and harder and deeper.

'The condom!' I reminded him.

'It's all right,' he said. 'I'm nowhere near.'

'I don't care,' I told him. 'Put it on if you want to fuck me.'

'What about if I do it like this?' he said, rolling me onto my stomach.

I was just about to say that was even more important, but he avoided my anus and rubbed his cock up and down the crack of my arse instead. I gripped him between my cheeks and wondered how hard it would be to crack a walnut. Maybe I could start with squashing a ripe peach and work my way down, I thought.

Tom started moving himself quicker and quicker. 'I'm coming!' he called. 'I'm coming!'

He sounded like he was late picking up the kids.

'I'm coming!' he called out one more time and then blew all over the small of my back, rubbing it over me with his hand.

He had a grin on his face from ear to ear when I emerged from the pillows and laid my face on his chest.

'I'm sooo happy, Hollee,' he said blissfully. 'I sad until now. My wife, she Australian. She leave because I with other woman. Only once but my wife, she find out anyway. She leave me straightaway. No forgiveness. I not understand! Fifteen years we married. I make one mistake and she no forgive. She think I love woman but I love only wife! Eight years I wait! Now she meet other man and want divorce. I no divorce! My wife not understand. She no realise I am man. She no want sex after second son. Why she think I no love her? Eight years long time to wait. New man will make her understand. She will realise all men same. Then she will forgive.'

His words brought a chill to my heart. I too had closed my legs at times. I too had broken up with men who had been unfaithful to me. At the time, I had thought it the ultimate act of betrayal. But now I was becoming convinced that cheating was an act of nature and not a lack of love. Had I been too hasty? Had I broken up with potential soulmates merely because they were doing what they were programmed to? Please, Goddess, I prayed silently, let me be wrong about this.

'Maybe you could find another woman while you're waiting,' I told him. 'A Chinese woman. They understand, don't they?'

'Chinese women better,' he replied. 'But she mother of my sons. I will wait. She will forgive.'

I couldn't help feeling a tad jealous. I wondered if I would ever meet a man prepared to wait nearly a decade for me to realise a mistake.

As Tom got dressed, I hardened my resolve and rattled off my terms. Although I was getting better at it, it still felt awkward.

'I want $1000 a week in advance,' I reminded him. 'And I want two weeks' notice if you want to stop the arrangement through no fault of my own. Severance pay,' I added sternly, by way of explanation.

'That fair enough,' he agreed, nodding at me.

I gave him the security pass, hoping it would encourage him to cough up the money.

'We start Monday?' he asked me, pocketing the pass and turning to leave.

'Sure,' I said, berating myself for giving him a freebie, but totally unable to ask for the money all the same.

As he walked down the hall I tried not to dwell on the fact that somehow Tom felt wrong. But I quashed the feeling of unease. It was getting harder to trust my instincts. They'd betrayed me so often in the past. If only I'd realised it earlier.

# CHAPTER 20

I spent most of the weekend trying to convince myself that Tom was genuine. I wasn't sure why I mistrusted him – perhaps it was the mood swings or his childlike nature. But I couldn't help feeling something wasn't right.

I expected him to call sometime over the weekend and confirm what time he would see me, but by midday on Monday I still hadn't heard from him. I sat on the couch trying not to think about money. I had been so jubilant with Dick. Compared to Jacques and Tom, he'd been perfect. I missed his gentlemanly demeanour and our intelligent conversations. Hell, I even missed reading the *Financial Review*!

But since then, all I had known was financial uncertainty. I was supposed to be doing this to pay my bills, not worry about them! Somewhere along the line I had lost sight of my original intentions. I wondered if I would ever find them again. What had started as a means of survival had become many other things. Was I doomed to sit on the couch every Monday wondering if I'd be paid? When I thought about it, depending on the whim of the penis for my mortgage payments wasn't the cleverest thing in the world.

Once again, I found myself turning to my diary in order to sort things out in my head. The words flowed like they'd never flowed before. I wrote all day, never daring to re-read, frightened that if I did, I would have to stop everything and go back to normality again.

Tom rang at eight that night.

'Hi, Hollee, I'm sooo sorry,' he said cheerfully. 'I forgot I had yoga. What you doing?'

I was lying in bed, watching TV and trying not to feel anxious, that was what I was doing!

'I'm watching the rain over the city,' I told him calmly. 'I love the rain – it's like looking at the world through a Picasso painting. It makes me remember how beautiful it is.'

'Ahhh,' he said. 'You are lucky woman. Can I come tomorrow afternoon instead?'

'Sure. It will be lovely to see you,' I said. 'We need to confirm our arrangement.'

'See you then!' he said joyfully and hung up.

I scolded myself for doubting him. I was just being paranoid. So this was what wives felt like.


Tuesday. Mortgage payment day. I wasn't going to make it. Again. Even if Tom came through with the money that afternoon, I wouldn't be able to get to the bank until the next day, which was too late. I'd incur a financial penalty for the attempted debit from my account. Curse the whims of penises!

Interestingly, the world didn't collapse around me. Normally, I would've sat around frantically worrying about the failed payment and about whether Tom was dependable. I would've agonised over where I had gone so hopelessly wrong and berated myself for embarking upon such a foolish plan. I would've contemplated giving up and going back to the office and a safe fortnightly salary paid into my bank account. I certainly wouldn't have logged onto my computer and started frantically typing away in my diary.

Yet that's exactly what I did. For the second day in a row. The novel could wait, I thought. Transcendence must come first. Above all, I told myself, don't stress. Remember what Theodore Roosevelt said. What was it again? We'd learnt it at school. Something about it being far better to dare mighty things, to win successes chequered by failures, than to be someone who neither enjoyed nor suffered much because they lived in a twilight that knew neither victory nor defeat.

Well, I'm certainly not one of them, I thought.

By 3 p.m. Tom still hadn't called.

I texted him: *How are things? We need to confirm our agreement or personal circumstances require me to make other arrangements. H*

Then I went back to my writing.

By early evening I still hadn't heard from him so I decided to use the time productively. I called my friend David for some urgent advice regarding the matter of Tom's foreskin.

David is bisexual and gorgeous inside and out. I knew he considered himself somewhat of an expert in 'uncut' men – a man dedicated to turning on other men will always have more tricks up his sleeve than a man turning on women, or vice versa.

He invited himself over for dinner in exchange for an assurance that I would henceforth be able to deliver the best uncut blow job in the world. Knowing David as I did, I believed him.

Once we'd polished off a couple of glasses of chardonnay and a bowl each of my specialty king prawn laksa, I told him about my sexual encounter with Tom and the disastrous head job I'd given. There isn't a topic in the world that I can't broach with my gay friends. I'd picked up a lot from them over the years. They talked about sex a lot. When you think about it, gay men make the best instructors in the world.

'Before you tell me where I went wrong can I ask you a really personal question about something else?' I said.

'Of course, you know that.'

Bless his cotton socks!

'Are you a top or a bottom?'

David looked amused. 'I'm actually both. Why?'

'Well,' I said cautiously, 'I've always been a bit confused. Why would a bisexual want to fuck a bottom when he can fuck a pussy? I mean, if I stick my finger in my arse, it's kinda boring – it's just a cavity. But if I stick my finger in my pussy it's all tight and wet and there are all these wonderful muscles I can use. It also smells a lot better! To be honest, I think bums are boring compared to pussies.'

David laughed. 'That's because you don't use your anus for sex. Men's anuses are like your vagina – we can use the muscles in the same way. With practice, you can make the muscles in your arse just like the ones in your cunt.'

I was horrified. Here I was, approaching middle age, and there was an erogenous zone I'd never known existed! I couldn't believe I'd wasted all of those years!

'So how do I make my rectal muscles as good as my vaginal ones?' I asked. Naturally.

David chuckled again. 'With practice. Why do you think gay men sleep around so much?'

We laughed.

'So what about this foreskin business?' I said. 'What did I do wrong?'

'Think of a foreskin like the flaps around your clit,' he replied. 'The head is more sensitive because it's covered by the foreskin, just like your clit is. Be gentle with it. You can use the wet insides of the foreskin for stimulation. Draw the skin up over the head when you wank him or give head. Run your tongue or your fingers around the inside. Nipples are good too. It actually self-lubricates, you know.'

So that was why Tom couldn't maintain his erection. I'd probably over-stimulated the poor thing!

David laughed to himself. 'Dick snot,' he said.

'What?' I asked, puzzled.

He laughed again.

'Dick snot – that's what they call the stuff uncut dicks make.'

Charming!

'So what about this gag reflex thingy? What's the big gay secret there?' I asked.

David looked mysterious. 'I'm not sure I want to give that one away. After all, if I tell you everything, straight men mightn't want to see us any more!'

'Come on,' I cajoled. 'Call it in the interests of humanity.'

He laughed. 'OK, if you want to stop your gag reflex, try sucking it from the right angle for starters. Hit the oesophagus and bypass the trachea. Stay away from the sides too – that's where most of the nerves are. Try tilting your head more, or facing his toes – same as you would for a sixty-niner. Some people think it's better when they're lying down. Other guys I know use lozenges to numb the nerves or avoid sucking cock on a full meal. Maybe that's why it's better in the mornings – when your stomach is empty, I mean.'

I shook my head in wonder. Why wasn't all this on billboards?

'I've always assumed I need personal and spiritual growth, but I never realised I need sexual growth as well!'

'Women's libidoes often act as a natural brake in relationships,' David explained. 'Gay men don't have that so we get to evolve more. People who are sexually exclusive experience what we call sexual sacrifice. They don't get to develop sexually. Usually it's women because they don't cheat as much.'

I couldn't help giving a big sigh. I was ignorant about so many things.

'If I'm single and struggling with all of this, just imagine how people in marriages cope,' I said. 'It's no wonder there are so many divorces. Married people are actually stunting their growth. The worst thing is, they probably don't even realise it.'

'The knowledge is out there, Holly,' David replied seriously. 'Look at the internet, for starters. People just don't want to search for it.'

'Yeah, but it should be mainstream,' I declared. 'Every single person in the world is probably "doing it" yet I can't think of a single advertisement about improving your sexual delivery. Vitamins and drugs maybe, but not technique. Besides, you need knowledge to be able to ask questions. If I hadn't fucked Tom the other night, I wouldn't be asking these questions either.'

'You're probably right,' he replied. 'But do you want to be the one who stands up and tells the straight world that they're doing it all wrong?'

I got defensive.

'We're not doing it wrong,' I retorted. 'We're just not doing it as well as we could be. Look at anal sex for starters – most of us are only operating at 50 per cent capacity and we don't even know it! Why aren't women regularly using dildos on their partners? How is it that a woman can get to my age and not encounter an uncut cock? What's wrong with us? This is pleasure we're talking about! How did we ever get to be so prudish?'

David smiled.

'Well, the Rugby-Player-Can't-Touch-My-Arse Syndrome has a lot to answer for, plus it's in the interests of society to keep people concentrated on work, not pleasure. What better way to do that than stigmatise some of the pleasures? Especially the best ones.'

I shook my head. 'A conspiracy to make people work more and play less? I doubt it.' Yet as soon as the words were out of my mouth, it made horrifying sense. It was certainly more believable than most of the conspiracy theories I'd heard.

'Well, you tell me why violence is preferred over sex on telly, then,' David said. 'You get a lot more fiscal activity out of a violent rape than you do out of a loving fuck.'

Call me thick-headed, but I still couldn't believe it. Maybe I didn't want to.

'So what do we do?' I asked him in bewilderment. 'How do we point people in the right direction?'

'Well, you're a psychologist. You're probably in a better position than most.'

'I'd probably be sacked if I told my clients this!'

'Well, if gay saunas are any indication, the husbands are probably already doing it anyway,' David said. 'Maybe they'd be grateful. You might even appease a lot of guilt.'

'I doubt it,' I said gloomily. 'Husbands realise their wives fuck for love, not sex. Unless that changes, women would always be unfaithful for the wrong reasons.'

David shook his head sadly. 'And you straight people think *we're* fucked up!'

After David left, I felt a terrible sense of unease. What had started with my own issues was becoming so much more. Worse still was my growing compulsion to expose what must surely be one of the largest under-the-carpet-sweeps of all time.

Then I wondered what my Pilates instructor would say if I told her I wanted to develop my rectal muscles alongside my pelvic floor.

# CHAPTER 21

I woke up at dawn on Wednesday with a strong inclination to walk away. What I'd mistaken for deluded thinking based on self-justification was becoming irrefutable fact. I was more comfortable with the deluded thinking! Then I told myself I was just a simple woman with an over-active social conscience. Someone else could stop the cheating. I had bills to pay.

So I wrote a big sign – 'DON'T LET YOUR FEARS GET IN THE WAY OF YOUR DREAMS' – and put it near my computer. Then I resolved to sack Tom and hire Philip instead.

At 7 a.m. I got a text from Andre: *I'm hard and thinking of you. About to play.*

I wondered if his wife was in the shower. I texted him back: *I'll join you. Think of me in the morning sunshine. H*

Then I went back into the bedroom and got out my vibrator. So much for paying my bills!

Andre texted me again: *Hmmm would luv my tongue between your legs . . . sun beaming through your window.*

Naturally I thought of exactly that for the next few minutes.

But when I got up to write down those very words, I began to wonder whether I was writing the diary or the diary was writing me. Was I a whore investigating journalism or was I a journalist investigating being a whore? And what the hell was I doing text-masturbating with an admittedly gorgeous Argentinian when I had missed a mortgage payment yesterday and had barely a cent to my name? Worse still, why on earth was I sitting at my computer writing it all down? I was becoming obsessed! Was the diary starting to justify my entire existence? At least the ending will be a surprise, I thought.

In the interests of politeness, I left another voice message for Tom: *Please let me know if you've changed your mind. I deserve to know. H*

No response. I couldn't say I was surprised. Bloody instincts.

At 9 a.m. I went to the internet café in the hope that perhaps he'd lost his mobile phone and an apologetic email was sitting in my tray. No such luck. Instead, there were four newsletters and a note from my managing real estate agent to say that my single mother was defaulting on her rent.

So I went ahead and emailed Philip.

I think I've been duped. My gent was meant to start after Easter but I've hardly seen him since. I feel a tad stupid for believing him. It just goes to show – always go with your first choice. Are you still interested? Please ring me. Cheers, Holly

At 11.30 a.m. Tom rang. My heart pounded.

'Hi, Hollee,' he said. 'I'm so, so sorree! I've had all dramas – I'm very sorree I haven't ring you. I still want to continue. I'll tell you tonight. Can I come see you at nine?'

He sounded very agitated but the cynical side of me thought it was the easiest thing in the world to fake.

'Sure, I'll look forward to it,' I said confidently, trying to sound as if the prospect of no income and losing everything was as far from my mind as cleaning the toilet with my tongue. 'See you tonight.'

Maybe I had over-reacted. What if Philip rang?

Tell him the truth, I told myself. Tell him Tom was proving unreliable but I'm seeing him tonight. Tell him that I'll ring tomorrow and let him know what happened.

I didn't hear from Philip but Tom breezed in at nine on the dot. I say 'breezed' because it was exactly the way Tom moved, just like a big kid. He was beautifully dressed in a dark blue calico shirt and linen trousers.

I'd been determined not to so much as smile at him until I saw his money. I'd also resolved to give him a little lecture about what was pleasure for him was business for me and that it was essential he pay on time. But he kept rubbing his forehead and his eyes as if he had a tension headache. So I asked him if he wanted a neck and shoulder massage instead.

All during the massage I berated myself for not being firmer with him. Here I was, massaging a man who quite possibly didn't even have $1000, let alone have it to spend on me each week. Not only had he got free sex out of me, he was now getting a free massage. He probably thought I was the stupidest bitch he'd ever conned! But you've got to remember, I was new to this. Up until now, I hadn't even worked in retail. Asking someone for money in exchange for loving was about as alien to me as cleaning the sump of a Mack truck. Sure, I knew wives did it all the time (the loving not the cleaning), but maybe that was why I was approaching middle age and wasn't married.

Needless to say, it wasn't my best massage. Tom kept his shirt on and didn't want me to use 'smelly oils'. The trouble was, my massages tended to be mostly aromatic, highly sensual and hopefully ending in sex. Things got considerably worse when Tom rolled over onto his back and asked me to massage his face. My only experience of such a thing was at the beautician's, so I mostly rubbed his drainage points. Then I lay down beside him and gently stroked the area he'd been rubbing between his eyes earlier.

Finally I'd done the right thing. Tom put his head on my breast and I gently fondled his entire head, secretly marvelling at the difference between his short spiky Asian hair and the unkempt stuff most of my boyfriends had sprouted. At last. Fondling was something I did well. I could caress for hours. One boyfriend had even removed my hand from his back once, complaining I was rubbing the skin away!

'Feel better?' I was finally brave enough to ask.

'Much,' said Tom, his face nestled against my breasts.

Now was my chance.

'I thought you'd reneged on our deal,' I told him. 'I didn't think you were going to show up.'

What was really going through my mind was, I thought you were a Chinese con man who used me to get free sex, and now you've got a free massage and breast rest as well.

'I no do that, Hollee,' he replied contentedly. 'I had forgotten was school holiday and yoga on Monday. I'm very sorree. I always keep word.'

'You're here now,' I said soothingly. 'That's the important thing.'

'Not for long,' Tom said, glancing at his watch. 'I must pick up sons soon.'

So this was it. A half hour of distracted massage and a couple of sentences.

He got up and sat on the lounge to put his shoes on. 'I'll come around same time tomorrow night,' he told me. 'Things difficult while school holidays on.'

He reached into his pants and removed his wallet. Then he threw a wad of hundreds wrapped in a rubber band onto my coffee table. I nearly wept with relief. Once again the sheriffs were diverted from my door.

Instead of grabbing it with joy, I picked up the bundle and casually threw it on the chair beside me, as if it were a discarded bus ticket. Tom caught the feigned casualness of the movement and gave a little start. So I picked it up again and placed it deferentially in one of the vases on the table in front of us. I wondered if I was supposed to count it.

'Remember, I need two weeks' notice if you want to stop,' I muttered to the floor, unable to look Tom in the eye.

'I won't let you down,' he said.

He gave me a long hug and left in a rush. I closed the door behind him, feeling like I'd been run over by the Mack truck whose sump had needed cleaning.


On Thursday I still hadn't heard from Philip. I felt decidedly glum so I took up an offer from Andre for 'afternoon tea'. He was up for anything so I suggested the pub.

'You look gorgeous,' he whispered in that sexy voice of his. 'Look at all the men perving. I love being seen with you. I know I can't have you but I just love the tease.'

I grinned.

'I've always enjoyed a bit of tease myself,' I confided. 'When I was younger I used to go out with my boyfriend and we'd chat up other people in full view of each other. If someone else was interested in him, it'd turn me on. There's no point in having someone no-one else wants! Then we'd dump them and go home and fuck like rabbits.'

Andre laughed. 'Me too! I still go out and flirt like crazy – all of the most beautiful women in the room. I love being around them, smelling them, watching them. But sometimes I don't want to get physical. I just go home and fuck my wife. She loves it. Everyone wins.'

I stared at him in amazement. 'It's another taboo!' I said excitedly. 'We're brought up to think teasing is wrong, but it's not! If both parties are willing, what's the problem? It's only . . .' I groped for the words. 'Surrogate foreplay!' I concluded elatedly.

'Surrogate foreplay,' Andre repeated to himself. 'Maybe you're on to something!'

He shook his head. 'If only other women could be more like you. Some of them are so hung up! Take my wife, for instance.

She thinks I leave her stuck at home with the kids all the time. I tell her that's what the in-laws are for! I tell her to get out more but she doesn't listen. She thinks I'm having all the fun.'

I refrained from saying he probably *was* having all the fun. I imagined his wife at home minding the kids day in, day out, while Andre went out to his 'business meetings'.

'Does she work?' I asked.

'She's got a great job!' Andre said. 'She's an accountant. Works for a law firm. Loves it. She's got a degree and every-thing. She's really good at it too.'

'Is it full-time?' I asked, wondering if she was one of those superwomen who seemed to be able to work eight hours at the office and then return home and look after demanding families.

'Nah. Part-time. Her choice. She doesn't *have* to work – it's not as if we need the money. She can do whatever she wants. But it doesn't matter – she still reckons I leave her by herself all the time.'

It sounded like she was lonely. That she was living her life through a cheating husband.

'Maybe she senses what you're up to. Maybe she's jealous,' I suggested.

'She's not really interested in socialising. She'd prefer to curl up with a book than go out.'

'It sounds to me like she'd prefer to curl up with *you*,' I told him. 'Maybe you've been neglecting her.'

'Well, that's not going to happen. I'm not interested in the couch. I want to go out and have fun while I still can. I want to live my life – not spend it closeted at home.'

Curse instinctive determinism!

'Maybe you could get her interested in swinging,' I said. 'That way you could have your cake and eat it too. You wouldn't have to lie to her any more. Hell, maybe you could introduce *me*.'

Andre shook his head, looking wistful. 'She wouldn't go for

it, Holly. She's taken our vows to heart. She fully expects us to be monogamous for the rest of our lives.'

He shuddered. So did I. Monogamy was becoming a dirty word.

'I wish I could be like you,' he whispered in my ear, nibbling my neck ever so gently. 'You're free – you can do whatever you like. Men aren't supposed to be married, it's not natural.'

I changed the subject and told him about the scare Tom had given me earlier in the week.

'Why didn't you hassle him more?' Andre asked, puzzled.

'Discretion's one of the most important things,' I replied. 'They like me because I've got no strings attached. Girlfriends and wives nag. I don't. I'm merely a service provider. I'm not entitled to information about their lives – like when I'm going to see them again. Nor do I enquire after their families. I don't whinge if they've been neglecting me, or talk about my own problems. That's not what I'm all about. But it's bloody hard. I don't know what I'm doing half the time. Everything seems so uncertain. If it wasn't for the diary, I think I'd have stopped by now. I've got to be honest – this mistress business isn't that dependable. I'm supposed to be paying my bills!'

Andre laughed.

'It doesn't surprise me. You're trying to formalise the informal, that's all. It's no wonder your gents are baulking. You're not exactly a harmless bit of fluff. Men want as many women as they can attract, with as little commitment as possible. Women want the reverse. If you want your gents to be dependable, you're still just a woman expecting them to act unnaturally.' He laughed again. 'I don't think I've ever heard the guys going on about a woman's dependability. All they're interested in is getting laid. He looked me in the eye. 'But you're making it legit, Holly. You're bringing it out of the closet. You might even save a few marriages.'

His gorgeous Latino eyes shone with open admiration.

I sighed. 'But is the world ready to hear such things?'

'Holly, Holly, Holly,' Andre said, shaking his head. 'That's my whole point! No-one has the guts. If someone doesn't put their hand up, the divorce rate is just going to keep on climbing. One dysfunctional generation after another all passing on the lesson that cheating for the sake of the children is better than re-examining monogamy. It's a bloody disgrace, that's what it is.'

'What about your own wife?' I countered. 'Why doesn't she realise what's going on with you? I can't imagine you'd marry someone unintelligent. Surely she must know you're spending time with other women?'

'We're soulmates,' Andre told me. 'I love her more than anything in the world. But I'm still a man. She knew I loved women when she met me. She knows I'll never change. Besides, it's expected. The way things are these days, it's easy for men like me. That's what expense accounts and weekdays are for. I can spend $400 on "lunch" with a client and the company won't bat an eyelid. They'd be worried if I didn't!'

Another word that keeps popping up, I thought. *Expected.*

He laughed wryly. 'But I must admit, I don't abuse the system much. I'm too honest – that's why I can't afford you. To my deep regret, I might add. But I know a lot of men who do. It's the norm, Holly. All of your men would be the same. You're probably being listed as a business expense right now. They're probably claiming you on their tax.'

'You wouldn't believe some of the stories I've heard,' he continued. 'About mistresses, I mean. One of my mates was telling me about his – they both work together in the same office and the stupid dickhead invited her over for dinner with his wife. His wife had no idea he was seeing this woman. All during the dinner and afterwards he and Tanya were texting smutty messages to each other behind his wife's back. They all started watching telly after dinner. When he got up to go to the loo, he accidentally left his phone behind. One of Tanya's text messages came through late and his daughter picked it up and read it. The daughter showed the mother. They were outraged but they couldn't figure out who the mistress was. Meanwhile, poor Tanya's lying there on the carpet in front of them, watching telly and shitting herself! So then they decide to ring the mistress's number. Tanya's frantically trying to turn off her phone but can't get to it in time. Her phone rings and they realise the mistress is her! All shit hits the fan. My mate comes back and his wife and daughter have got Tanya in a headlock!'

He roared with laughter. It was awful, but I couldn't help laughing too. 'How embarrassment!' I said. Then I realised Andre knew Tanya's name but not the wife's.

Andre rubbed my leg.

'You're so beautiful,' he told me again. 'You know I'm hot for you. I can't help it. Every time I masturbate I think of you. The taste of you. It's driving me crazy.'

I giggled nervously. It was so hard to resist him.

'I'm sorry, but I can't have sex with you. I'm supposed to be exclusive, remember? Sometimes I'm not even allowed to kiss people!'

'But, baby,' he said, 'you can't live on a grand a week. What if you get dumped again? Your clothes alone probably cost more than that!' He gestured at the olive silk coat that I had carelessly flung on the chair beside me. He was right. It had cost a small fortune.

'Well,' I relented, 'maybe. I'll talk to him about it. But I want to wait a while. Wait till we settle down into a pattern. Then I'll ask him.'

The trouble was, Andre was right. I had as much job security right now as a tea lady in a vending-machine factory.

I looked at my watch: 4 p.m. Tom was dropping by at eight. Call me old-fashioned, but I needed space between them.

'Sorry, but I've got to go,' I told Andre. 'I need to go shopping and get some treats for my man.'

I walked him back to his car. He insisted on holding my hand. 'Can't I come up for just a little while?' he pleaded.

'Sorry, Andre, but you're far too tempting,' I said.

He tried to kiss me but I pulled away.

'I'm so hot for you, baby,' he said again, rubbing his crotch. 'I want to taste you.'

I was very glad when he got into his car. He made me feel so sexy! Much more of that treatment and I would have succumbed. Tom was going to be a lucky man tonight.

Resisting the urge to masturbate when I got upstairs, I fussed with the cushions a bit to calm myself down, kept myself away from my diary, then I went shopping. Retail therapy. Bliss.

Tom arrived right on time, dressed in the obligatory polo shirt with navy slacks and loafers. He had on a lovely aftershave.

He'd said he didn't want dinner, so I produced dessert instead. I'd walked down to the patisserie in Victoria Street and allowed my inner child to select two enormous sour cream and black cherry strudels, a carton of King Island white chocolate cream and a Toblerone, which I'd chopped up and sprinkled over the top.

Tom's eyes lit up with greedy pleasure. He grabbed a spoon and hoed in with the gusto of a small child. He even got cream on his face. And all the time he smiled. A huge grin from ear to ear. He forgot about his wife. His work. His life. He just ate delightedly, beaming up at me with gratitude. Such simple things made these men so very happy.

The sex wasn't good that night. I didn't even get a chance to use my new tricks. I think Tom had already come once – during dessert. Not literally, of course, but mentally. He had a soft-on for most of what was a very unenthusiastic effort. We both gave up after about five minutes.

I was pleased when he left. Once again, I couldn't ask when or whether he'd be back.

# CHAPTER 22

In the morning I went for a wax at the beautician's. I contemplated surprising Tom with a Brazilian, then thought about what Roger had said about sadomasochism, so I got my usual instead. My beautician called it a 'G-string', which meant a narrow line of hair from brickie's cleavage to camel toe (as Andre put it) ending in what was described as a 'racing stripe' at the front.

I looked at the red skin and wondered how Tom would react.

'I've got a hot date tonight,' I said. 'Have you got anything that'll take the redness away?'

'Put a cold compress on it right away and I'll give you some oil to put over it. Then, after you have a shower tonight, put on some of the oil again. It'll be fine.'

I was back home checking my snail mail when I got a phone call from Henry.

'Hi, Holly, I'm just checking in to find out how you're going,' he said.

Henry. The respectable job where I got to fuck the boss in his wife's own home. The wife who'd want to swing with me eventually. Or so Henry believed. But it was a real job. With superannuation and a legitimate pay packet that came with rights. *No, Holly, don't do it,* I thought.

'Henry!' I said. 'It's great to hear from you. Things are going really well. Although I must admit, I've been thinking about you.'

It was true. Almost. I *had* been thinking about legitimate work. He was the halfway step. So, three-quarters true.

'Yeah, well, I've finished those deals I was telling you about. I've got enough work for the next six years. I need to get my staff together. Are you sure you're not interested?'

Six years. It sounded like music to my ears.

'Well . . . er . . . I'm just trialling someone at the moment. But I've got to be honest – it's not the most secure work in the world. I'm not sure what I want to do, Henry. I'll admit, right now it's tempting to go back to an office and do a proper job. But . . . well . . . I'm just not sure yet.'

'Well, you're a beautiful girl, Holly. You know I think that. We've got the right chemistry. It could really work out for both of us. How's the book going? When'll that be finished?'

'The book is writing itself,' I said truthfully. 'I've done nearly a hundred pages since I saw you. I'll be finished in another month or so.'

'That's great news!' he said. 'Maybe then you could come and work for me!'

'Perhaps. But we either make the job legit or we tell your wife straightaway. Your choice.'

'Sure,' he replied. 'Anything you say. You know I think a lot of you. Give me a call any time. Maybe we could just go out for a beer or something?'

I nearly laughed out loud. One Andre was enough for any girl, I decided.

'That'd be lovely,' I lied. 'I'll be sure to keep you in mind.'

I rang off and saved his number. Just in case.

At midday I finally heard from Philip via a text message: *I'm still interested . . . delayed response is because I haven't been checking that account. Although you have to make it up to me since I am second best.*

I texted him back: *First best, as it turns out. But there's been a development. When you get a chance, call me so we can have a chat. H*

Then a message arrived from Andre: *I want your aroma.*

I texted him back: *Aw shucks . . . and me just freshly waxed and tingly . . . Lunch Fri? H*

Andre's reply was immediate: *Hmm . . . that could be arranged . . . I am hard . . . Also clean-shaven so it's smooth for your lips.*

I wondered if exclusivity included dirty texting. Cyberdelity.

*Smooth on smooth . . . mmm . . . Love a face against my lips. H*

*I'm not completely shaven just trimmed at top and stem and balls are smooth . . . Are you completely brazilian? I want to run my tongue over your lips.*

*My lips are fat and bald but, alas, only for single play today. H*

*Do you want to watch each other play?*

I imagined Andre coming over and us not touching each other. Yeah, right.

*Not today, my friend, but soon. H*

*OK, baby, will let u know about Fri . . . I should be able to clear my appointmts.*

I couldn't help grinning. Confucius say beware of man clearing appointments.

My mobile rang. It was Philip.

'Philip!' I said. 'Thanks so much for calling. I'm so sorry about what happened. I feel like a complete dill. I knew you were the right one! There I was, telling you how empowering all of this was and then I went ahead and picked the only person who probably wasn't genuine. I had coffee and arranged to start Monday and then didn't hear from him again. I feel like such a fool . . .'

I trailed off. Philip chuckled.

'Don't take it personally,' he said. 'He probably just changed his mind, that's all. Men do that sometimes. Maybe he was frightened of being ripped off or something.'

'But I'm the one taking all the risks,' I protested. 'I've got everything to lose and he's got nothing!'

'Maybe he thinks you're a honey-trapper or something.'

'Honey-trapper?' I said. 'What the hell's a honey-trapper?'

Philip laughed. 'Don't you know? Geez, you'd probably be great at it! A honey-trapper is paid by women to test the faithfulness of their partners. I was reading an article in one of my wife's magazines about a woman who does it. Apparently she's never, ever had a husband who's refused her advances! One hundred per cent of subjects were convinced to stray. She wasn't even that good-looking! Then she dobs them in to their wives.'

I scowled. That such a role even existed was yet another nail in the marriage coffin.

'Well, the fact that someone is hiring them in the first place probably means the sample's pretty skewed,' I said. 'I can promise you, I'm not a honey-trapper – I'm just trying to pay some bills, that's all.'

Philip laughed again. 'Don't worry, I don't think you're a honey-trapper. My wife has no idea anyway. So, when do we start?'

Confession time. Sometimes I wish I was a Catholic and could get a clean slate every week. How suspiciously convenient.

'There's a problem,' I said. 'When I didn't hear from you I thought you weren't interested. So I've been trialling someone else. Trouble is, I'm not sure it's going to work out. This sounds terrible, but is it possible you could be my reserve? I'll know by Friday. I'm so sorry about this. I wish I'd gone with my first choice – with you, I mean.'

I cringed. I'll bet no-one had ever asked him to be on their reserve bench before. But Philip just chuckled again.

'It's OK,' he said. 'I should've called sooner. I've been away. Yeah, Friday should be OK. I realise you want to do the right thing. Just let me know as soon as you can.'

I sighed in relief. 'Thanks, Philip. I'll let you know ASAP, I promise. Thanks for being so understanding about this.'

I rang off, feeling exhausted. Then I went and put a cold compress on my pussy and oiled it, just like the beautician had told me.

By 6 p.m. I still hadn't heard from Tom. Once again I found myself wondering why I was still doing this. If only Dick had worked out – he'd been perfect. Now I was living on the edge. I didn't think I could stand much more.

That night I cooked up six fat sausages for dinner and ate every last one. It took me a week to get the smell out of my apartment.

By the next morning, I had decided Philip was my man. I would tell Tom the truth – that I needed another Dick, so to speak.

At nine Henry rang again and wanted to know if he could take me to lunch.

'Er . . . I'm sorry, Henry, but I'm busy right now,' I said.

'Well, maybe we could have brunch this weekend?'

'I'm sorry, I'm busy. Maybe in a couple of weeks.'

I rang off and continued to write my diary.

At 1 p.m. Andre texted me: *I can't do lunch 2moz – want me to bring you coffee later?*

I wrote back: *Sorry – can we make it next week – too many commitments right now. H*

I started to giggle. Tom and Philip and Henry and Andre. Served me right for wanting Dick!

I texted Philip at 9 a.m. on Friday. *No-one can beat my number 1. H*

His reply was almost immediate: *Purrr. It's nice to be wanted. Are you still interested? H*

*Sounds good. Looks like you will have to be extra nice. When do you want to start?*

*How does Mon sound? Same deal as before. H*

*Sure. What do you have planned for me on Mon? What are you into?*

*Whatever you desire plus a few surprises. Especially lingerie, corsets, threeways and role play. H*

*Corsets . . . Excellent. Big yes on that. Can you send a photo? What role play outfits do you have? Geez I'm getting v. hard.*

I shook my head. I'd get RSI at this rate. Had cyberspace increased cheating? I'd heard somewhere that flurried texting was one of the first things private investigators looked for when examining suspected infidelity. Some suspects even used two phones, maintaining a 'clean' one for their spouse. I mentally thanked Andre for giving me texting practice.

*All fetishes catered for, including some of my own. I'll have bodily surprises in store to delight and surprise you – have you quivering with anticipation or moaning with pleasure. All will have you wondering, satisfied and longing for more. H*

*So Greek and facials are in? I am feeling so aroused. How can I work for the rest of the morning when you are occupying my thoughts?*

I wondered what Greek and facials were. I resolved to Google them when I got a chance. Then I remembered that Philip was into 'anticipation' so I texted back.

*Nothing better than a Grecian yearn . . . tee hee . . . plus my big fat lips are perfect for facials . . . but above all I look forward to having an erotic surprise waiting for you every time you walk in the door. H*

It was pure bluff. His response arrived in about five minutes:

*Sitting here thinking of you, the anticipation of my hands caressing your body for first time, my lips on your skin. Your breasts behind lace tempting my touch but not fully naked. Imagining your hand caressing my hard member while the other explores your own body. Resulting climax of juices being shared as true enjoyment of sex . . . I am waiting for you.*

Wow. And I thought *I* was supposed to be the writer! But I was getting cynical – was this original or had he sent it to all his girls?

I sent back: *Have read your message 3 times and am fully aroused. Resolve not to touch myself until Mon, when I can hold your hard cock in one hand and myself in the other. I will be clad as you suggest. Untold pleasures await you. I will have damp dreams until then – hope yours are wet. H*

It did the trick. I didn't hear from him for at least an hour after that. I hoped his office was private.

Later, there was another flurry of texts organising lunch on Monday, commencing at noon. I learned that two of Philip's 'favourite' things were Coke and lemonade. Great. A tee-totaller. Just what I needed.

When I went down to the internet café that afternoon and delivered my email there was a lovely long message from Dick, asking what I'd been up to lately.

*Still searching for another you*, I replied honestly.

I checked my snail mail on the way home. Buried amongst the bundles of restaurant menus and real estate offerings lay an envelope clearly containing my plastic security tag. A barely decipherable note read: *Dr has prescribed rest due to anxiety. Tom.*

I didn't feel angry. Just relieved.

Monday. Philip day.

Once again, I purchased an assortment of fine cheeses, dips and meats. I drank a glass of leftover red wine as I prepared the platter. I wished Philip drank something harder. Give me an alcoholic over a teetotaller any day. Although, come to think of it, a lot of alcoholics *are* teetotallers. AA is very successful, but cessation doesn't make the disease go away.

I hoped Philip was a good lover. If his emails and texts were anything to go by, I worried he might find me too 'vanilla'. I hoped Greek facials weren't painful.

He knocked on the door right on time and handed me an

envelope as soon as he walked in. I carefully placed it on the desk. By now I knew what it contained.

'What would you like to drink?' I asked, listing his options.

'Lemonade would be great,' Philip replied.

'Diet or real?'

'Real, please.'

I looked at his considerable belly and tried to be glad it wasn't created by beer.

I gave him the tour of the platter but he scarcely glanced at it. He'd told me that Italian and Asian were his favourite foods, but I'd wanted something portable – something we could take into the bedroom during a long afternoon of glorious, lazy sex with my accomplished lover. Instead of trying the smoked salmon, caper and cream cheese parcels or the beautifully crumbling blue cheese, he went straight for a chunk of cheddar that had been sitting in the fridge for a while. I'd only included it in the interests of cleaning out the shelves. Instead of the organic semi-dried tomatoes drenched in rosemary oil or the ricotta stuffed peppers, he carefully picked out a bit of iceberg lettuce that had somehow found its way into the exotic leaf mix and a piece of fresh tomato leftover from last night's dinner. Then he put it all between two hunks of sourdough baguette and squashed it down into a sandwich with the palm of his hand. So much for a refined Dick!

I asked if he wanted some Dijon mustard.

'Nah,' Philip replied. 'I don't like hot things.'

He ate his sandwich quickly, then skolled his lemonade in a single mouthful.

'Would you like some more?' I asked.

'No, it's fine,' he said, looking at his empty glass. 'I'm sorry – I'm a bit nervous.'

I couldn't help looking at my own full glass and wishing it was a double shot of vodka. I resorted to an icebreaker that had worked well in the past.

'So, what's a nice guy like you reading Persona for anyway?'

Philip instantly relaxed and laughed.

'Geez, you'll love this!' he declared. 'The Persona site is owned by one of the media corporations I consult with. I was sitting at a meeting with about twenty other dudes when some IT guru came in and gave us a talk about how to use the net to target different consumers. Help identify whether they're legit or not. He showed us a couple of examples of ads that had large hit rates and yours was one of them!'

He laughed again but I was horrified!

'Wait a minute,' I said. 'You mean this guy had my ad – my picture in the mask – up on one of those big screens and it was shown to about twenty men? You've got to be kidding me!'

Philip was enjoying himself.

'Don't worry, everyone was very impressed. I probably wasn't the only one who contacted you!'

I didn't know whether to feel flattered or appalled.

'So the men . . . did they like me? What did they say?' I asked, my vanity getting the better of me.

'They were drooling over you,' Philip said. 'One of the reasons I'm here, really.'

Then he closed his eyes and leaned forward to kiss me.

I responded in kind but it was a 'nothing' kiss. His lips went through the motions, but there seemed to be no sensitivity there – no mouth full of nerve ends, no lips exploring my own; rather, it was steady, medium pressure and a tongue that dutifully went in and out of my mouth.

Within moments he moved to my breasts and started groaning at the mere sight of them cupped in his hands. Then he tried to pull off my shirt and John's expensive bra together without even undoing the straps. So much for the tantalising underwear beneath the flimsy garment! I pulled off my shirt then undid my bra. He ripped it off with barely a glance.

'What are your fantasies?' I whispered throatily. 'What could I role play for you?'

He hesitated.

'A school girl?' I prompted. 'A bondage mistress? Appear at the door in suspenders?'

'A nurse,' he finally replied, rubbing his face in my now naked cleavage and groaning louder and louder.

I wondered what Greek nurses wore.

'Would you like to go into the bedroom?' I asked.

'Sure,' he said, heaving himself off the couch.

We walked into the bedroom.

'Sit down,' I commanded and he obediently sat on the edge of the bed.

I slowly undid his shirt buttons to reveal beautiful skin marked here and there with the occasional mole. His stomach was very large, but so beautiful was his skin that it was a bonus – a glorious expanse of something to kiss tenderly.

I kneeled on the fluffy mat and undid his trousers. I was becoming used to business attire by now! Up until the past few months, I'd mostly encountered jeans. Business slacks were much harder to negotiate, sometimes incorporating a little slide thingy that was almost as difficult to undo as a bra. Give me denim any day.

He stood up while I slid his pants off. I could see his erect penis underneath his jocks. *Medium*, I thought. I peeled down his undies and it sprang out (as they do). I was glad to see it was covered in the same gorgeous skin that contained the rest of his body.

I kissed it very gently on the tip and Philip collapsed on the bed, groaning even more loudly now and saying my name over and over again.

I must admit, I was a tad mystified by his intense reaction. Perhaps I was better at this than I thought I was – all of the women he'd seen so far must have been duds, or he was a lot more naive than he'd made himself out to be. Naturally, I decided to go with the first possibility.

He was cut, so I deep-throated him like David had recommended, driving my mouth down over the complete shaft of his penis and changing the angle of my airway to accommodate him. There was no sign of my gag reflex. It worked!

I thought Philip was going to have a seizure with the pleasure of it. His eyes were screwed shut and he kept convulsing, groaning louder and louder.

'Stop!' he said, within mere moments. 'I don't want to come.'

I moved up his body, kissing him tenderly over his beautiful, hairless belly, holding his nipples gently in my teeth as I tongued them.

'Sit on me,' he whispered, not opening his eyes and still groaning loudly.

'OK,' I replied. 'But remember the condom.'

I leaned over to the bedside table and got out my little pocket clit-tickler, some lube and a condom. I opened the wrapper and left it sitting where Philip could access it quickly. Then I sat astride him with his cock between my legs, moving my hands along it and rubbing my cupped palms ever-so-gently over the head. At the same time, I ground my clit into the base of it, wiggling from side to side to make myself horny.

Philip lay on his back where he had first flung himself, still with his face screwed up, still groaning loudly, saying 'God' over and over again.

So loud had his moans become that I started to get worried he might come. I moved off him and whispered, 'How would you like to fuck me?'

He opened his eyes for the first time and seemed to take stock of his surroundings.

'From behind,' he whispered hoarsely, heaving himself up.

'Remember the condom,' I muttered, putting my face in the pillows and applying lube to myself to counteract the drying rubber.

Within moments he was entering my pussy. I groped for the clit-tickler and put it against the both of us. Philip gave a yelp and then fucked me hard. I put my hands on the wall and timed my pushes back so that each thrust of his penis drove it as deep as it would possibly go. I felt my own orgasm begin to mount.

It came quickly and, knowing I was good for several more, I went with it, gasping out loud at the pleasure and telling him not to stop.

Philip complied and within moments he was coming too, shouting, 'Oh God, oh God, oh God!' before quickly pulling out and collapsing on the bed beside me.

A tad concerned that he'd left the condom within me, I groped at myself and pulled my face out of the pillows. To my horror, I saw the condom still sitting within easy reach on my bedside table.

'You came?' I asked him, disbelieving.

'Sure did,' he said contentedly.

'But the condom,' I said. 'Did you have your own?'

'Oh,' was all he said.

'You didn't use it?' I said, slightly hysterical. 'Why do you think I put it there? Don't you know that people can carry diseases? That I could get pregnant? This isn't the marriage bed, you know!'

'I'm starting to get nervous again,' he stammered.

I thought about Philip's poor wife. Then I thought about my ultimatum. I had failed. Something inside me snapped.

'Nervous!' I shouted at him. 'You should be more than nervous! You've just fucked a woman you don't even know and you've got a wife at home! Do you plan to tell her you've had unprotected sex? Or are you just going to use condoms for a while in case you've caught something? It's people like you who are spreading AIDS! You haven't been with other women! You couldn't fuck your way out of a wet paper bag! You're worse than a cheater. You're a fucking social menace!'

Still naked, I stomped into the lounge room, got his envelope, ripped it open and threw the money all over him. 'Get out!' I screamed. 'Get out of my house, you moron! Take your fucking money! Nothing's worth this! You're not a Dick, you're an oafish fool! Go home to your wife and stay there where you belong!'

Philip gathered his clothes and money, looking completely stricken. He left with his shoes still in his hand.

As soon as the door closed, I let out a scream of frustration.

And you know what the really ironic thing was? I'd probably finally helped a marriage. Philip was unlikely ever to stray again.

# CHAPTER 23

I rang Henry the next morning and asked if the offer of a legitimate job was still available. To hell with the diary. Whistle-blowing wasn't my style.

'Sure,' he said. 'I promise, I won't touch you. Why don't you come and meet my wife on Saturday? We can all have lunch together. If all goes well, you can start on Monday.'

Then I made an appointment with my GP. A couple of my friends were HIV positive, and thanks to them I knew the testing procedure had changed. Doctors now had a significant chance of detecting seroconversion within three to five days. I gave myself a week to be absolutely sure.

After that I rang Kev and asked if he'd be interested in a liquid lunch. Unsurprisingly, he didn't let me down.

I met him at the Institute of Molecular Biology as usual. The staff knew me by now, and I found it rather pleasant to sit in the enormous foyer and watch the scientists scurry past. Not many people seemed to use the little reception area; in the whole time I'd been having weekday lunches with Kev I'd never seen another person there. It surprised me – the seats were comfortable and there were plenty of benefactor boards to read.

Sometimes I'd see a rich old lady being led around; I always wondered who she was – a particular breed, those ladies. They always wore lots of gold rings, big round stud-style earrings and had carefully foiled blonde bobbed hair. They dressed in flashy Italian designer labels with high heels. Stockings were a definite must. The handbags held in the crooks of their arms were wearable art – elegantly crafted and understated Chanel or Prada.

Kev and I were steak sluts. There were at least ten different restaurants and cafes nearby offering lunch specials and we were working our way through the beef options. Today we'd chosen the French restaurant across the road from the Institute. The steak wasn't that good but the barista sure was. Kev and I took turns giving him the eye because we still weren't sure which side he was batting for.

'So, how's Dick going?' Kev asked me, after we'd seated ourselves and the obligatory glasses of house red were in front of us.

'Oh, off and on,' I said evasively. 'I saw him yesterday. Very plain vanilla, a bit naive in the sack.'

'So how are you coping with all of this vanilla then?' (Don't you hate friends who get right to the point?)

'Well,' I said, trying to stick to the truth as much as I could, 'you can have vanilla lots of different ways, you know.'

Kev laughed. 'But it will never be chocolate.'

I laughed with him, but I couldn't help thinking that it *had* been chocolate for a while there. Well, cappuccino, anyway.

My mobile rang. It was Dick.

'I got your email,' he said. 'I haven't stopped thinking about you since. Would you like to have dinner?'

I thought about the possibility of having contracted HIV.

'Er . . . I'm sorry, Dick . . . I'm having lunch with Kev. I can't really talk at the moment. Could I ring you back?'

'Sure,' he said. 'No problem. But don't forget!' He rang off.

'Dick,' I said to Kev unnecessarily.

He grinned at me. 'I figured that.'

I changed the subject, falling back to another age-old question.

'So, what've you been up to lately? I haven't heard from you in a while.'

'Marcus has been sick so we haven't done a lot. Watched telly, mostly. We've hardly been out at all. Getting too cold for that anyway.'

I nodded in commiseration. 'Yeah, I haven't been up to much either. Quiet time of year, really.'

More lies of omission. I seemed to be telling them a lot these days. How sad that my previous existence never seemed to require them. I gave a big sigh. Maybe an office wouldn't be so bad after all. Photocopying and multi-tasking and singing happy birthday at morning tea-time.

'I'm thinking about starting proper work again,' I said. 'I'm sick of sitting around all day trying to look beautiful. I want to make some money for myself. I want to be financially dependent on *me* again.'

Kev just nodded and ate his steak.

Nothing we did seemed to surprise each other any more, I thought. That was the good thing about growing old together – we became so predictable. Now we catered to each other's neuroses instead of accidentally provoking them. We were still the same people as twenty years ago; we'd just had different input.

I ploughed on. 'This sugar daddy business might seem glamorous and wonderful, and it is sometimes, but there are also all the times I'm left on a whim. I need a proper income. I need super and long-service leave. I can't keep doing this for the rest of my life. I think I want to be on my own again.'

'Somehow I just can't imagine you'd be happy going back to a normal life, Holly.'

I gave another big sigh. 'I'm a bit over it, to be honest. It started out as a way to pay my bills. Then I started writing the diary. I was convinced completion of the manuscript justified the job, but now I think the job is justifying the manuscript. I don't know if I can keep going. Going back to an office is my only option. It's the only thing I know how to do.'

'I'm just not so sure an office would be the right thing for you,' Kev said. 'Especially after everything you've been through. Maybe there's something else you can do from home. Maybe something *artistic*.'

'Shit, Kev, is that what I've become? An "artistic" type who can't blend with "office" types? I might be incredibly happy back in an office. It won't matter to me if my colleagues are a wife, a single mum or a BDSM fetishist who likes little old ladies with blue hair – I'll be able to appreciate them for who they *are*, rather than what they *say*.'

Kev didn't look convinced.

'It's bizarre,' I went on. 'You're one of the few people who knows what's going on in my life, and you know absolutely jack shit! I've never had so many secrets before. But I have to confess, despite its shortcomings, it feels kind of good to have a secret life . . . Maybe it brings out my inner child. Makes me feel young and naughty.'

'Why do you think Marcus and I have sex outside our relationship?' Kev replied. 'It keeps us on our toes. Keeps us competitive. Stops us growing stale. We learn tips from other people regularly, then take them home with a secret little grin and deliver them like a gift. Marcus learnt a doozy the other day from a guy at the sauna; best wank he's ever given me! It's really good for the relationship, believe me.'

'Open relationships, eh?' I mused. 'Maybe that's the solution. I know one thing – traditional marriage needs an upgrade. It needs to move with the times.'

'At least straight people get to make mistakes,' Kev complained. 'Thanks to Howard's rightist cronies, we don't even get a chance. It's not fair that the breeders get all the misery.'

'Why don't you try and improve it?' I said. 'Maybe you could re-negotiate the terms to suit gay people and conduct regular performance reviews. If you hire an employee to do something and they can no longer fulfil the requirements, you can fire them. Why not a spouse? It doesn't matter whether couples agree to remain monogamous or they want to danger-fuck strangers in front of the Sydney Opera House, just so long as the marital expectations are agreed to beforehand. Partner A wants sex, dinner, a well-maintained figure, conversation and sports on the couch. Partner B wants a bread-winner, regular oral sex, romantic getaways, conversation and no beer bellies. A performance review is held after five years. If one of them no longer meets the other's service standards, they become financially disadvantaged in the allocation of property. If they deliver only three out of the five marital expectations, they only get three-fifths of fifty per cent. Financial incentives for marital performance standards – that'd be a way to ensure marriage works!'

Kev laughed. 'Not a bad idea. Same-sex marriage could be called a *civilised* union, instead of a civil one. Something the breeders can envy. We've already done it for fashion; why not for marriage as well?'

I made a face. Gay men always claimed the good stuff.

'Yeah, but that's if they even recognise a problem at all,' I replied gloomily. 'I've never seen so much rampant denial in my life. I think just about everyone in the whole world knows what's going on, but no-one wants to do anything about it.'

'Why would they? Everyone's instincts are being satisfied. The women are at home worrying if their mate is OK out there in the big, bad world, and the mate is out hunting and sowing his seed under the pretext of work.'

I shook my head.

'Our instincts don't want us to rock the boat,' Kev explained gently. 'Only genetic mutations do that. Freaks. People like us, Holly.'

Was that what had happened? I had found my inner freak?

I tried playing the devil's advocate. 'Yeah. But you're a molecular biologist! You're supposed to say that,' I argued. 'You just can't go round calling us primates with instincts that sabotage advancement. Surely we've come further than that!' I glared at him.

'Sooner or later society will have to accept what science has known all along – that we'll always behave as our DNA intends. Then we'll have to admit we got it horribly wrong in the monogamously-ever-after department. Human beings are cyclical. Marriage should be too. Scientists wouldn't expect *any* living creature to follow an identical cycle to any other – why should humans be exempt?' He snorted with contempt for us all. 'Why can't people believe the bloody statistics?' he growled, finishing the rest of his wine in an angry gulp.

He made me feel like a gluttonous rutting pig that had been caught with its snout in the trough. Curse Kev. It wasn't what I needed to hear right now.

I left soon after the second round of red. Somehow no amount of alcohol was going to change anything.

I stopped at the chemist on the way home and asked for the morning-after pill. I whispered my request in shame and hoped the gay man beside me was into bare-backing. Then I saw he was buying a giant syringe with a thin rubber hose attached to the nozzle. Chemists are probably the least judgemental of us all, I thought.

When I got home, I returned Dick's call.

'How have you been?' he asked. 'I must admit, I've been worried about you. I've been thinking about you quite a lot, actually. It took me weeks to write that email. Is everything OK? How's your new man?'

I winced. 'How about I tell you all about it over that dinner you promised me? I hate talking on the phone.'

'Sure,' he replied. 'But I'm out of town for a couple of days. How does Sunday sound?'

I nearly laughed. The day after my 'job interview' with Henry and his wife.

'Sunday would be absolutely perfect,' I told him truthfully. 'I'll call about lunchtime to confirm.'

I had arranged to go out with two of my long-time girlfriends on Friday night. I tried to cancel, pleading poverty, but they insisted – we'd been planning the evening for months.

Naturally, they wanted to know all about my current work and how my love life was going. So I told them about what had happened with the first John and how I thought I'd been in love for the very first time. Then how Charlene had threatened to kill herself and the kids, and how John had gone back to her.

They fed me marijuana and patted me on the shoulder saying, 'How terrible.'

Sara said that her garden was now producing vegetables and she and her partner were considering having a baby in the following year. I'd known Sara since high school, where she'd always been the rebel and me the admiring follower. Isabella – think thin, gorgeous with natural red hair – confided she'd been on a blind date that hadn't worked out. With an Elvis imperson-ator she'd met in a Chinese restaurant. There was no way I could tell these women that I had just fired my fourth sugar daddy and these men paid me $1000 a week for a few hours of companion-ship. Nor could I tell them I might be HIV positive.

Instead I grinned sympathetically and rolled my eyeballs whenever the conversation required it.

We had arranged to meet a group of Sara's friends at a bar in Bellevue Hill. I'd dressed carefully for the occasion, in my white snug-fitting pants and a pretty pink top with a cowl neck. I put my olive green jacket over the top and my faithful Birken-stocks on my feet. Just about every girl in the pub was dressed in $1000 designer frocks with killer high heels or Sass and Bide jeans tucked into leather boots. I couldn't help thinking they'd become the society matrons I'd seen during my lunch with Roger.

I felt like an alien in their midst. But every man in the pub turned to stare as I walked past. Most of them found some sort of reason to brush against me on their way somewhere. It was extraordinary. It was as if I was emanating pheromones or something. I wasn't meeting anyone's eye, and I was in thongs, for Goddess's sake!

By 2 a.m. I'd had enough of the men's stares and the girl-friends' glares and so I snogged the alpha male. He was a very tall African–American who had an endless parade of women approaching him. He often walked around the room, touching various girls (who knew him) on the arse as he walked past. He had approached our table twice, pausing in front of it dramatically, staring at us and then leaving again without a word. The third time he draped himself across an adjacent table, talking on his mobile phone and gesturing at me to come over.

'No,' I said rudely. 'You're on the phone. If you want to talk to me, I suggest you hang up.'

He hung up immediately and pulled me across to him.

'What would you say if I told you I wanted to fuck you?'

I nearly laughed out loud. I wondered what he'd think if I told him I was approaching forty, possibly contagious and very nearly a whore.

Instead I coolly replied, 'Not tonight, my friend. I'm promised to another.'

He contemplated this a while and looked around the pub, trying to see who was watching us. I winked at Isabella and Sara.

'I'm married anyway,' he declared, showing me his mobile phone. 'Look, seven messages from my missus!'

I look at his inbox. He even had his wife listed as 'Mrs' in his address book. There they were – a list of unreturned messages from some poor woman just called 'Mrs'.

His timing could not have been worse. He was so cock-sure I felt a strong need to deflate his ego. I couldn't help myself. I would save the missus's face by making her man lose some of his.

'I've changed my mind. Let's go, I want to fuck you after all,' I said, kissing him in full view of the bar. 'Let me tell my friends.'

Sara and Isabella were standing nearby. 'I'll be five minutes,' I whispered to them. 'Don't leave without me.'

I took his hand and led him out the front door. Several of his mates gave him good-natured punches on the shoulder as we walked out. The girls just gave me filthy looks.

When we got outside I shoved him into the nearest dark alcove. 'I'm on a promise but I'd love a snog,' I told him throatily.

He pulled his face away and tried to put my hand on his cock.

I went to leave.

'Wait!' he cried, pulling me back. 'OK. A snog then.'

Once again he pulled his face away and grabbed my hand more forcibly this time, pulling it down towards his crotch.

'Sorry,' I said, turning away. 'I told you, just a snog.'

'OK, OK,' he said grumpily.

I leaned forward and kissed him teasingly on the mouth, running my full lips over his. It lasted about three whole seconds. Then I walked away without a backward glance and returned to the pub. I'd been gone about three minutes.

I gave his mates a wink when I walked past. An indie guy who I'd boogied with on the dance floor gave me an approving smile that I'd got rid of him so fast. 'Cool,' he said.

When I got back to Sara and Isabella, I told a joke that made us all giggle loudly like schoolgirls. By the time my man returned by himself half an hour later, the entire pub knew something about my three-minute experience had amused us greatly.

He found me later on the dance floor and tried to save face by dragging me into a slow dance. The indie guy and I had been dancing up a storm. I pushed him away and told him coldly, 'Go away. I told you, I don't want to fuck you.'

I turned my back on him and resumed dancing – my way. The indie guy just watched, smiling. When we were leaving, he was standing near the door with his other indie mates. I nodded farewell.

'Where you headed?' he asked.

'Home,' I said.

He smiled again and nodded, sticking with his mates. 'Cool,' he said again.

Sara, Isabella and I took separate taxis. I charged my ride home on my Visa, knowing the portable swiper couldn't tell if the card was maxed. I grinned to myself as we sped through the deserted streets towards Darlinghurst. It was the most satisfying night I'd had for months.

# CHAPTER 24

At 11 o'clock on Saturday morning I drove out to Erskineville in Sydney's Inner West and followed Henry's careful instructions to his combined home and office. It was remarkably easy to find – a tower building perched under the flight path. Karen wasn't there when I arrived and I felt a small pang of anxiety. I hadn't alerted any of my friends to this expedition; if I were to disappear mysteriously, now would be a good time.

Henry looked exactly as I'd remembered him – dark jeans, black T-shirt, blond hair and goatee; fit, lithe and hot for me. Whilst he didn't try to touch me or make lewd suggestions, by now I could recognise the longing. I was glad I'd worn my business attire – a white-collared shirt and tailored pants.

Henry proudly showed me around their apartment. It had matching cream leather couches and dining chairs and some misguided surrealism adorning the walls. The pictures looked too gaudy, too bright – as if the artist couldn't be bothered mixing his paints and had regressed into off-the-shelf primary colours and childish scrawls.

Everything was immaculate – right down to the fresh hand towel in the main bathroom. Their balcony looked across most of western Sydney, with the airport clearly visible. Planes took off regularly. We didn't even hear them.

In pride of place was an ornate cage holding two brightly coloured African parrots. Double-glazed glass stood between them and the outdoors. All day, every day, these birds looked out at aircraft taking off into the endless expanse of blue sky complete with white fluffy clouds.

I gazed at Henry's birds. For a second I felt like throwing the closest chair through the double-glazed window and releasing them into the wild. Instead, I sat down as far away from Henry as possible and launched into conversation. When Karen arrived, I was discussing the pros and cons of a religious upbringing for children, with a cup of tea perched primly on my lap.

Henry had given the impression that Karen would be the first wife in history not threatened by my appearance, so, at the risk of sounding hideously vain, I had expected a woman with unflinching self-esteem. Instead, she was very tall, very thin and very agitated.

Top points for my business attire at least.

Karen gave me the look I dreaded, the look all wives give when they discover I've been alone with their husband. A momentary start as they take in my full lips and long auburn hair, and then a quick assessing glance at their partner to ensure that he hasn't been wallowing in my presence. I couldn't help thinking that I deserved that look now. I had become everything that wives feared most.

But I wanted to right the wrongs with Karen. I wanted to wave myself under her husband's nose and make him suffer for wanting me. I wanted to deny him the chance to cheat on his wife. Maybe I'd even tell her what he had proposed. It was important that she liked me. I began to trowel on the charm, mostly ignoring Henry and trying to make her feel secure.

'You have a beautiful home,' I told her. 'Your artist has certainly found his inner child.' I nodded at the collection of originals on the white walls around us, each with its own little down-light, so obviously lovingly placed and viewed with reverence.

She barely glanced at them and busied herself with unloading her groceries. She did it with her head bowed, slamming cupboard doors, not talking to us.

When she pulled out a bottle of cranberry juice I saw an opportunity to connect with her.

'Ahhh,' I commented. 'Cranberry juice. I've got to admit, it's a terrible weakness of mine. Mixed with vodka, that is. And did I mention beer and wine? In fact, when I come to think of it, I've got a lot of weaknesses . . .' I trailed off with a look of mock concern.

Karen laughed at my self-deprecation. 'Yeah,' she said. 'The dreaded alcohol. Lovely stuff. That and chocolate. Where would we be without them?'

'Healthier,' I said, and we all laughed.

I broke all my rules that day. Maybe it was to make up for the guilt. We left my car in their security parking and went to lunch in theirs – the same immaculate ute Henry had driven when I first met him. Three of us in the cab. Wife in the middle. Not the most pleasant situation to find yourself in. I couldn't help it. I got the giggles. Just a little one escaped but it was enough.

'What are you giggling about?' Karen asked with a smile on her face.

'The last time I was in a ute I was about sixteen,' I told her. 'I got the giggles then too. If I only knew then what I know now . . .'

Karen laughed. 'I'd be locked up!' she exclaimed.

Yep. Everything's a matter of perspective, all right.

After some debate, we settled on lunch at their local pub – mostly because I had about $3 in my wallet and there was a strong likelihood they would accept credit cards at the bar. I ordered a steak and mushroom pie (the cheapest thing on the menu) and a schooner of VB. Henry insisted on paying and I didn't argue as much as I usually would.

We ate outside. Henry and Karen were particularly impressed with a small aviary full of budgies in the middle of the beer garden. They discussed the pros and cons of giving their own lone budgie to the publican so it could make new friends. In the end, they decided the cage was too small.

'Would you like our budgie?' Henry asked me.

Maybe I should accept, I thought. Maybe I could take the budgie home and then release it from my own balcony. But at the back of my mind was the thought that a hawk or a magpie or something would seize it and I would learn what really happens when you give domesticated things their freedom.

'Sorry, no pets allowed at my place.' I shrugged regretfully.

By the end of the lunch, Karen was hypothetically renovating their home office to suit me better. She was so nice that it made me feel awful just to be there. I might have been able to prevent Henry fucking me, but there was no way I could make him be mentally monogamous as well. I felt like taking her aside and revealing that her husband had wanted to engage me as a fuckable personal assistant right under her very nose. Instead, I kept my mouth shut and resolved never to see them again.

We dropped her off at her work, then Henry drove me back to my car. 'She likes you,' he said.

'Yeah,' I replied glumly. 'Too much. That's the problem. I'm sorry, Henry, but there's no way I can take this job, even without the sex.'

'You're absolutely right,' he said, to my surprise. 'I've come to exactly the same conclusion. I've been going about this thing so wrong! Seeing Karen side by side with you has put it into perspective. You don't compare at all. I must admit, I thought you were the most gorgeous woman I'd ever seen, but seeing you stand next to my wife, I've realised how beautiful she really is. I'm not interested in other women any more, Holly. I want my wife back. She's the one I love! Thank you for coming today. I thought I was going to be able to change your mind, but I've changed mine. I'm already married to the most beautiful woman I know!'

It was another misfire, but somehow I'd helped them after all. Two marriages in the one week. Three if you counted 'the missus'. I was on fire!

'I'm glad about that,' I said, climbing out of the ute's immaculate leather interior and looking at my own dusty little Barina. 'Hey, Henry,' I said through the window, nodding at my filthy car. 'If you leave the dirt on, it provides a natural barrier. Maybe you shouldn't hide it in future.'

Henry just grinned.

Dick picked me up in his BMW on Sunday evening. 'Hey there, Holly-girl,' he drawled. 'You're lookin' mighty nice!'

'When in Rome . . .' I replied, gesturing at my very corporate black pants and tailored jacket. Underneath was a beautiful white fitted shirt with a bow at the front. 'You don't look so bad yourself.'

It was true. He wore an open-necked striped shirt with a black jacket and trousers. The same beautiful blue eyes gazed at me.

'It's so nice not to have to drive such a distance,' he told me. 'Now I can arrive looking like I did when I left home.'

Dick had recently moved his family from the outer to the inner suburbs. He reckoned it won him another three hours each day. I was impressed. He looked like a new man.

We drove to the Wharf restaurant at Walsh Bay, which abutted the Sydney Theatre Company at the very tip of one of the wharves. It felt more like a warehouse than a restaurant, but the views of the Sydney Harbour Bridge were amazing.

'What would you like to drink?' Dick asked when we were settled at our table.

'A vodka and soda would be lovely, please,' I replied, studying the people around me.

Most of the other patrons were my age or older, the men in shirts and ties, the women in dress shirts, many of them crisp white like my own. There was little of the mutton-dressed-as-lamb that I had encountered at Woollahra – most of these people probably worked for a living. Many of them looked like husbands and wives who worked senior jobs in the city and pulled dual incomes that paid off large mortgages on houses in the inner west. Children negotiable.

Dick spotted me studying our companions. 'You'd be surprised how many of them are exactly like us,' he said with a wink.

I stared at him. 'You mean, they're not married? They're . . . like us?' I whispered.

I looked around again. Come to think of it, most of the women were slim and well-dressed. The men were often bald with large beer bellies. The women were also considerably younger than their male counterparts. I was aghast! Dick laughed.

'Not quite like us,' he said. 'A lot of them probably work together.'

The more I thought I knew, the more I realised I didn't know. Andre was wrong – I wasn't doing anything new.

Where were the wives? Surely they weren't all at home fussing over Sunday roasts? I longed for their input on all of this.

'So how's that book of yours coming along?' Dick asked.

It took me a moment to remember my tale about the old ladies. 'Oh, great!' I replied. 'My characters are really starting to develop well.'

'How long till you're finished?'

'Oh, probably another month or so,' I said vaguely.

'What are you going to do then?'

'I dunno.' I looked gloomy. 'Maybe go back to the office.'

Dick raised his eyebrows. 'You?' he said. 'In an office? I can't see you in an office any more, Holly. There's no way you'd fit in.

The women will hate you and the men will want to bed you. There's something about you now. It won't wash off with water, you know.'

'What do you mean?' I said sharply.

'It's raw sex appeal,' he replied. 'You ooze it. It's in the way you carry yourself. In your eyes. It's an aura.'

I rolled my eyes. 'It's called Pilates and it's taken me three years to get this far,' I said jokingly, not at all sure I wanted to go around putting out some kind of sexual emission.

Dick shook his head. 'You won't be able to go backwards, Holly,' he said ominously. 'You might not have any money but you're still living the high life. You're an adventurer. You'll never be happy within four walls. You'll always want to break out again. You're not meant to be caged, Holly.'

'Well, I can't rely on the kindness of strangers for the rest of my life,' I quipped. 'The trouble is, I don't belong anywhere any more.' I gestured at the people around us for emphasis. 'I'm in-between everyone's worlds. I'm not gay, but I'm not exactly straight either. I'm not young, but I'm certainly not over the hill. (And as long as I don't change my name, I never will be!) I'm not really a sex worker but I get paid for sex some-times. I'm not rich but I live like I am. I can't pay my mortgage, yet here I am, sitting in a fabulous restaurant with you. I don't know who I am. I can't define myself. Nothing is true any more.'

'Maybe that's got something to do with the judgement that you're always going on about,' Dick observed. 'Maybe you *need* judgement in order to find a slot for yourself.'

I repressed a shudder. I didn't want to become predictable. I didn't want to be defined by a 'slot'.

'Well, lack of judgement has certainly made my life easier,' I argued. 'I used to have a whole heap of self-analysis going on. Normally it was about various things I'd done and whether I'd offended anyone or not, or whether it was good or bad. But now I've discovered that every person will have a different view so there's not much point worrying about 18 billion varying opinions. Writing this book has certainly helped me appreciate the lighter side of life – maybe flippancy will become my new black. It's definitely easier to wear than morbidity!'

'I hadn't realised it was so deep,' Dick said looking thoughtful. 'I thought you wanted it to be commercial?'

'Deep. Commercial. Same thing,' I muttered dismissively.

It was the pre-dinner vodka. I had to stop quaffing it.

Dick looked sceptical that a book about little old ladies could challenge society's ideas about right and wrong. I was almost tempted to tell him the truth, but he was one of the main characters. I wouldn't have fancied being observed like a rat in a cage. It made me feel incredibly guilty.

'So does that mean you might only be doing this for another month?' he asked, sounding a tad alarmed.

'You mean the sugar daddy thing? Probably.' And if my test results were negative, I thought.

Dick looked upset. 'Why did I ever let you go?' he said, touching my face wonderingly. 'You're so beautiful. Your new gent must be treating you well. You're looking positively radiant. You have the most amazing aura. When you walk into a room it's incredible. Has anyone ever told you that?'

'Er, yeah . . . but I'm turning forty this year, remember, so it gets better every time someone says it.'

The waiter hovered.

'What would you like?' Dick asked.

'Are you going to have an entrée?' I said. 'I wouldn't mind some oysters.'

'Sounds great. You Aussies have the best oysters in the world. I'll have some too.'

'OK, well, in that case, I'll have the baked snapper afterwards,' I said.

'I'm going to be really boring and have the beef fillet medallions with béarnaise sauce,' Dick said.

He reached for the wine menu with relish. 'Red or white?' he asked me.

'Oh,' I said, 'you'd prefer a red. So would I, actually. Let me change my order.' I quickly scanned the menu again and selected my second choice: the deboned rack of lamb with eggplant parmigiana.

Dick looked pleased and took a long time to peruse the extensive wine list. He came up with something called a fifth-pick pinot and asked the hovering young wine waiter (olive skin, brown eyes, gorgeous) what 'fifth pick' meant. I snuck a look at the menu – it cost $420 a bottle!

'It's the fifth time the grapes have been harvested,' the waiter replied. 'It stems from the 1800s and isn't very relevant today. It's a good year, though.'

It was interesting to watch the exchange – the millionaire money man being taught by a stunning young Eurasian man.

'It's got a kind of funky taste,' the waiter concluded.

Dick raised his eyebrows. 'OK, let's give it a go,' he drawled.

I tried not to think about spending a mortgage payment on a drink that was 'funky'.

When the wine was decanted and eventually poured into giant red wine glasses, it was indeed as the young man had described. There was something unusual yet gutsy about it that we couldn't quite put our fingers on. 'A new descriptor for you,' I said to Dick jokingly. 'Your investors will love it.'

'To quote you, Miss Hill,' Dick said, 'there are lessons for everyone from everyone.'

He leaned forward and touched my face again. 'You've changed my life, Holly-girl. The weeks we spent together were the happiest I've ever had. I know how to have fun again. You taught me that.'

If he were an ex-boyfriend I could have asked, 'So why did you break up with me?' But just like 'When are we going to see each other again?' and 'Do you love me?', I knew it was the wrong thing to say.

'The right people come into our lives at the right time,' I said instead. 'We wouldn't notice them otherwise.'

'You're a very special person, Holly,' he said, kissing me chastely across the table.

The oysters came and were some of the best I'd ever eaten – in a restaurant, that is. None could ever beat the stolen ones pulled fresh by my sister's boyfriend and washed in the river.

We talked about Dick's work and Dick's marriage and Dick's new-found leisure time. Like Andre, he was horrified that I was trying to survive on $1000 a week. 'You can't live on that!' he declared.

'It's only for the short-term,' I said. 'I'm paying the bills. It's the cream that I can't afford. Things like this.' I gestured to the restaurant around us and the half-eaten main courses on our plates.

'Would your gent allow you to see other people?' he asked.

I inwardly cringed. I had been down this very path with Andre. 'I'm not sure I want to do that,' I said again. 'It's just not me.'

'But you need cream,' Dick said. 'Look at you – you can't look like that without cream.'

If it were Andre talking, I'd be wondering what kind of cream he was referring to. Perhaps Dick was doing it unconsciously. Then it struck me – Dick and Andre had both been concerned with how much cream I was getting. Roger too, although he called it juice. It was all a bit too Jungian for me.

'Would you like dessert?' Dick asked.

'Maybe just a coffee,' I replied. 'No cream.' I winked at him.

He gazed at me for a long time after he'd placed our orders.

'Why did I ever let you go? What's going to happen to us? What's the ending of all this?' he said again, shaking his head. He leaned across the table and kissed me again, on the lips.

I found myself thinking about John again. Dick was so much like him. Maybe Dick could be my John, after all. I wished someone would let me stay on for the long-term. Even the medium-term would do. But then I found my resolve. I was going to get a proper job this time. No more sugar daddies. Dick was entitled to be safe from the likes of me. I smiled at him instead.

'Endings are never happy-ever-after,' I told him. 'That implies things don't change. We get bored, for one thing. Better that we grow, move on and seek new forms of happiness.'

Dick took my hand and kissed the back of it gently, staring deep into my eyes. 'As long as we realise our mistakes along the way,' he said.

The waiter arrived with our coffees. I extracted my hand. The homemade sweets that came with the coffee were delicious and I gobbled them down. Dick's too. There was a little bit of Tom in us all, I thought.

'Thank you for a wonderful dinner,' I said as Dick paid the bill.

He looked at me and smiled. 'It's an absolute pleasure.'

He helped me into my jacket as we left, and took my arm as we strolled back to the BMW. A chilly breeze blew across the harbour. Dick opened the car door for me and I was careful to keep my knees together as I swung in.

'You're very special, you know,' Dick kept saying as he drove me home.

I was beginning to think that maybe that was the problem – I was too special. Maybe I needed to start acting like a square peg in a square hole.

He pulled up outside my apartment and gave me a perfunctory kiss on the lips. I was good for a pash and dash so was a little disappointed. But then I realised that men of Dick's generation didn't pash just for the hell of it. A couple of quick kisses across the dinner table and dashboard were all he was good for outside the bedroom.

As I approached my building door I realised a girl had been watching us closely. She probably thought my daddy had a Beamer. I laughed to myself. If only she knew how close she was!

# CHAPTER 25

If you ever have to get your blood tested and you're queasy about needles, make sure you get it done in Darlinghurst. My doctor took four whole phials and I hardly felt it. I didn't even have to wait weeks for the results – most of them would be available within twenty-four hours. Unfortunately, they wouldn't deliver them over the phone, just in case I was HIV positive and tried to neck myself or something. So I made another appointment for midday on Friday.

I spent the rest of the day worrying. I told myself my fear of AIDS was justified by the ongoing headlines in local newspapers and the large number of people I knew who were positive. They didn't die as frequently now, but I'd seen some of the early ones go. Providing palliative care to a friend so he can die at home is an experience that imprints on your soul. Although Ken had been HIV positive, it was his secondary melanomas that got him in the end. Skin cancer doesn't slowly cover your skin, as I had once thought – instead, what can look tiny on the outside can rapidly eat away your vital organs from the inside. It was the lung cancer that got him. Suffocation is an urban myth. We watched him slowly *drown* in a bright yellow foam that gradually filled up all his cavities. On the final day, I sat by his bed for hours, wiping it away as it came out his nose. It had the consistency of hair mousse. Imagine that filling up your airways. As soon as I cleaned it away, more would appear. The home nurse shook her head at me but I just couldn't stop wiping. I did it for hours. Wipe. Wipe. It was the only thing I could do. You don't get to say goodbye to people in a coma.

I tried to stay calm by rationalising the likelihood of Philip being HIV positive. Truthfully, he had as much chance of having a sexually transmitted disease as Bin Laden did of becoming godfather to George Bush's children. No-one got to be that bad at sex without lack of practice. Chances were Philip only made love on his birthdays or when his wife was drunk. Maybe that's why he was a teetotaller – he always got to drive. Well, after the way I'd yelled at him, his testicles had probably receded never to be seen again. I wondered if his wife would approve.

The only thing worse than being flat broke was being a bad liar with a colourful imagination.

When my real estate agent rang to tell me my rent was in arrears I was too proud to tell them the truth. Instead I said the money wasn't a problem, it was finding the time to get into the city to pay.

'Why don't you use our BPay system?' she said. 'It'll only take you a few seconds – much better than visiting the office in person.'

'Ahhh . . .' I replied, frantically searching for an excuse. 'The trouble is, I'm currently doing some confidential writing work for the Australian Federal Police. You know all the stories about terrorists? I wrote most of those. Well, I've got a top security clearance, which means they monitor all my accounts and who I pay money to. I'm happy to do the BPay, but first you'll have to sign a release to let them examine all your records to make sure you're not a terrorist organisation. Maybe you should put all your requests in writing from now on – that way you won't have to undergo a security clearance.'

'Er . . . well . . . continuing to pay cash would be fine then,' she said hastily. 'You must have a very important job. When do you think you can get in here?'

I gave a mental sigh of relief and wondered if they cooked their books. 'Well, I'm on call 24/7 for the next month or so while we're on high alert, but I'll ask the minister if I can dash out during a spare moment. Keep an eye on the newspapers; if things get quiet, I'll be on my way!'

It was the lips that made me say it!

Then I went to the internet café and applied for as many jobs as I could. Given my shifting belief system, a return to psychological counselling seemed both hypocritical and un-ethical. So I applied for corporate 'client relations' positions instead. I got five whole Seek applications sent off in 45 minutes!

While I was online, I took a quick look at my bank account: I had a balance of seven dollars. I was so broke that it felt like I had won a small lottery.

The internet café cost $6 an hour and I'd been online for 55 minutes. I had the sum total of $5.20 worth of coins in my wallet. My heart pounded as the girl behind the counter did the calculations. They didn't take EFTPOS – I was short.

'That will be $5.50,' she said.

I blushed. 'I'm 30 cents short,' I confessed.

'Don't worry about it,' she replied with a wink.

Funny how the kindness of strangers can make your day.

Then I walked to the bank with dread. Curse the $10 minimum on automatic teller machines! I would have to ask for my $7 over the counter.

There was a long line inside the bank and an awful smell. As we shuffled forward, I realised the smell was coming from a battered-looking homeless person with unkempt hair and a long straggly beard a couple of places ahead of me. He was pitifully thin and his dirty mismatched rags hung from him. He stank of urine and there was a large stain on the seat of his trousers. Poor man, I thought. If I'd dreaded this visit, imagine how he must feel!

When I got to the front of the queue, a woman ushered me over to the merchant banking room. 'Sorry about the wait. The merchant tellers are available.'

I went to the vacant window and handed my card to the teller.

The homeless man stood at the other counter. 'How much do you want to withdraw?' a clerk asked him in a loud voice that implied he thought the man was deaf as well as homeless.

'Four hundred and eighty dollars,' the man murmured. 'My pension.'

My teller rolled her eyes at him and then smiled warmly at me. 'How much are you after?' she asked, busying herself at the computer with my card.

'Seven dollars, please,' I said. 'That's all I've got.' I turned to the homeless man and gave him a friendly grin. 'You've got more money than I have.'

He gave me a bewildered toothy smile. I think it was my turn to make someone else's day.

Thus enriched, I returned home and searched through all my handbags for shrapnel. I also raided the silver coins I'd put on the window sills for the faeries. I'd learnt about the custom on my grandmother's knee and had followed it ever since: it was supposed to attract good spirits to your home. Then, realising this was no time to be upsetting faeries – silly superstition or otherwise – I returned a five-cent coin to each sill and hoped they wouldn't notice the cost-cutting measures.

I carefully counted out the proceeds of my foraging. I now had a whole $10.60 in cash, a maxed-out credit card, a $180,000 mortgage, and was behind in my rent to a real estate agent who thought I had a very important job.

I climbed on a chair and examined the shelves of my pantry.

Among the highlights was a large bag of rice and some chicken salt. I also felt a new appreciation for my spice rack. In the fridge was one egg, some leftover cheeses, plus an assortment of gherkins, olives and relishes.

I walked over to the supermarket and bought the cheapest loaf of bread I could find, a bag of granny smith apples, a packet of real butter (much cheaper than margarine), a tiny jar of Vegemite and a dozen slices of devon, the cheapest protein I could find. I now had the potential to make a variety of meals served on toast or rice. Then I remembered the parsley plants on the balcony. Add a few sprigs to plain rice with lots of butter and chicken salt and I'd have a dish fit for a queen!

I sat down on the couch with a squishy Vegemite sandwich on fresh bread with real butter (yum) and wondered how long the selection processes would take for the jobs I'd applied for. Failure to secure an interview was unthinkable.

Benedict rang in the afternoon and invited me to his birthday party the following evening. He said he was 'laying everything on'. I was too embarrassed to tell him I didn't have the bus fare, so I used the 'gay excuse' instead – that I had a date with a hot new lover. He enthusiastically agreed that that was *much* more important and rang off wishing me luck.

Finally, I had to make the call I'd been avoiding. I rang the bank, 'fessed up to my poverty and was advised to let my mortgage go into arrears. I wouldn't be eligible for any assistance schemes otherwise. I hung up and bawled my eyes out. So much for pride; it seemed it was something only the solvent could afford. Whoever coined the phrase 'humble pie' didn't know the cost of pastry.


Friday was D-day: when I'd find out whether I was a drama queen, contagious or both. My appointment wasn't until midday so I resorted to the chief distraction of women everywhere: housework.

Bored women tend to have immaculate homes. I lived in a shoe box so the only thing left to do was wash the windows. I didn't want to use one of the tea towels so carefully hand washed in anti-dandruff shampoo, so I broke open a packet of disposable nappies that I'd bought in preparation for a visit from my sister and her baby that never eventuated.

I dipped the first nappy into the bucket and began washing the window with it. To my surprise, the glass remained relatively dry. Frowning, I dipped the nappy in the bucket again and repeated the procedure. Same result. I'm ashamed to say that I did it a third time before I twigged: the advertisements aren't idle boasting – nappies do actually draw liquid away from the surface. There was half a bucket of water in that nappy and it wasn't even dripping!

I was suitably impressed. But then it struck me: *kids no longer had to deal with their own shit.* Could this be the explanation for society's increasing intolerance of anything outside the norm? Whole generations were avoiding shit. No wonder the world was getting messier every year.

In the end, I raided the skip bin downstairs for old newspapers and used them to clean the windows instead. Searching through the bin made me remember the homeless man at the bank. We are indeed merely at different points on identical lines.

My last domestic chore completed, it was time to set out to receive my verdict. I arrived at the doctor's surgery forty-five minutes early. At least they had good magazines to read. I guess that would be a priority in an inner-city doctor's surgery where the clients are unlikely to come in for scrapes on the knee.

By the time the doctor called me in, I'd become convinced that the pounding in my chest was an early symptom of sero-conversion. I'd have to ring Philip. He'd have to tell his wife.

The doctor flicked through the reports in front of her. As well as a full blood count and the HIV test, I'd also asked for 'whatever else was available'. Apparently, this included chlamydia, gonorrhoea, syphilis and Hepatitis B. She'd also done a pap smear for good measure.

She looked up and smiled. 'Everything's negative,' she said. 'There were no atypical cells in your smear. Even your blood count's fine. That's unusually good. A lot of women your age don't get enough iron. Whatever you're doing, keep it up!'

A slightly hysterical giggle of relief escaped me. Keeping things up had been difficult, lately.

I walked back to my unit in a relieved daze. It felt like I'd been given a second chance. I wondered how to use it wisely. When I got inside, the fridge was still empty, my bills were still unpaid and I still had no source of income, but it was home and I was very glad to be there.

# CHAPTER 26

I received a text from Dick just after lunch on Saturday: *How's the book going?*

I rang him back immediately.

'The book's nearly finished,' I told him truthfully. 'With some luck, I might get the ending written soon. After that I'll spend another month editing and trying to get an agent.'

I didn't tell him that I didn't know what the ending was. I didn't say that my 'novel' had turned into a non-fiction exposé based on my diary. I wondered if Dick would be the ending – a second chance for a second chance. Maybe I would get a fabulous new job and the ending would be a warning to readers about not trying this at home.

Whatever the case, I could sense the ending was near. I would keep the diary as true as I could make it and just write in the end when it came. I hoped it was a happy one.

'How are you going, Holly? I've been concerned about you.'

'I'm fine, Dick, really I am.' I didn't sound very convincing.

'You're not fine, are you?'

I gave a big sigh. It was time to tell him the truth. Some of it, anyway.

'Oh, it's just the finances again – my last gent wasn't really suitable and I haven't had anyone since.'

'That's not good enough, Holly. That's not good enough at all! You don't deserve to live like that. You deserve better! How long has he been gone? How long is it since you've been paid?'

I winced. 'Er . . . well . . . I haven't been paid for a couple of weeks actually.'

Dick was outraged.

'What did you have for lunch?' he demanded.

'Cheese on toast.'

It was actually a lovely cheddar and some leftover Brie that I'd discovered at the very back of the fridge behind a jar of mouldy jam. It's amazing how dried-up cheese still melts the same.

'Bloody hell, Holly-girl – you're thin enough as it is.'

'It's OK, Dick, I'm not going to expire or anything.'

'What kind of man would leave you without an income all of this time?' he asked angrily.

'Well, it was my decision actually. The whole thing just didn't seem to be working. I'm sorry I didn't tell you at dinner – I guess I wanted to sort it out by myself first.'

'I knew there was something wrong, I could feel it.'

'Oh well, you know how it is – darkest before the dawn and all that.'

'Don't give up, Holly. Not when you've come this far. Never give up!'

I rubbed at my face. I had a second chance – maybe Dick should have one too. I took a very deep breath.

'Please say no if you want to, but would you consider recommencing our arrangement?'

They were the words he'd obviously been waiting for.

'Holly, I would leap at the chance! I've got so much time on my hands now; I don't know what to do with myself. You deserve the best. Don't give up now. I'd love to come back.'

I gave a big sigh of relief. 'OK, let's do it.'

'Let's start tomorrow,' he declared. 'I've just bought myself a new pushbike. You've got a bike, haven't you? We'll go for a ride in the park. I'll come round in the morning. We can have brunch afterwards. Someone needs to look after you. Some sunshine will do you the world of good!'

He rang off after extracting a promise to text him in the morning to confirm. The moment I hung up the tears started. Tears of sheer relief.

Andre called in the afternoon. He too had been worried and asked me how I'd been surviving. How bizarre. My first truly miserable day and I'd received calls from two of my men, both of them wanting to help me! It was almost enough to restore a person's faith.

Not long after, Dick rang a second time.

'You're not going to change your mind, are you?' he demanded. 'We can make it work this time, I know we can.'

'OK . . . OK . . . I won't,' I said. 'I'll see you tomorrow.'

'Promise me,' Dick said. 'Promise I can have you for the next month, at least.'

I was slightly alarmed. I really, really liked Dick, but this didn't sound like him – he was normally so casual. He was being incredibly pushy and it seemed very out of character.

'I promise,' I replied.

As I rang off, a pervading sense of disquiet began to sneak up my spine. Dick was acting strangely. Was he being obsessive or was I having delusions of grandeur?


Apart from a quick visit to Kev's to borrow his bike, I spent the rest of Saturday cleaning. It was very symbolic: I wanted to give Dick a clean slate. It also stopped me from thinking about how much I needed this to work.

I dressed carefully in a pair of jeans with a tight belt (to stop bum-crack displays) and a couple of layered fitted knits. I had to practically dust off my gym shoes. I wondered if Dick would wear a tracksuit. I hoped not.

At 9 a.m. on Sunday he rang to say he was on his way in the Range Rover with his bike in the back. I must admit, I felt nervous. Dick had rung more times in the past day than in the entire time I'd known him. He was also convinced that I'd been treated dreadfully. Surely he couldn't be jealous of my other gents? Maybe he was just lonely. I was also a bit worried about whether he'd want sex. Admittedly, he'd been a great lover – especially in comparison to Tom and Philip – but fucking me in the daylight after a bike ride didn't seem his style.

When I met him in the security parking area, we gave each other a good, long hug. It was so nice to be in his arms. All of my reservations disappeared. He was just a nice man with chivalrous tendencies, that's all.

But my worst fashion fears were realised. Dick wore a flashy blue tracksuit with matching cap and spotless gym shoes. Although it hadn't seemed so obvious when we were both dressed in smart casuals or dinner wear, our age difference was now unequivocal. I looked like his daughter. I wished I'd dressed in a tracksuit as well. If I had one.

He came upstairs to help get Kev's bike and handed me an envelope. Opening it seemed uncouth, so I just thanked him profusely and put it carefully amongst the papers on my desk.

Both of the tyres on my borrowed bike were flat and there wasn't a pump, so we walked the bikes to a store in nearby Paddington. I selected the cheapest one available – one of those shoulder-action ones with the fabric nozzle that we probably all used as kids. I paid for it with my maxed-out credit card and held my breath until the computer said yes.

In the meantime, Dick went outside and started inflating my tyres. The shop assistant looked at him working away and gave me a grin.

'Got him pumping, eh?'

I smiled. I couldn't help wondering if he meant more than the bike.

Finally, we got underway, riding up Oxford Street towards

Centennial Park. I hadn't noticed it was uphill before. There's something about riding a pushbike that brings out your inner child. It felt wonderful to be riding along, looking at the scenery, the wind in my hair. I probably hadn't been on a bike since my teens and yet here I was, riding along on a Sunday morning with my 'daddy' again. Who cared what people thought? We were enjoying ourselves. Wasn't that the most important thing?

I looked around us. Paddington was at its early best too – most of the shops were closed and it was still quiet. There was an occasional mother with children, or a DINK (double income, no kids) walking along, papers under one arm, fresh bread under the other. The trees around the church and town hall were golden and our wheels crunched over a carpet of fallen leaves. One or two party-goers from the night before were staggering home, but it was nothing compared to the streets of Darlinghurst. Even the traffic was sporadic, rather than the usual dull continuous roar. It was a side of Sydney I hadn't seen before. I had had no idea so many people got up this early on Sunday mornings.

I watched Dick on his bike ahead. He turned to smile at me. I didn't think I'd ever seen him look so happy. He slowed down so I could catch up. I was embarrassingly out of breath.

When we arrived at the park, yummy mummies and dashing daddies were everywhere – albeit rarely together. Most of them had one or two children, although there were a couple of harried-looking nannies with half a dozen or so. The nannies were easy to spot because there was no way you could have that many children and still be so thin.

I studied the mummies with interest. I now knew that more than 70 per cent of them had cheating partners. They certainly didn't look stupid. Like me, most of them wore designer jeans with fitted tops and expensive gym shoes. Unlike me, they had faces full of botox and sensible hair.

When we stopped at a coffee shop for brunch, we locked up

our bikes and sat amongst the gathered throng. The mothers seemed to congregate in groups while most of the fathers appeared to be alone. The kids played with one another and hassled their parents for drinks and cakes.

Dick gave a big grin. 'Well,' he drawled, looking around. 'We've certainly found the right spot.'

I laughed. 'Your next pick-up destination? Centennial Park on a Sunday morning? Who'd have thought? There's certainly a good selection . . . your age too.' Give or take a decade or so.

Dick blushed. 'That's not what I meant.'

I gave him a smutty grin. 'I know that,' I said. 'I'm just teasing you. But if *I* wasn't happy with *my* partner and *I* wanted to pick up, this is where I'd come.'

Dick looked around again.

'Maybe you could give me some tips on that,' he said seriously. 'I haven't picked anyone up since my wife. I wouldn't know what to do.'

I grinned and gazed around again. Surely it couldn't be that different from a pub.

'It's all in The Eye,' I told him. 'If you fancy someone, simply look them in the eye until they bust you. Then hold it a moment before you look away. If they're interested, they'll keep glancing back to see if you're still watching them. They might even move into your line of sight. Gay men take it further with the three-step method. Walk past them, count to three and then turn back and look at them. You're in if they're looking back too.

'Then, once the two of you are exchanging meaningful glances, try and get closer. Don't do it as if they're the reason – try and make it look as if chance has brought the two of you within talking distance. At pubs and clubs it's easy – you can pretend to brush past them on the way to the bar or the loo. I've done it myself. It works, really.'

I nodded towards an attractive woman who was sitting by herself. Dick looked sceptical.

'How are you at lurking?' I asked jokingly.

'I'd look like a deviant hovering here!'

I laughed. 'No, you wouldn't! Stay close to your bike. Throw some rollerblades over your shoulder. Talk on your mobile if you're afraid of just sitting there. Better still, borrow a cute dog from one of your friends. Make sure it's not a butch dog or they'll avoid you like the plague – they might even think you've got penis issues! Just make sure you've got an excuse for sitting there; otherwise you'll look like a pervert. Then just wait for their kid to throw a ball in your direction and hand it back to her, or make some fatherly joke about Sunday mornings. Hell, you could probably even say something about the weather if you were really desperate. You're a businessman – I bet you have a whole file full of shallow talk.'

'Asking for someone's phone number isn't exactly shallow talk,' Dick replied.

I rolled my eyes at him.

'You don't ask for their phone number straightaway, you engage them in conversation first! Talk for a while and get them interested in you. Charm them with that accent of yours. Tell them you want to continue the conversation. Start small with a coffee or a movie – that way, if they turn out to be a dud, you don't have to spend too long with them. Save the expensive dinners for when you know them better. Only ask for their phone number if they're interested in seeing you again. Otherwise it's creepy.'

I looked around at the women again. 'You could do this,' I told him encouragingly. 'They'd probably think you were a real catch. If it makes it any easier, imagine they're a customer or a client that you have to woo for the company. I bet you're great at that! These women aren't any different – in fact, they probably have a lot less savvy and relationship experience than you do. You'd probably be able to walk all over them if you wanted to.'

Dick was smiling at me.

'You're an amazing woman, Holly-girl,' he said. 'I'm so glad we're doing this again. I'm ready for it this time. You're almost like a halfway step to finding someone else. Someone I don't have to walk on eggshells with. You're getting my confidence back already! I'll be a new man in a month or so. I'm so glad I met you.'

I swelled with pride at his words. It felt so good to be helping people like this, much better than it ever did as a psychologist. Then I could only restore things like self-esteem and motivation. Now I could fix just about anything.

As we rode the bikes back to Darlinghurst, you couldn't wipe the grin off my face. For one thing, it was all downhill; but mostly it was because Dick looked so darn *happy*.


My nervousness returned as we put the bikes back in the garage. It was the sex thing again. Would Dick expect to make love to me today? Would he be nervous? Should I make the first move? I'd worn my sports bra. Maybe he'd think I didn't want to fuck him.

'So, are you coming up?' I said cheerfully.

'Yeah, that'd be great,' Dick replied, as if sex had never entered his mind.

When he'd made himself comfortable in front of the view, I poured us some water and sat down beside him. I was glad I'd put fresh sheets on the bed.

He finished his water quickly and gave me a kiss. Yep, he wanted sex all right. I recalled that this was a man who didn't kiss unless he intended to take it further. He'd probably been looking forward to it all morning – all week, for that matter.

Well, I was in no situation to disappoint him. I was in a bigger financial mess now than ever before. I might have felt as horny as a beach ball, but I kissed him back – slowly at first and then more passionately. Within moments he suggested we move to the bedroom.

Lucky for me, I'd mastered the big O at any time. Refusing one of them is a bit like not being in the mood for ecstasy. You change your mind once the pleasure starts. So I swallowed my reservations, walked into the bedroom and stripped off all my clothes. I don't think he even noticed the sports bra.

Dick took off his tracksuit and shoes. He already had a hard-on. I smiled when I remembered he had such a lovely penis – clear-skinned and perfectly shaped, with clipped balls and pelvic area. 'Ahhhh,' I commented, stroking him. 'I'd forgotten what a lovely cock you have.'

Dick looked pleased. 'Yes, well, that's probably because it's rarely been used,' he joked.

'What a terrible shame,' I replied, taking it in my mouth.

Dick gave a little whimper every now and then but was otherwise silent. After a few minutes he pulled me up. 'Will I perform oral sex until you come or shall I fuck you?' he asked me, smiling.

I smiled back. Such talk was a big step for him. While I'd always loved dirty talk and plenty of feedback noises, I recalled that Dick was a quiet lover. It must have been wonderful for him to say such a thing out loud.

'You can do whatever you want,' I whispered, kissing him.

While he was thinking about it, I straddled him (although I would have probably preferred to roll on my back and put my legs in the air). There was none of the erectile dysfunction borne of guilt – he was hard and willing and his cock reached me 'just so'. I watched his face intently as I moved up and down him. His eyes didn't leave mine once.

'You're such a horny girl,' he said. 'How long is it since you've had sex?'

It was one of those awkward moments when your mind sorts through mountains of data in the milliseconds before an answer is required. In my case, I debated whether to tell the truth or to err on the side of caution. Sitting with his cock inside me probably wasn't the best time to tell him about the

HIV scare or that the sexual highlight of my week had involved a vibrator and a fantasised bondage scene with a 'quivering bottom'. Instead I stuck mostly to the truth and said that I hadn't fucked anyone for weeks. Then I changed the subject and made him notice how wet I was. And I *was* wet. Very! If I had achieved anything over the past months, it was the realisation that our bodies could become aroused by anyone. When I thought about some of the sex I'd knocked back because they were too old or too fat or too strange, it was damn near tragic. I'd been self-limiting my experiences for years and I hadn't even realised.

Dick's cock felt fantastic. I made sure I included my clit when I ground into him, his penis deep inside of me. He seemed to love the additional rubbing of skin on skin and gave little groans of pleasure each time our pubic areas mashed together.

I leaned over and kissed him. 'How do you want me?' I asked, still thinking about the aforementioned cunnilingus.

'Turn over,' he replied gruffly.

What was it with these men? I wasn't complaining – it was one of my favourite positions – but their appreciation for doggy style seemed almost universal!

I reached over and got out my little pocket rocket from the bedside table. When Dick entered me, I put it against his balls at one end and my clit at the other.

'Oh my God, that's good!' Dick gasped as the little vibrator moved against his testicles.

'You ought to try it from my end,' I told him as I held it firmly against my clit.

'I'm going to come,' he warned.

'You're supposed to.'

He drove against me hard and called out as he climaxed. He'd come such a very long way. My own orgasm was mere moments away.

'Keep going,' I told him. 'Fuck me hard.'

Then I was coming too and the both of us were gasping and collapsing on the bed beside each other.

It had been good. Very good. Dick knew it.

'You're one sexy lady,' he told me. 'That was fantastic. Better than fantastic.'

'You're not so bad yourself,' I replied truthfully.

Yeah, I know. Clichés. But I'll bet there aren't too many original lines people say after fucking each other's brains out.

We lay there a while and gazed out at Oxford Street below us. I snuggled my head into Dick's wonderful chest and stroked his body softly.

'You're looking really good,' I told him.

And he was. He'd lost about five kilos since we'd first met and the down-trodden look was gone. He'd been working out at the gym regularly and was playing tennis twice a week. His skin was brown from the weekends he spent sailing and his thighs were hard and sculpted. He'd even clippered all of his body hair. I didn't have the heart to tell him I liked hairy men.

'Holly, thanks to you, I'm starting to *feel* really good,' he replied. 'I'm taking a new interest in life. I'm accumulating *hobbies*, for Chrissakes! I'd forgotten what happiness was. I haven't felt like this for years. Funny how one door opens . . .' He laughed.

I felt on top of the world. This was how it was supposed to be. It wasn't about cheating or being dirty – it was about helping people enjoy life again. We'd allowed wowserism to reign for too long. Men had been ashamed of how nature had made them, and women had helped them feel that shame. We'd closed our legs and expected them to still be happy. It was like telling someone to get over their need for oxygen. There was nothing shameful about wanting to have an orgasm. If you took away all of the value judgements, that's all sex really was. If only I'd realised it twenty years ago.

After Dick left, I tidied the unit and had a cup of tea. Then I remembered the envelope. Inside was $4000 in crisp one

263

hundred-dollar bills. A month's payment in advance. No wonder he'd been so insistent about promising him a month. I immediately felt guilty for doubting his intentions. I texted Dick: *Oh my goodness. Thank u so much. You are indeed a legend. H*

Then I sat down and bawled my eyes out. Again. I could pay my rent. I could pay my mortgage. I could even afford protein again, and nicotine patches. I guess <sheepish grin> that I hadn't mentioned I'd started smoking again. The shame. It was just that a $13 pouch of tobacco was cheaper than a $30 pack of patches, and a lot better for the nerves.

I wondered about Dick, then. He'd just paid four grand for a bike ride and some bloody good sex. And you know what? I got the strong feeling it had been one of the highlights of his decade. Just a ride in the sunshine in Centennial Park followed by lovemaking . . . for him, it was worth the money.

Maybe I was on the right track after all. I could continue to work with Dick right up until the point that he found the *new* love of his life – and even past it, if their libidos didn't match. I would finally have long-term employment in a job where I would always be making my 'client' happy. I chided myself. This whole sugar daddy gig was going to my head. But there was a smile on my face when I went to sleep that night. The man himself would be a fitting end to my Life of Dicks, whatever the length of my employ.

# CHAPTER 27

When I sat down to write on Monday the words didn't come as easily as usual. It was strange. Up until then, I'd written frantically, pounding away at the keyboard as if my sanity depended on it. Perhaps it had.

I filled in some of the gaps instead, going back over the times that had moved so fast I hadn't had a chance to record them fully. I've never been very good at tenses and writing about my experiences retrospectively was difficult. I also carefully proofed everything I had written about Dick. I wondered if I could ask him to check what I'd written to make sure I hadn't given him away. Although I hadn't used anyone's real name, I worried that I hadn't disguised him enough, so I mixed up some of his characteristics and background with other men who had responded to my ad. I just hoped his occupation wouldn't make it obvious; it was too hard to fake such a high-flying job.

I wasn't surprised by my feelings of protectiveness. Although I would never love him, he was my knight in shining armour. Call me old-fashioned, but you don't bite the hand that feeds you. Perhaps I could make it up to him by dedicating the book to him. I knew one thing for sure: I wouldn't have got this far without him.

Dick came to see me at lunchtime and I laid out a beautiful spread of deli treats with some of his favourite wine.

'Would you be interested in being one of my first test readers?' I asked him tentatively. 'Not all of it – just a couple of chapters.'

Dick looked reluctant.

'I'm sorry, Holly-girl – I have so much reading for work that it's a chore for me. Sad but true. Would you mind terribly if I waited until I got a signed copy first?'

'Sure,' I replied, not knowing whether to feel relieved or disappointed. 'But you've had more influence on it than you think.'

'Well, it's nice to know we're a good influence on each other,' he said, smiling, and kissed me on the forehead.

I felt incredibly guilty. Dick deserved to know what he'd declined to read. I hoped he'd find it flattering but I couldn't guarantee his reaction. It was the deception that worried me most. Admittedly, I had written the diary for myself at first, but now I was considering publication, my all-American hero was looking more and more like a social experiment.


By Wednesday I'd paid most of my outstanding debts. Dick was coming around for dinner, and by the time I'd paid my bills and bought groceries and treats, I'd spent well over half his money. He was very impressed with my efforts. I cooked gourmet lamb sausages with mushroom risotto followed by the sour cherry strudel I'd tried with Tom. He practically licked the plates clean. And he liked the wine. I'd paid $38 for a bottle of 2003 red and decanted it three hours earlier, just as Dick had advised me to.

We also had great sex – I came twice, although Dick didn't come at all. He said it didn't matter. He said it was still the best sex he'd ever had. Afterwards we lay in each other's arms and chatted drowsily. It felt great to be cuddling someone again and Dick seemed like an old friend. I asked him to stay the night but he left shortly after.

When I sat down to write about our evening, the words wouldn't come again. All I could do was summarise. It suddenly seemed wrong to repeat our conversations or describe our lovemaking. Maybe it was because he wouldn't be checking my work, but it was more likely to be that big, fat conscience of mine determinedly clawing its way back from wherever I had squashed it.

Later that night, I got a text from Andre: *I am still horny and wanting to do you hard.*

I sat on the couch and laughed and laughed. Then I texted him back: *We might have to talk about this inclination of yours. H*

*Join me and the boss for drinks tomorrow night? We might go salsa dancing.*

*Sounds great. C u then. H*

We arranged the details and I went to bed shortly afterwards. But I didn't go straight to sleep. Curse the image of sexy Latinos – I was spending far too much money on double A batteries!

Dick called on Thursday and said he wouldn't be able to see me again till Monday. This time there was no sense of not earning my keep – the smile on his face after the bike ride would stay with me for a very long time. Trouble was, I was still finding it difficult to write about him. It worried me enormously: how was I going to finish the book if I couldn't write about one of its main characters? Did exposing the deception of millions of women I didn't know warrant betraying the confidences of one man who'd been good to me? I struggled with my conscience. I knew one thing for sure, my earlier comment that journalism and psychology were compatible was wrong. I was coming to see you couldn't get two more different sets of outcomes. In one profession, you tell as many people as you can as much as possible. In the other, you don't record a person's most intimate secrets for fear the secretary will read them or the file will get subpoenaed.

Which one was I?

On Friday night I faced my biggest dilemma yet: whatever was I going to wear?

'How do salsa dancers dress anyway?' I asked Kev over the phone.

'Skank Nouveau,' Kev replied instantly. 'Definitely Skank Nouveau.'

He had to be kidding me. Yet a picture of teased dark hair and bare midriff in designer calypso worn over a well-maintained body with perfect breasts entered my mind.

In the end I ignored Kev's advice and chose my little black dress that hinted but never revealed. Every girl needs a dress like that. I wore it with the highest heels I had. I was glad Andre was tall; it made it so much easier in the shoe department. God bless Nicole Kidman, I say.

Andre arrived to collect me early. I should have guessed. He was a master at seduction and probably realised women usually got dressed last. Arrive half an hour early and it's quite likely she'll be in her lingerie. Luckily, my make-up was done and I only had to throw on my LBD. Bare feet were better for evading his clutches; once again, I had to practically fight him off. He loved every minute of it. It was almost like a farce, with the main characters running around the dinner table. But I didn't have a dinner table; I only had a very small unit and Andre was a very obstinate man.

Yet so determined was I not to be seduced by him, I somehow managed to avoid his advances. I mostly did it by jumping up, clapping my hands together and exclaiming that some obscure thing needed doing in another part of the unit. Andre would be left with his arms hugging an empty space.

Finally we were in a taxi and on our way to pick up his boss from his hotel in the CBD. Five star, naturally. When Pedro got into the taxi, I couldn't help staring at him. Andre had told me that his boss was a relative but that was all the information he'd supplied. Pedro was stunning. Short and wiry, with a foxy goatee and the devil in his dark eyes. He had big, gorgeous dimples when he smiled and brilliantly white teeth. His cheek-bones looked like they'd been sculpted with an angle grinder. The whole gorgeous package was draped in a beautiful black silk shirt tucked into an elegantly crafted pair of black trousers.

I couldn't believe my luck. I had been expecting a grouchy old uncle with thinning hair and glasses who drank beer all night. It was a fantasy come true! I was out with two gorgeous, sexy Argentinian men. I wondered what would happen if I showed up at Port Stephens with them. <Insert evil laugh.>

Andre introduced me as a friend, with emphasis on the platonic. Even though we were in the back of the taxi and he was in the front, Pedro somehow managed to kiss the back of my hand. My heart was pounding.

We started out at the Establishment, an upmarket bar in the CBD, where they had arranged to meet a couple of their major customers. The introductions were interesting. Like Pedro, the three men seemed to accept my presence as a 'friend' of Andre's with no surprise.

'So how did Andre find you?' one of them asked me at one point.

'On the internet,' I said truthfully. 'We exchanged details and have been friends ever since.'

'Ahhh,' he replied with a wink. 'Internet friendships are often the most satisfying.'

I'm ashamed to say that I took advantage of the situation and teased Andre mercilessly that night. Although I suspected the men all knew that I wasn't just a friend, Andre still had to maintain the platonic façade. As a result, they flirted with me outrageously, despite the fact that they all wore wedding rings.

Pedro, the boss and alpha male, was worst of all, and Andre couldn't do a thing about it. Poor Andre: the tease of the tease of the tease. I loved every minute of it.

When we were all pleasantly inebriated, the discussion turned to women.

'Why don't we go to Tiffany's?' one of the men suggested.

I was confused. They wanted to buy their wives gifts at eleven o'clock at night? Would Tiffany's even be open?

The others looked at me pointedly. I mocked a hurt look.

'But I've got good taste in jewellery!' I joked, wondering what was going on.

They all roared with laughter.

'Tiffany's is a sex venue in Surry Hills,' Andre eventually managed to splutter.

Strike one for Holly Golightly!

'Why don't we go to a titty bar instead?' another suggested. 'Maybe Holly could learn a few tricks.'

'*Earn* a few tricks more likely,' I quipped, trying to cover my gaffe and ensure there were no misconceptions about me at the same time. 'Not my scene, I'm afraid. I'm sorry, gents. Call me old-fashioned, but at this point I think I might turn into a pumpkin and bid you good night.'

Out of the corner of my eye I saw Andre and Pedro give each other The Look. I was clearly cramping their customers' style.

'I tell you what,' said Pedro, producing a credit card and extending it to the men. 'Why don't you gents go and have some fun on us while Andre and I take this lovely lady salsa dancing?'

Wow. Who'd have thought sex could be a corporate gift? If only wives knew what their husbands didn't have to pay for.

We caught a cab to the Latin Bar in Liverpool Street.

'Come on, let's go and have some fun,' Pedro said. Pedro hopped out and opened the door for me while Andre put the fare on yet another company card.

As we entered the bar, they each took one of my elbows.

Would people think we were together? I realised I didn't care if they did.

The club was packed to the rafters with other South Americans and I'm pleased to report none of them were dressed in Skank Nouveau. It was an amazingly sexy atmosphere full of men and women enjoying the rhythm of the dance. Women danced with women, men danced with women, and there were a couple of groups just like ours.

Andre and Pedro were very attentive – they seemed to take turns at flirting with me. At times I felt like a tennis spectator, turning from one to the other as they stayed on either side of me, and it was difficult to hear them above the music unless they shouted in my ears. Despite my escorts, lots of people gave me The Eye. Couples too. It was easy to tell if a couple was trying to pick you up: one of them would engage you with their eyes and then direct you to their partner's eyes.

While Andre was at the bar, a dark, lean, wiry man slid towards me and caught my eye within talking distance. Now I would have to say hello or be regarded as rude. Nightclub etiquette.

'Hello,' I said reluctantly. I felt Pedro stiffen at my side.

'Helloo,' the man replied in a heavily accented voice. 'Enjoying your evening?'

It was difficult to hear him above the sound of the music so I just shook my head, pointed at my ears and shrugged expressively. I waited a respectful second or so, then turned back to Pedro with an angelic smile on my face.

Pedro laughed.

'I wonder how you'd handle me,' he said, gazing at me intently.

I laughed and headed out on to the dance floor to avoid things going further. Although I have as much musical inclination as that Mack Truck I'm always talking about, I am an excellent dancer. Maybe disinhibition does that to a person! Whatever the reason, I rarely suffered a lack of willing partners

271

and Latinos turned out to be no different from gay men and clubbers.

Among my new friends were a couple of transsexuals. They told me I was the only person in the room who knew they were mostly men. I did a great salsa with one of them, with everyone thinking we were two women dancing beautifully together. We carved it. Her name was Sunny and she was the most beautiful woman in the room: a drop-dead gorgeous blonde with a tall, thin body and great tits. I warned her not to disclose; I wasn't sure how the South Americans would have taken it.

Andre was very impressed after that and wouldn't let go of me. Pedro just hovered. We danced the last couple of songs together, the three of us: Andre, Pedro and me. Naturally I was in the middle. I was glad they didn't play the lambada. Shame on me. I was getting so good at being naughty!

'This night will cost the company about $5000,' Andre whispered to me as we were leaving. Pedro had gone ahead to get his coat. 'Multiply that by every major company in every major country in the world. Even occasional cheating costs big companies big money. Without so-called monogamy, huge savings would probably be made. Put that in your book.' He laughed bitterly. 'How ironic that the cost of infidelity could feed a small nation.'

'But whole industries thrive on the dashed hopes of monogomists. Waiting rooms everywhere are full of people with relationship problems. Psychologists would go out of business. And I'll bet cheating is responsible for a huge part of the income of just about every beautician on the planet. Not to mention the exorbitant price of a haircut these days. When you think about it, a lot of business is generated when people are unfaithful!'

Andre frowned theatrically. 'So big business strikes against chemical weapons once again!' he declared, laughing uproariously at his own joke.

It was 4 a.m. and we'd all had far too much to drink so we

sensibly decided to go our separate ways. Decisions like that are one of the benefits of age. Only junior burgers enjoy drunken sex. Besides, if I was going to have two stunning Argentinians at the same time, I wanted to remember it.

Andre took a cab headed west and I dropped Pedro off at his city hotel in my taxi. As we pulled up outside, I realised I wanted desperately to kiss him. I turned and instantly employed the Lips Technique. For all you pash and dash virgins, the Lips Technique is almost infallible and can get results within seconds. It is also distressingly easy.

'It's been a pleasure to meet you,' I said, looking him in the eye.

'Ditto,' he said. 'I haven't had this much fun in years. I think we've really clicked tonight. I don't suppose you'd like to come upstairs?'

As he spoke, I flicked my gaze to his lips. I kept looking at them until he'd finished speaking.

'Alas,' I said wickedly (and loving the chance to say it again), 'I'm promised to another.' I returned my gaze to his eyes and smiled.

'This is goodbye then,' he said, raising his eyebrows and tilting his head.

'It is,' I replied, returning my gaze to his lips and slightly pursing my own.

(It was the lips that made me do it, I swear!)

Hence make or break time for the Lips Technique. It hasn't happened often, but I must be completely honest and confess that at this point, some have been known to turn and flee. Not so Pedro. By now he was looking at my lips too.

We kissed passionately there in the back seat, while the taxi driver waited and the hotel's bellhop backed off a respectful distance.

Pedro was an amazing kisser. He looked me in the eye the whole time, and somehow managed to engulf my entire body with his sensitive lips and flirtatious tongue.

'Goodbye,' I eventually said, pulling away and cursing his five bloody stars.

'Look, can I have your number?' he said, getting his phone out.

After a kiss like that I would have given his name to my first child! 'Sure,' I said, reciting it for him.

He keyed it into his address book then gazed into my eyes. 'Are you sure you won't come up?'

I shook my head sadly. 'I can't, I'm sorry. I've made an agreement with someone.'

'I understand,' he said, putting a kiss on my lips with his fingers.

He gave a nod to the bellhop hovering outside, gave me another quick kiss, groaned and got out of the cab.

I wondered what I'd said 'no' to.

As the cabbie drove me home to Darlinghurst, I leaned back in the seat and looked out at the city and thought about what a blissful place the world could be if you let it. What a fabulous, spur-of-the-moment, amazing evening!

But it was not over yet!

Barely had we cleared the block when my mobile rang. It was Andre.

You've got to be kidding me.

'Where are you?' he demanded.

'I'm on my way home.'

'I'll meet you,' he declared.

'Where?'

'Anywhere. I have to see you.'

I repressed a sigh. 'Meet me in front of my apartment,' I told him reluctantly.

We pulled up in front of my building and Andre was standing waiting for me. He opened the door of the cab with a flourish and kissed me. Passionately. The cab driver was still waiting for his money. The same cab driver who'd seen me kiss Pedro.

How embarrassing.

If I had any morality left, I sure couldn't find it. Andre paid the driver, then I took him upstairs.

We were barely inside when Andre asked me if he could get naked. Who was I to refuse?

I watched from the couch while he did a long, slow striptease. I hadn't seen him naked until now. He had a wash-board stomach and pecs with nipples just the way I like them. The whole delicious package was wrapped in clear, olive skin. No wonder 'the ladies' liked him so much!

Then he took off his underpants. His cock had a medium-on. Oh sweet Goddess, he was uncircumcised!

Grinning maniacally, I practically threw him on my bed. Every time he tried to touch me I roughly pushed him back. Andre loved it. He had a grin from ear to ear, as if he couldn't believe his luck. Then I tried every single one of David's sugges-tions and a few others for good measure. I had a lot of new tricks to experiment with. Andre just lay there whimpering, sometimes sobbing softly, convulsing every now and then. Tears rolled down his face when he finally blew.

Poor Tom never knew what he missed out on.

'I want you to be mine,' Andre whispered, when I snuggled down beside him.

'I belong to everyone and no-one.'

'Then you have everything.'

'You're the one with everything,' I said. 'You've got me; you have your marriage; your children; your job. You've even got a great boss. You're the one who has it all, not me.'

'But I don't have *you*, Holly. I'm in love with you. I can't stop thinking about you. I can't have sex without you in my head.'

Well, I probably won't be able to give a blow job ever again without David in my head, so we're even, I thought.

'It's the booze,' I told him. 'It exaggerates things.'

'I'm serious, Holly! I've fallen in love with you.'

'I love you too, Andre, but I'm not *in* love with you,'

I replied, stroking his arm. 'We've become close. That's probably what you're feeling.'

There is indeed no better weapon than denial. Otherwise known as looking the other way. Arguing about the existence of something means you don't have to examine its pros and cons.

Andre kissed my hand.

'You're probably right – but I still can't help thinking you're the only woman I've ever met who understands me. I've got to tell you, Holly – the lads are all blown away by the fact that you're even *thinking* about publishing this book of yours. Some of them think it might even save their relationships.'

'Relationships aren't the problem, cheating is.'

'Yes, cheating *is* horrible; but men aren't,' Andre said drowsily. 'We might blunder along sometimes, but we really *do* try our best to do the right thing. We're not bad people – we *want* our marriages to work.'

I gazed into the dark. I wanted marriage to work too. I was tired of morningless sex – now I wanted a body to spoon when the nights got cold or the aloneness got too much.

Andre gave a little snore. I snuggled into his borrowed body and resolved to get my own one day.

# CHAPTER 28

It wasn't until Andre left the following morning that I realised I had technically been unfaithful to Dick. To make matters worse, it was my first time. Ever.

Although I took full responsibility for helping John and my sugar daddies be unfaithful to *their* spouses, I had never actually done it myself. I realised Dick wasn't a 'spouse', of course, and that many would argue that oral sex didn't count, but unfortunately my conscience didn't agree. Nor did it think much of the excuse that I had cheated on a cheater with a cheater. It told me I had made an agreement with Dick and I had broken it. That 'sexual exclusivity' included head jobs.

I wrestled with the concept for most of the day. How could you define sex anyway? Was it cheating if you spooned someone? Were you being unfaithful if you had a gentle flirtation behind your partner's back? Was kissing someone else infidelity?

In the end, I figured that cheating wasn't about the definition of sex; it was about deception. Nor had I any right to decide what constituted sex for Dick, just as he had no right to define it on behalf of his wife. What constituted sex had to come from the person being cheated – they were the only ones who could decide on the boundaries and whether their partner's behaviour had transgressed them.

Above all, I realised that no matter what the sexual act might be, lying about it was irrefutably wrong. Oral sex wasn't the culprit; I was. I should have negotiated the term 'sexual exclusivity' with Dick from the very start.

Perhaps this wasn't about the movement of boundaries, after all; maybe it was about the need to identify them properly in the first place.

I got a text from Dick at 7 a.m. on Monday:

*Are you interested in some debauchery this afternoon?*

I felt flattered that he'd thought of me first thing on a Monday morning. I wondered if he had something planned or just wanted to make love all afternoon. Knowing Dick as I did now, either option was good for me.

I texted back:

*Absolutely! H*

He replied:

*I'll be there about 3.*

Once again, I enjoyed his visit immensely but my betrayal of him was at the forefront of my mind. He would recognise himself in the book regardless of my disguises.

During his Thursday visit, Dick was very businesslike. He kept asking me what I was going to do when the book was finished. I'd been wondering the very same thing. Once I published the diary, not a single one of my relationships would ever be the same again.

He studied the job vacancy clippings I'd collected from the weekend papers. I hadn't heard a thing about the applications I'd submitted online – perhaps big business thought psychologists weren't good at relationships. Like a lot of people, they probably thought relationships were all about marketing, not honesty.

Dick screwed up one of the clippings, saying it was a dead-end company. Then he insisted on looking at my resume. I couldn't help feeling disconcerted. Did Dick want me in a job so no-one else could have me?

'I love you,' he said while we were sitting on the couch.

I was fussing over a fresh round of drinks so wasn't looking at him. I pretended I hadn't heard. I figured if he wanted to talk about it, he'd need to be able to say it again.

He didn't.

After he'd left, I sat down and tried to write, but once again the words wouldn't come.

Pedro rang the following day. He was planning a trip to Sydney in a few weeks and wanted to see me. I said it wasn't possible. When he asked why, I told him it was to preserve his reputation; that maybe being seen with me wasn't such a good thing any more. He rang off puzzled. I didn't care. The thought of one day publishing my diary had made me wary. I kept accidentally procrastinating. As soon as I sat down to write something I noticed that the washing up hadn't been done.

I saw Dick again on Monday and cooked him Chateaubriand. We had fabulous sex but something had changed. Somehow my heart was no longer in it. Funny that. I never thought it had been.

I still couldn't write in the diary. My mind was too busy fighting with my conscience. I wondered which one would win.

Besides entertaining Dick, I spent the next week doing little else but struggle with my moral dilemma. I finally decided to regard the diary as just another job: an honest account of my undercover observations as both counsellor and journalist. I was still me; I'd just been doing different tasks, that was all.

It was strange how a melancholy mood seems to make you

more sensitive to the change of season. The inevitable chill of winter seemed to be personally directed at me. I was looking through my wardrobe for warmer clothes when I found John's jacket hanging at the back. Without thinking too much, I sent him a text:

*Found your dark brown leather jacket. Please collect. H*

Then I couldn't stop thinking about him all day. I kept checking my mobile to make sure a message hadn't found its way into my inbox without me hearing it. What was he doing? Did he still love me? Did he ever think about me? Maybe he hated me. Maybe he thought the happiness we'd had together was just a mid-life crisis. How sad. Mid-life crises always sound like so much fun.

I went through the classical psychological stages. At first I couldn't believe he wouldn't respond, hence the phone fixation. Then I sobbed. The thought of still feeling love for someone who won't even answer your texts was a frightening thing. Then I got to the angry stage.

*Grow a spine and collect your jacket. Only thing worse than being a doormat is choosing to be a doormat. If you don't collect in 24 hours, I'll give it to a dero. H*

It was the nastiest thing I'd ever said to him. I proofread the SMS three times. I even used correct grammar. Correct grammar is serious. That's when you want to be absolutely clear.

Then I took a deep breath and pressed the 'send' key.

Thanks to mobiles, waiting by the phone isn't such a big deal any more – not physically anyway. You can still do it in your head though.

I got down my dusty copy of *Elsa: The Story of a Lioness* and flicked through the pages. I realised it was John who'd identified with Elsa; it wasn't about me at all. John was the Leo who'd been brought up in captivity and I was the one who'd taught him the skills to cope with the wild. I wondered if Joy Adamson would've been as disappointed as I was if Elsa had chosen to remain caged.

Still, I couldn't help thinking it took courage to be a coward. Only the bravest of people could sleep beside a black-mailer and allow her to raise his children. Or the dumbest.

I tried to send him a telepathic message. *Ring me,* I urged with my mind. *Ring Holly now.* I visualised him getting up out of his seat and going to the nearest phone, struck by the image of Holly.

As if. But we've all tried it.

I had to face it: I still missed John dreadfully. In fact, not a day went by when I didn't love him as much as the last day I saw him. I truly loved him, regardless of what he did or said. It was such a gift to give him. It was the biggest I could offer. It hurt so much that he'd rejected it.

His wife had made a tactical mistake, though, when she forbade a farewell. A love without goodbye never ends. You are haunted by 'what might have been' for the rest of your life.

It took me six valerian tablets to get to sleep that night. Thank the Goddess health food shops are still legal.


I checked my phone first thing next morning. Nothing. Then I went to the internet café and checked my emails. There wasn't even any spam.

So I moved myself into the acceptance stage. John wasn't coming.

I sent him a final text:

*Jacket shall remain until collection. It will keep me warm on my deathbed. H*

Then I put on an old shirt of his (one I'd kept deliberately) and curled up on the bed. It is indeed the clothes you wear that attracts the company you keep.

I lay there and thought for most of the day. Mostly about John, but Andre and Dick and Pedro were in there too. Plus a couple of friends who shall not be named. And you know what the really spooky thing was? I realised *all* the men in my life were unavailable in some way. Somewhere along the line I'd developed a preference for men who needed chasing, and when other men threw themselves at me I ignored them.

Some of my friends had commented on this, and I'd told them that I wanted to be the chas*er*, rather than the chas*ee*. I told them that there was no 'challenge' in the men who sought me. But today I realised that chasers are, in fact, predators. My lioness had come back to haunt me. I hadn't transcended my biology at all – I was still hunting for a man to support me, just like all the girls did. The only difference between me and the girls who became wives was I had disregarded the limitations set for me and discovered that it was easier to ignore the rules of marriage than it was to change the nature of man.

A pervading sense of gloom settled over me as the weekend beckoned. I still had no source of income beyond Dick. I had two weeks to find alternative employment.

I declined all social invitations in the interests of my dwindling bank account and made an investment in the weekend newspapers instead.

I broadened my job search to include positions on the fringe of the psychology industry, where I wouldn't have the chance to 'taint' clients with my controversial new beliefs. These mostly included supervisory or management roles, and I got quite excited about one of them – going in to bat for people with psychiatric disturbances under the new mental health initiatives. I felt a curious affinity with them: as if I'd undergone a mental illness myself and was only now recovering. When I went back to an office, it would be a bit like returning after a long period of sick leave. Only it'd be easier for me, as my experiences wouldn't show on the outside.

I duly typed up my applications, addressing the selection criteria, then went over to Kev's to print them out. But my heart wasn't really in any of them. It seemed to me that none of them utilised my full potential like my sugarbabe role did.

I reminded myself that I had to grit my teeth and put up with a job that wasn't really me, just as thousands of other people did.

In a way, my grand scheme had failed. Although I suspected I could be happily entrenched for the long-term with Dick, my motives had changed. What had started from a position of financial desperation had become a desire to explore the nature of cheating; but now that had been superseded by my difficulty with keeping up the diary and my instinctual unwillingness to expose the Dick I had captured. Perhaps I'd already learnt the lessons meant for me. Now I just had to live with them.

# CHAPTER 29

I went to the football with Dick on Sunday. Thousands of people saw us together. I was glad it was freezing: I wore four layers, a scarf, a hat and very dark sunglasses.

Would I really be brave enough to publish my findings? I was losing faith in myself, becoming frightened by my own words. But I was a writer who'd been blessed with an amazing true story. I should consider myself grateful and stop cursing so much.

I resolved that I would be true to myself. That I'd be true to my belief in the diary. I wouldn't fear the ending. Above all, if I did publish it successfully and it actually managed to help someone, I'd finally be able to stop resenting my ongoing love for John. If he hadn't left me jobless and broke, none of this would have happened. I'd learn to love my scars. I'd even be grateful to him for making them so deep. John would have helped me become an author despite his worst intentions and every time I sold another book there would be a new reason to be grateful for my unrequited love.

Sometimes not getting what you want is a wonderful stroke of luck.

Delusions of grandeur or not, when I got home I printed out the first fifty pages of my book and wrote a synopsis to send with the extract to a literary agent. The trouble with synopses is they need endings. I was still vague about that. I concentrated on the themes instead, wanting to give the agent some sense of what the diary had become for me.

I printed it all out at the internet café with a pounding heart. Then I put on my best clothes and set out to hand-deliver the pages to the first literary agent in the phone book within walking distance. I didn't have any rubber bands to hold the pages together, but I found one on the street along the way. I considered that a lucky omen.

When I got there, I was startled to find the office full of women. Although I had started writing the diary for myself, somewhere along the line I'd begun hoping its main readers would be women. Even if it got no further than this office, would the reading of my diary change these women's lives?

I timidly handed my package to the receptionist and scuttled out the door before she could even ask my name.

I'd just accomplished stage one in my aspiration to be an author, but it didn't make me feel as good as I'd hoped. In fact, I felt rather frightened. I had just gone public with a wide-spread secret fuelled mostly by denial.

I gritted my teeth and went to Dick's place with a smile on my face that evening. It was our last official night together. He hadn't mentioned extending our arrangement and I wasn't sure I wanted to any more.

I wondered whether to confess all about the diary, then decided to wait to see if the agent was interested in it. There was no point in worrying Dick about secrets that might never see the light of day.

It was the first time I'd seen him at *his* place – his new place. He'd finally separated from his wife. Unofficially, anyway. The flat was located in the CBD near the bank. He'd made a cheese platter. Plain water crackers with supermarket cheese.

I wondered where he found supermarket cheese in the inner city. I suspected I was his first ever guest.

I tried to be enthusiastic but the flat was a shoe box. He'd just bought a multi-million-dollar property in Glebe and was now living in a dump. Dick described it as a 'boarding house' but in reality it was a studio apartment with a kitchenette. A small television was mounted on one of the walls, along with a VCR (not a DVD player) – with a sign that said 'See management before use'. A synthetic floral quilt graced the queen-sized bed and there was a pathetically small wardrobe for his clothes. There were no ornaments or flowers – *he'd* given *me* roses – just a cheap Picasso print screwed into the wall above the bed. The tiny balcony looked out upon a blank wall with rust stains seeping down it. He said the place cost him $360 a week. So this was what it meant to leave your wife.

I sat down on the well-used lounge and enthusiastically helped myself to the large cubes of cheese and Jatz while Dick prepared our drinks. I tried not to think about my cactus glass when he handed me a bourbon in what looked suspiciously like a jam jar. It even had a cartoon character embossed on the side. At least I'd moved beyond recycled glassware – maybe I was the rich one after all.

'So, how are you?' I ventured, taking a large sip of my bourbon and wishing it was vodka.

'Surviving,' he said, sitting down beside me. 'I might not have my marriage any more, but my integrity is still intact.'

I seized upon what was probably a flippant remark as if it was a life jacket in a rolling ocean. 'So you think your integrity is more important than your marriage?'

'How can you have a marriage without integrity?' he replied. 'If our relationships aren't built on truth, then they must be built on illusions. I don't want to raise my children on falsehoods, Holly. My love for them shouldn't be conditional on my love for my wife. They're separate entities. They deserve to be disentangled from my failing marriage. It's not right to take them down with us. Using your kids as an excuse to be dishonest isn't the most admirable quality in the world. Even *this* is better than that.' He looked around at our meagre surroundings and took a sip out of his jam jar.

'But surely there must be another way,' I said, almost in tears. 'This is so . . . drastic. What if you and your wife could live together as friends and have separate lives? You loved her once; you could love her again but in a different way.'

Dick shook his head sadly.

'The world would have to change for that to happen, Holly-girl. Customs would have to be broken. Rules would have to be rewritten. There's no hope of that, I'm afraid.'

'But what if there was hope?' I said excitedly. 'What if someone came up with a new way of doing things? If they invented a way to manage relationships so they wouldn't end in divorce? What if that person could facilitate a review of the marriage rules?'

Now was the time to tell him about the diary. Finally I could confess!

'Then that person would need a miracle,' Dick replied softly. 'And I don't believe in miracles.'

I came down to earth with a thud. Curse my delusions of grandeur. There was no way people would even consider rethinking monogamy. And the agent wouldn't call. Those women in that office probably thought I had more front than a grand terrace.

'But why this?' I said despairingly, looking around. 'You can afford a million-dollar home. Why are you living like a pauper? You can *buy* yourself a good time – you don't need a miracle for that!'

Dick took my hands and looked deep into my eyes.

'Don't you think I'm already doing that?' he said.

I avoided his gaze and stuffed another large cube of cheddar and a Jatz into my mouth.

Dick gave a big sigh and took a sip of his drink. He hadn't touched the cheese platter.

'The trouble is, if I start divorce proceedings, I couldn't even have you any more. If she wants more than half – and she might – they'll investigate everything I earn and everything I spend. They'll put me under a microscope, Holly. She might even hire a private investigator. If she can prove I've been unfaithful, the courts will be more sympathetic to her. I don't know how I'd be able to cope without you, Holly-girl.'

'Why don't you try and find a woman in the same situation as your wife?' I said cheerfully. 'You could move in with her and have an instant home again. There must be plenty of husbands and wives who've separated out there – I guess it'd mostly be the men who move out – it's a shame you can't all get better organised and just swap with some other couple. That way, you wouldn't have to waste all this money establishing bachelor pads. You could just move in with a woman who's been left in the same way your wife's been. You'd even know exactly what she's been through! It's a pity we can't set up a register, or something.'

Dick laughed. 'That's not a bad solution! We could set up a "displaced husbands" service, looking for matches with recently separated wives. You're right – there's got to be hundreds of us poor souls, none of us very good at the cooking or the cleaning. And the women aren't much better off – living alone in big houses like mine, far too accustomed to having someone to care for. We could put it on the internet: a displaced husbands and wives matchmaking service. We'd make a fortune!'

We dined at an exclusive Italian restaurant in Elizabeth Street. For the very first time, I didn't stick my nose in the air and walk in like I owned the place. Instead, I kept my head down and walked like someone with surprisingly bad posture. I didn't want Dick to be seen with me. I wanted to protect him as much as I could. I didn't even go to the toilet.

Afterwards we went back to my place and had sex. Dick took

some kind of drug to maintain his erection, but he said it also decreased his sensitivity. I was finding it increasingly difficult to perform anyway. It didn't matter that he was an exceptional lover; it was my guilt, this time. Still, in the end, I was probably more enthusiastic than I normally was. I came not once, but twice. The coming was the easy part; it was the going that was a problem. I hugged him for ages before I could let him go.

# CHAPTER 30

At 7 a.m. I got a text from Dick.

*I've got a real spring in my step today – thanks to you. Have a nice life, Holly.*

I burst into tears.

Not a single soul in the world knew what I'd been through. Even Kev thought I'd been living the high life. It had started with Dick and now it was going to end with Dick but that didn't undo all of the people in between.

Late that afternoon, the agent rang. The moment of truth had finally arrived. Did the world want to hear my story?

'I passed your submission around the office,' she said. 'We all want to know more. When can you bring in the rest of the manuscript?'

I didn't tell her that it didn't have an ending yet. I didn't tell her that I was still living it. 'Give me a fortnight,' I stammered.

After I hung up, I hugged my legs close to me and wept into my knees. Great shuddering sobs that made no sound at all.

The agent might have been a complete stranger but the relief was enormous. At last, someone knew everything about the life that had risen out of the love of my first John.

More importantly, there was an office full of women who wanted to know more.

At 7.36 a.m. the very next day The Ending called.

Naturally I was having a read on the loo when the phone rang. Lucky for me, large handbags have forced me to set a long ring tone on my mobile. I managed to grab it and answer, noticing the 'withheld' number as I did so.

'Holly Hill,' I said curtly.

'You don't know me,' said a female voice on the other end. She sounded upset. 'I'm Mark's other half. We've been together for eighteen years.'

Sweet Goddess! Had I finally been sprung for my crimes against women? Mark, Mark, I urgently thought. Who the hell was Mark? Two of my best friends were called Mark, and I'd recently been reunited with an old acquaintance called Mark but I certainly hadn't slept with any of them.

'Mark?' I said dumbly. 'Which Mark?'

She gave a snort that easily translated as 'hussy'.

I thought about the Mark I'd met most recently. Surely it must be him!

'If it's blond Mark, the Mark who's recently lost his job – I swear to you, we only had drinks. He's an old acquaintance. We ran into each other by accident. I've got absolutely no interest in him whatsoever,' I gabbled, not letting her get a word in.

'How many Marks have you slept with?' she asked mockingly. 'He's not blond, he's dark. You slept with him about two years ago. He confessed everything the other day. I haven't been able to stop thinking about you. I had to talk to you – ask how you could possibly do this to another woman. You're supposed to be a psychologist. You should know better!'

My mind searched frantically. I'd been in Port Stephens two years ago. Mark . . . dark hair. The penny dropped. *That* Mark! The Mark who was visiting from interstate and we'd had a brief fling. The Mark I'd run away from in a nightclub because he danced like a chicken. Yes, a headless chicken.

'In Port Stephens?' I asked, thinking surely it couldn't be him. I'd only fucked him twice and he'd never mentioned he had a girlfriend. 'The one who was working away from home?'

'Yes, that Mark,' she replied sarcastically. 'The one who was doing the plumbing work from Adelaide. The one who couldn't keep his hands to himself.'

'But I didn't know he had a girlfriend!' I declared. 'It was a nothing relationship. I assumed he was single.'

She snorted again. 'You knew. Mutual friends have told me you knew.'

'Mutual friends?' How could I have mutual friends with someone who lived in Adelaide? Besides, most of my friends would be more interested in whether a man who couldn't dance could still fuck.

'Look, I swear to you,' I said, 'I had no idea. We never had the conversation and I didn't ask. I probably should have. That was my only mistake. He certainly didn't offer the information.'

'You knew,' she said again. 'He told me you knew all about me. He told me you seduced him. How could you do such a thing? Women are meant to have solidarity. Sluts like you are ruining the relationships of people like me. You should have more sense. You're a psychologist – you're supposed to know about these things, about the harm you cause other people. About how damaging it is.'

I took a deep breath and thought hard about what I could say. I'd had some ironic things happen in my life, but this had to take the cake!

'Look,' I said, 'the onus was on Mark to tell me, not the other way around. What was I going to do – suck it out of him?'

'But you should have asked,' she said, breaking into sobs. 'You should have *respect* for another woman.'

'Lies of omission are still lies,' I said quietly. 'You can't cure gullibility. Even if I promised you I would never sleep with another "attached" man again, there are millions of other women who haven't learnt that lesson yet. And even if they had, I can guarantee most of them wouldn't be as good at detecting lies as I am. There is *always* going to be fodder for cheating men. Can't you see that? It's in our biology. We've all given into our bodies in one way or another. Just ask overweight people or someone with an addiction – it doesn't matter if it's unhealthy or wrong, we still do it anyway. I'm sorry to disagree with you, but most of us have no right to point the finger at someone who wants more sex. That's just hypocrisy!'

She was really weeping now. 'But you should be leading by example,' she cried. 'How could you do this to one of your sisters?'

Now I felt like crying myself. How could I indeed? Women had endured this kind of pain for hundreds of years. Men's infidelity turned us into shrews. Instead of blaming the partners who lied, we blamed each other. Men sometimes blamed us too. Mark had told her I'd seduced him. He probably even gave her my phone number. Talk about divide and conquer!

'Please,' I said. 'I'm sorry if I've caused you any problems. I've learnt a lot in the past two years. It's horrible that what meant so little to me a long time ago can mean so much to you now. That's half the problem. In fact, I'm writing a book about it. About cheating. I could learn a lot from you. Maybe we could meet and talk about this?'

She gave another one of her snorts.

'I don't want to have coffee with *you*,' she said viciously. 'I want to stop women like you. I want to cheat-proof the world and people like you can't stop me.'

Then she hung up.

I burst into tears. But I wasn't crying for me, I was crying for her. The poor woman – I felt so sorry for her. She believed in lifelong monogamy. She would be vulnerable to betrayal for the rest of her natural life. Even if she met one of the uncheating minority, people can change after precious wedding anniversaries and all those kilometres. What was to prevent him from giving his statistical unlikelihood to some other woman? It would certainly be sought after.

I rang Kev and told him what had happened. As usual, he was suitably sympathetic.

'The sad thing is, the people who fear cheating most are the ones most likely to be cheated on,' Kev said.

I frowned.

'What do you mean?'

'Well, if a person is jealous and possessive they're going to place restrictions on their partner's freedom. They might not even allow the little things – like gentle flirtation and cuddles. Yes?'

'Yeah, I suppose so.'

'And what's the first thing most of us want to do when we realise our freedom has been threatened?'

'We want to break out.'

'And how do we break away from someone who is jealous?' Kev prompted.

'We cheat,' I said glumly, the tears starting again. 'But if it feels this bad when I *unknowingly* helped someone cheat, how will it feel if one of the wives of my *real* cheating lovers rang? I *hate* having the power to hurt someone. It was easy when John portrayed his wife as a bitch and when I desperately needed money; but this is different. This is a real, live, hurting woman and I'm at least partially responsible.'

'Well, why don't you just become ethical about it?' Kev replied. 'Make sure you always ask your sexual partners what their social privileges are. If the boxes aren't ticked, the dick gets kicked. But by the same token, you can't be expected to have ESP, either. If a man is prepared to lie to his wife, he's probably prepared to lie to you – just like Mark did.'

'But that means I might inadvertently do it again!' I sobbed. 'I'll bet everyone we know has been injured like this – there's got to be *some* way to cheat-proof the world.'

'Sure, if you want to cut off men's testicles or relinquish monogamy.'

'Yeah right,' I said bitterly. 'We could call it "Noughty Feminism" and let everyone fuck whoever they like.'

'Well, feminism began with the sexual revolution of women – why not end it with the sexual revolution of men? The boys could finally stop fighting and go out to play!'

I laughed in spite of myself.

'You might even be eligible for the Nobel Peace Prize!' he chuckled.

'Well, there's one thing I *do* know,' I replied grimly. 'People who bury their heads in the sand put their butts in the line of fire. I don't know how I'm going to do it yet, but there's no way *I'm* going to be lied to when *I* get married.

Kev gave a big sigh.

'Why is it we can figure out rocket science, but we can't come to terms with each other?' he said sadly.


Late that night, I stood on the balcony of my apartment and absorbed the view of the city laid out below. It was a breathtaking sight. One-thirty on a Saturday morning in Sydney's hippest entertainment strip. People crowding in and out of clubs. The fragmented shout of a drunk who'd fallen behind his mates. Buses speeding up the street. Ambulances flying by, sirens wailing. Helicopters rushing places. The occasional stray bat on its way to Moore Park. A thousand lights twinkling at me – a thousand questions without answers.

I breathed it all in and offered the Goddess a prayer.

'Please help us,' I said. 'I know our customs don't reflect the biology you gave us and you're probably insulted or something, but please help us live in harmony.'

No answer. But the night became unusually still.

And then I said it. I offered the Goddess the biggest trade I could.

'I will trade everything I have for true and enduring love.'

There was no blinding flash or revelation. Instead the intentions of the night rushed on like they normally did.

So I went inside and lit candles so that I wouldn't have to turn on the lights and spoil the city spread out before me and I typed my wish into the diary.

It was the biggest wish I could make and certainly not original.

I would trade all of this, all my experiences, all the knowledge I'd gained, just to have a soulmate in my arms. Someone I could trustingly marry without fear of ever losing them.

But as soon as I typed the words, I realised I had asked for a miracle, not a boon. Marriage had reached an impasse and there wasn't a man, woman or child not steeped in its decay.

This wasn't about being a sugarbabe.

It wasn't even about the ongoing sex war.

It was about being able to grow old with the people we love.

And the words slowed down.

And the gaps between the typing lengthened as the diary caught up with life and life caught up with the diary.

And then I lit an old cigarette that I'd hidden from myself and wondered what the hell I was thinking.

# EPILOGUE

John came and got his coat. When he buzzed unannounced on a Tuesday night, I forgot all my reservations and raced downstairs with a pounding heart. Our eyes met and suddenly we were sobbing in each other's arms. I really had loved this man, with all my heart. We stood in the foyer and held each other for ages before going upstairs.

Apparently, he'd been through hell.

John said he lived with a woman he didn't love and spun illusions of happiness for his beloved children. He was expected to maintain a façade of cheerfulness for his wife's friends even though he didn't like most of them. They rarely went out together and on the few occasions he did socialise with his mates, she always waited up for him. She didn't trust him any more after the affair with me so she often made nasty little quips about unfaithfulness. As he frankly put it, she closed her legs three months after he returned, but before that she fucked him good and hard, just to let him know what he'd be missing later. It was also an ideal opportunity to show him all the new tricks she'd learnt from other men while he'd been with me. She sneered at him when he'd had too much to drink and belittled him in public. She always found fault with his cooking. In front of the children she was adoring – too adoring. He said he wanted to feel something for her but it was like being caressed by Golem. If she did engage in sex, it was only as a reward for something and rarely, if ever, spontaneous.

Despite all this, there was no fairy-tale ending to my story. I was no Sleeping Beauty, and John was no Prince Charming. The more he told me, the more repulsed I felt.

John was committed to his family and told me he'd only leave his wife when his youngest child left home. Bobby was seven at present; so John figured he'd only have to endure another ten years or so.

I lost a lot of respect for John when he told me that. Dick was right. The only thing worse than not admitting a mistake is purposely teaching it to your kids. Children see, children do. It doesn't take a genius to figure that one out. To be honest, I was relieved when he left. Turned out John had been right all along – rich men can have poor lives.

It just goes to show a good Dick is better than a bad John any day. I'm giving Dick 'how to meet women' lessons now. Gratis. I confessed about the diary and he said he was glad that someone was finally telling the tale. He divorced his wife and she was more than happy with the $2 million settlement she received. She's even got a new boyfriend. Without his guilt, Dick's a changed man. He's responded well to my coaching and can write incredibly romantic replies to women he meets on the internet, although he still forwards me the more confusing ones and asks for a translation when he can't understand 'womanese'. His willingness to betray their confidences probably helped appease some of my own guilt in writing all this down. We continue to joke about forming a divorcees' swap service so people like him can avoid living alone. He wants me to put a marriage performance review on the internet and make a fortune, but I prefer to suggest it as a service to humanity.

Kev and Marcus are still going strong in the most successful partnership I know. They celebrate fifteen years next month. They're still fighting for the rights of same-sex marriage in Australia; I keep telling them they're under-achieving. We wouldn't accept even chances of failure for anything else; why is it OK for marriage?

Jason and Ivy broke up – no surprises there! I hope she finds one of the monogamous minority.

I still see Andre; we have a platonic lunch almost every week. He wants me to write a second book, this time from the point of view of women like his wife. He's got a thirty-year plan to make sex interesting for her; reckons he'll introduce clit-ticklers when they're about fifty. He's even 'collecting' a group of likely ladies for me to interview. He'd know – he's still adamant that just about every man he knows has had an affair or is in the throes of one. Women don't have secret business; men do.

As for me, I've become a tad obsessed with research. A survey by the New York City Health Department found nearly 10 per cent of male participants – who said they were straight – reported having sex with at least one man in the previous year. Of that 10 per cent, almost 70 per cent were married. I've also learnt that 80 per cent of detective agency work deals with the unfaithful, and half the divorcees in the USA cite infidelity as the most common cause. And did I mention that the average age of marriage is going on thirty and some of us can soon expect to live for over a hundred years? That's seventy years or 21 kilometres of the same penis!

I've also remained true to my vow to stay away from married men – as far as I know, anyway. I'd gladly hump a husband again if I had the wife's permission, but that will require the assess-ment of boundaries and marriages based on chemistry. So although I had a great adventure and peace negotiations work well in theory, I have to accept that it is currently far easier to deceive than it is to believe.

If there are some brave souls out there who want to put an end to the dishonesty in marriage, maybe these pages can provide some clues as to what could work. I suspect my own future relationships will be *negotiated* rather than open. If I meet my future soulmate and he wants sex three times a week and I only want it once, then maybe we'll compromise with another sex partner every so often for him and a new frock for me. To try and prevent attachments forming, we'll agree to have sex with other people only once and never with friends, exes or relatives. I envisage an apartment with two master bedrooms that permits the unobtrusive entertainment of other partners, and yearly performance reviews based on pre-specified criteria that can be changed if life's lessons change us. Oh, and a full service every 100 kilometres or so wouldn't go astray . . .

Above all, I'd like to think we won't be dishonest about sex any more. I won't make Mr Hill suffer for being a creature of nature. If I close my legs – and I might – I will *expect* him to seek it elsewhere, which is only fair.

I've already had several offers. Funny that.

But different horses for different courses. There are still some men out there who have managed to transcend their biology. I wonder if they're happy. I still think monogamy is possible, just not probable. But I've also realised I have no right to judge other people's choices. Nothing is really good or bad – it's just our judgements that make them seem that way. Next time you meet a gay man, a fetishist, a prude or a sex worker, try and remember they are merely at a different point on the same line you're on. A man with a tight cord round his neck has no right to point the finger at a man in a dress, even if the cord is tied in a Windsor knot. Be envious instead. By doing something unconventional, you free yourself of the yoke of other people's opinions. I now understand that the increased self-esteem I felt as a sugarbabe wasn't a result of my sense of attractiveness being reinforced; nor was it from having power over powerful men. Rather, it was because *I no longer cared what people thought about me.*

These days, I try to live by my actions, not my prejudices. The ultimate test of any experience is whether you would do it again. If the answer is 'no', it's time to move on. Would I ever be a sugarbabe again? Well, you never know. But first there's another experiment I'm interested in conducting. So, if you're ever browsing through the Classifieds and you find an ad for a forty-year-old woman looking for a toyboy, don't be shocked: the sugarbabe has transformed herself into a sugarmum. Stand by for the results.